FOREWORD

BY URI GELLER

CONTENTS

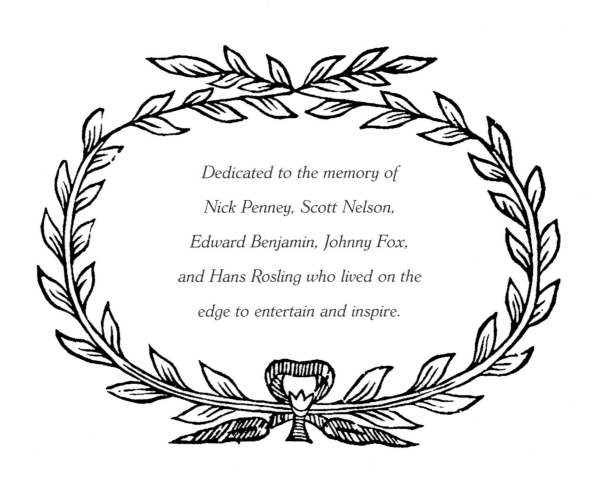

Dedicated to the memory of
Nick Penney, Scott Nelson,
Edward Benjamin, Johnny Fox,
and Hans Rosling who lived on the
edge to entertain and inspire.

Designed by Jack Chappell
Cover design by Jack Chappell

Type set in Minion/Frutiger/Dutch Mediaeval

ISBN: 978-0-7643-6882-0
ePub: 978-1-5073-0541-6
Printed in China

Published by Schiffer Publishing, Ltd.
4880 Lower Valley Road
Atglen, PA 19310
Phone: (610) 593-1777; Fax: (610) 593-2002
Email: info@schifferbooks.com
Web: www.schifferbooks.com

For our complete selection of fine books on this and related subjects, please visit our website at www.schifferbooks.com. You may also write for a free catalog.

Schiffer Publishing's titles are available at special discounts for bulk purchases for sales promotions or premiums. Special editions, including personalized covers, corporate imprints, and excerpts, can be created in large quantities for special needs. For more information, contact the publisher.

Warning: This book includes descriptions of sword swallowing and methods used by various performers throughout history. It is intended solely for informational and educational purposes. Under no circumstances should any content in this book be interpreted as instructional guidance or an endorsement of attempting sword swallowing. Sword swallowing is an inherently dangerous activity that poses a significant risk of serious injury or death. Do not attempt. Neither the authors nor the publishers assume any liability or responsibility for injury, harm, or death resulting from any attempt to perform or replicate the activities described herein. To the maximum extent permitted, the authors and the publisher disclaim all liability arising from the content of this book and its use.

TO THE HILT

A SWORD SWALLOWER'S
History of
SWORD SWALLOWING

Dan Meyer and
Marc Hartzman

SCHIFFER
PUBLISHING

4880 Lower Valley Road • Atglen, PA 19310

The impossible has never been impossible to me. For over fifty years, I've built a career of proving it, bending more than a million spoons through sheer mental power. My psychic abilities have even been studied by the CIA at the start of its remote viewing program.

But this is a book about a different kind of impossible—one I witnessed firsthand as a judge on *Got Talent Israel* in 2018. That's where I first saw Dan Meyer swallow swords. More than twenty inches of solid steel, straight down his throat. Dan Meyer is a master sword swallower—there are very few left around the world, but he is one of the best. How can someone possibly shove a sword to the bottom of his stomach and live to tell the tale? Even for me, this was astonishing.

As Dan began his performance, he approached me at the judges table and shared that I'd been an inspiration to him since his youth.

"As a child you bent my mind," Dan told me and millions of viewers. "Now it's my turn to bend yours and theirs. I'm going to swallow this sword, and I'm going to ask you to pull the sword out of my body. Not too fast or it'll slice the sides of my throat. And don't push—these are new jeans! And whatever you do, please don't bend it!"

I did just as he asked, not wanting to risk his life or his pants. After swallowing the blade, Dan pushed the impossible even further by towing a car across the stage—with our two hosts sitting inside it! This earned him a standing ovation, with me being the first to rise from my seat. Dan's performance amazed me and moved me.

After the show, I was eager to learn more about this man, so we met the next day at my museum in Jaffa, where I challenged Dan to swallow a sharp military bayonet from the 1800s. He did! Dan is incredibly nice, he's good looking, he has charisma, and he radiates positivity, so it's hard to believe that he pushes swords down his throat. We became fast friends, each pushing the limits of what's humanly possible in our own ways.

I can tell you with absolute certainty that sword swallowing is not a trick, though many believe it is. I've dealt with skeptics my entire career, but it's only driven me forward. Dan and every other sword swallower face similar disbelief. People think that surely the sword retracts into the hilt. No. It's 100% real and 100% dangerous. But the impossible is hard for most people to believe. Yet, without question, sword swallowing is proof that it's possible, no matter how unlikely it may seem. It's an art form passed down through generations to a very select, daring few.

This book is a tribute to all those who came before Dan—the performers who paved the steel path through sideshows, carnivals, dime museums, and wherever else they could exhibit their remarkable skills to amaze men, women, and children of all ages. Right now, as you turn these pages, that includes you. If you want to be astonished, shocked, and entertained, you must read this book. You will never forget it. Enjoy the show!

Uri Geller

World's Most Investigated Mystifier
Jaffa, Israel, 2024
urigeller.com

A SWORD SWALLOWER'S INTRODUCTION

MY PERSONAL

History of

SWORD SWALLOWING

The sharp pains in my stomach told me something had gone horribly wrong. After years of working as a professional sword swallower, was this how my career or, worse yet, my life would end?

It was October 2005—Friday the fourteenth, to be specific—and I was performing in a small local restaurant in Hartselle, Alabama. I had just pulled five long swords from my bag, wiped each of the blades with a soft rag doused in rubbing alcohol to sterilize the blades, and carefully felt the edges with my fingers for signs of nicks or burrs. Only a few weeks before, I had set a new personal record by swallowing four, then five, and eventually six swords at once while practicing at home. Then a few days later, at the annual Sideshow Gathering in Wilkes-Barre, Pennsylvania, nine of us managed to set a new Guinness World Record by swallowing a total of fifty-two swords at once, with me setting my own personal record of swallowing seven swords at once.

"This is extremely dangerous; it could kill me . . . I hope you enjoy it," I said to my audience with a wink. I stacked the five swords together, carefully arranging the blades to stagger the tips.

I slowly lifted the bundle of steel to my mouth.

"One for fun
Two for you
Three for me
Four is more
I'll strive for five
And if I survive,
You'll applaud like crazy
That I'm still alive . . ."

I opened my mouth and carefully maneuvered the cluster of blades down my throat,

hoping they'd all go in the same direction and not scissor against each other or splay outward. The weight and thickness of the blades almost made me gag, and my mind wandered as I wondered if the audience had noticed the reaction. I tried to open my mouth wider, but my jaw was extended as far as it would go and was starting to ache as the weight of the blades pressed heavily on my throat, prying my mouth open like a dentist's clamp.

Suddenly, before I knew what happened, my abdomen retched upward in an unexpected involuntary spasm so sudden that it felt like my stomach had exploded. The sudden spasm slammed my stomach up against the tips of the blades in an attempt to expel the foreign obstacles from my stomach. I didn't have time to react. The sharp pain in my stomach instantly told me something had gone horribly wrong.

"Stay calm," I told myself, as my mind raced. I could feel the pain in my midsection as my stomach throbbed. I knew something was not right. My watering eyes quickly inspected the moist blades for signs of blood, a regular habit after every swallow. No blood. Good. But I knew from experience that a lack of blood on the blades was often misleading—an injury below the epiglottis often will not show up as blood on the blades, and a false sense of relief could quickly turn a serious injury to a lethal one in a matter of hours if deadly bacterial peritonitis set in.

The audience sensed something was wrong. After a few moments of awkward silence, an audience member nervously blurted, "We need to keep our end of the bargain and give him that applause we promised for swallowing all five swords," followed by a meager smattering of applause that quickly faded at the audience's obvious apprehension as they wondered if my grimaces were just part of my act.

Fortunately, the "sword sandwich" was the finale for this show. Without speaking, I nodded in acknowledgment to the audience and, while still holding the five swords in one hand, waved feebly with my other, staggered a few steps, and slumped down next to my wife, while grasping my waist just below my breast bone.

After studying the physiology of sword swallowing on the human system for years, I knew just how serious an internal injury like this could be. The pains in my stomach told me that something was wrong, and I realized that my situation could quickly turn deadly. While grasping my stomach, I realized that what I had always hoped to avoid in my career as a sword swallower may have actually finally happened to me. After a few painful hours unsuccessfully trying to sleep, I ended up spending the rest of the night sitting up in the Emergency Room at Decatur General Hospital, followed by four weeks of bed rest and fasting from solid food. During those four weeks, I would often glance with disdain at my swords leaning in the corner, like a college kid who looks at the bottle after an all-nighter and thinks, "No way . . . Never again!" A month later, I forced myself to crawl out of bed to attempt to film an episode of Food Network's *Unwrapped* that had been in the works for several months, and I was back at it again until the next hospital visit.

If you're still holding this book and reading this far, you're probably as intrigued with the weird, bizarre, and unique world of sword swallowing as I have been, as well as most of the other sword swallowers in this book who have also been afflicted with this bizarre obsession. You might also have questions, such as:

"How did you discover you could swallow a sword?" "Did ya just wake up one day and decide to swallow a sword?"

I get asked these questions over and over again, word for word, day after day, as if they were tattooed on my forehead. I'm quite sure other sword swallowers get asked these same questions as well. Of course, we all have unique answers. After all, we are a unique group of people. There are only a few dozen full-time professional sword swallowers actively performing in a world population of over seven billion people, which makes each of us one out of every three hundred million people.

As for my personal answers—my reasons for deciding to shove a steel blade down my throat—well, it's not something I ever expected to do. Especially since I didn't even start until I was forty. But for the past twenty-five years, it's led me to places and experiences I never imagined. I've been blessed to have performed live in over sixty countries and have been featured on fifteen "Got Talents" around the world; as a finalist on *America's Got Talent*; as a Golden Buzzer Winner and finalist on Sweden's *Talang*; in Ripley's museums, books, and cartoons; at hundreds of state and county fair shows, festivals, Ren Faires, churches, and corporate events; and on hundreds of TV programs, interviews, and documentaries seen by over eight hundred million viewers worldwide. As president of the Sword Swallowers Association International, a forty-time world record holder, winner of the 2007 Ig Nobel Prize in Medicine at Harvard for medical research on sword swallowing (published in the *British Medical Journal*), Ig Nobel science and medical lecturer at dozens of top universities around the world, and global speaker with a viral TED Talk on sword swallowing that is the most translated TED Talk in the world, I'm also known as the world's leading expert in the four-thousand-year-old art of sword swallowing. As a matter of fact, as I was doing the ribbon cutting for the Ripley's Believe It or Not! Odditorium in Times Square, the president of Ripley's Believe It or Not! introduced me as "The World's Top Sword Swallower."

But I never set out to become the "world's top sword swallower."

I grew up a scared, shy, scrawny, skinny, wimpy kid in a very average noncircus family in Michigan City, Indiana. The first twenty years of my life, I grew up in extreme fear, afraid of just about everything: water, heights, spiders, snakes, doctors, nurses, needles and sharp objects, and, most of all, speaking in public. Because I suffered from inferiority complex, low self-esteem, and borderline social anxiety disorder, I found it hard to socialize with others. Grade school was living hell. I could barely talk. I would sit at my desk and constantly shake and tremble, nervously worrying about the next break and the teasing that would invariably come from the class bullies. I was petrified of the bullies, who wouldn't let me play on their sports teams and would constantly tease me and beat me up as the class "wimp" and "loser." Living in constant fear and due to the continuous cortisol my body was generating out of fear, I was constantly nauseated and sick to my stomach and spent my time as a loner without any close friends.

As a result, I vowed I wanted to someday do real magic, do real feats, do things the bullies could not do, to somehow run away and join the circus and amaze audiences, or be a superhero like Superman and fly around the world doing superhuman feats and saving lives. I wanted to find my purpose and calling, to know my life had meaning, to prove that the impossible is *not* impossible and somehow change the world.

When I was twenty years old, I got the opportunity to serve as a short-term Lutheran missionary in Tamil Nadu and Andhra Pradesh, South India, from 1977 to 1978. As a kid who had stared out the window in geography class dreaming of exploring the spires of India, I jumped at the chance.

In April 1978, the week before my twenty-first birthday, while living in Tamil Nadu, India, my good friend and mentor Greg Ormson told me about the concept of "thromes"—major life goals that can help reveal your purpose and calling in life, which is based on the book *The Throme of the Erril of Sherill*. Greg said, "If you could do anything you wanted to do, be anyone you wanted to be, or go anywhere you wanted to go, what would you do, who would you be, where would you go?" I said, "No, man . . . I can't do that! I've got too many fears!" That night, as I was thinking about my fears and considering the possibility of thromes, I came down with a severe 105-degree malaria fever, chills, and shaking that lasted five days and brought me to the point of reflecting on my life of fear. The malaria fever was my catalyst for change. On April 6, 1978, the night before my twenty-first birthday, I prayed a little prayer and said, "God, if You let me live to my twenty-first birthday, I will not let fear rule my life any longer. I'm going to put my fears to death, find my purpose and calling, know my life has meaning, take *on* risks and challenges, and somehow change the world."

That night, I made a list of ten "thromes" or major life goals—over-the-top, nearly impossible dreams that I doubted would ever come true. But I dreamed big, made up my list, and wrote them down: I decided I wanted to visit all the major continents of the world, visit the Seven Wonders of the World, live on a deserted island, live on a ship in the ocean, live with a tribe of Indians in the Amazon, work with a circus, work in the music business in Nashville, climb the highest mountain in Scandinavia above the Arctic Circle, see Mount Everest at sunrise, and jump out of an airplane. As a poor kid from small-town Indiana, I didn't really believe any of these thromes would ever happen.

Now I won't tell you if I survived until my twenty-first birthday or not . . .

But somehow that slight shift in my head took my focus off my fear and redirected my focus squarely to my dreams. Little by little, I quit focusing on the 99 percent that was impossible, and instead focused on the 1 percent that was theoretically plausible if even slightly possible. This slight paradigm shift changed my life.

After I returned from India, I got the opportunity to help a high school classmate's family develop their private island in the Bahamas, and I jumped at the chance. I had just received my Eagle Scout award at the age of eighteen, and I was eager to test out my survival skills. I ended up moving to a small island in the Berry Islands of the Bahamas called Little Stirrup Cay, where for five years I lived like Robinson Crusoe wearing a loincloth, living in a thatched hut, sleeping in a hammock, and spearing sharks and stingrays for food as an original "Survivor." Check. I managed to check my first throme off my list!

When I lived in the Bahamas, I got the opportunity to meet millionaires. So I decided to ask them their secrets for success. Almost without exception, they all told me basically the same answer: take opportunity when it knocks. So I did. For the next two years, I worked on a cruise ship as a scuba and snorkeling instructor and managed the island Little Stirrup Cay (now called Cocoa Cay), first for the owner of the island and later for Admiral Cruise Lines. Check another throme off my list. I later moved to take care of another set of islands in the Berry Islands and eventually moved to Cancún, Mexico, and eventually to Ecuador, where I lived with a tribe of Indians in Puyo Pongo on the Rio Pastaza in the Amazon rainforest. Check. Each time I would check one throme off my list, I would add another five or ten thromes onto my list, so my list of thromes continued to grow. Through a series of events, I discovered that if you don't focus on the 99 percent that's impossible, but instead actually focus on figuring out how to do the 1 percent that's plausible, that much of the time you can actually make the impossible possible.

While in college in the 1980s, I learned clowning, juggling, unicycle riding, and stilt walking. During my college years, I got into clowning so much that I would hitchhike off on the weekends to perform with circuses such as Hoxie Brothers, Clyde Beatty Cole Brothers, and other small "mud shows." Check off another throme. For two years, I taught classes at Indiana State University on the "FUNdamentals of Circus Clowning." During my time at Waldorf College in Iowa, I learned fire eating from a local magician, and I was hooked. That was as close as I could get to doing real magic! After this, every time I would check a throme off of my list, I would often add five or ten new thromes onto my list, so my list of thromes continued to grow.

In 1987, I moved to Nashville, where I worked in the music business for several years in copyright licensing, as well as a songwriter, studio engineer, and record producer. Check. During this time, I enjoyed juggling and passing clubs with the Nashville Music City Juggler's Club every Tuesday night at Centennial Park. On the weekends, I'd perform for corporate events at Opryland Hotel. I soon added human blockhead, glass eating, and the bed of nails to my repertoire of juggling tricks.

One Tuesday evening while we were juggling at Centennial Park, a van pulled up with a group of sideshow performers who were traveling across the country on tour. Among them was Tim Cridland, "The Torture King," and George "The Giant" McArthur. I found out that besides being a giant at 7 feet, 3 inches and doing the bed of nails, George was also the world's tallest sword swallower. I asked him for some tips. George said, "I'll give you two tips: Number one, it's extremely dangerous; there are fewer than twelve sword swallowers left in the entire world, and people have died doing it. Number two: *Don't try it!*" Guess what I did? I added it to my list of thromes!

In 1998, I set my sights on researching and studying sword swallowing so I could find each of those twelve sword swallowers and extract every tidbit of information I could find on sword swallowing.

But there were almost no books or videos on sword swallowing, and no formal way to learn. The only general book on the subject was Daniel Mannix's 1945 novel *Step Right Up*, which was later renamed *Memoirs of a Sword Swallower*. I studied Mannix's book, researched everything I could find, searched magic forums for tips on sword swallowing, and gradually began collecting tips from sword swallowers of the past.

During my research, I learned that sword swallowing had actually started in a tribe called the Khonda Dora in Andhra Pradesh, South India, which is where I had lived when I was twenty years old, and where I had seen one of the last sword swallowers in the local village. (To see the entire story, watch my 2013 viral TED talk, "Cutting Through Fear," at TEDxMaastricht.)

One of the tips I'd heard from an old sword swallower was to silver-plate a dagger and practice ten to twelve times per day. So, I bought a 13-inch dagger in Nashville, got it silver plated, and began practicing. (I later heard from other sword swallowers that the silver or nickel plating can flake off and cut your throat, so I quit silver-plating blades after that!)

I began practicing ten to twelve times a day every day while I worked in the music business in Nashville, from 1997 until 2001. I had been asking every sword swallower I could find—the Lizardman, Natasha Veruschka, Red Stuart, Todd Robbins, Slim Price, and others—figuring that if I got even just a tiny tip from each one of them, I might be able to put it all together and figure it out. Along the way I ran into a fellow performer named Roderick Russell, who was also studying sword swallowing. For several months, we emailed tips we picked up back and forth, encouraged each other, and helped each other out.

After about 14,000 unsuccessful attempts and a few major paradigm shifts, I changed my attitude and my posture and finally got my first sword down my throat on February 12, 2001. It took another four years for me to master it and to work my way up to curved swords, serpentine swords, and eventually multiple swords, and to ultimately put together an actual comedy show.

Once Roderick had gotten a sword down, we started the Sword Swallowers Association International (SSAI) together in 2001 and held our first convention in conjunction with the Sideshow Gathering in Wilkes-Barre, Pennsylvania, in 2002. I invited every sword swallower I had discovered in my research, as well as media such as

Dan Meyer performs as Belteshazzar early in his career. *Courtesy of Dan Meyer*

Jeanne Moos from CNN. We ended up setting a Guinness World Record when nineteen sword swallowers swallowed fifty swords at once and ended up on a segment of CNN. Eventually Roderick and I went our separate ways—he as a successful mentalist, hypnotist, and sword swallower—and I've run the SSAI ever since.

As my career in sword swallowing took off, so did the uniqueness of my adventures! In 2002 and 2003 I was honored to be invited to tour the US with country artists Brooks and Dunn on their *Neon Circus* tour. During the tour, I juggled, walked stilts, and performed the human blockhead on a small stage for audiences as they came into the concert area, then I would swallow a sword on the big stage with video projected onto the big jumbotrons. What an awesome sound it was to hear 25,000 people roar at once!

But something else was happening to me at that time. After years of desperately craving attention as an outcast, suddenly I was able to do something almost nobody else could do. I was so excited and proud of my new super-power that I became obsessed with it and loved talking about sword swallowing to just about everyone I met. If you were one of the people I overwhelmed with conversations on sword swallowing, I ask you to please forgive my enthusiasm in my new hobby. (Come to find out, this phenomenon was not something that was unique to just me. As I researched sword swallowing, I found a similar pattern among other outcasts turned sword swallowers who learned this incredible feat between the ages of eighteen and twenty-two and were so proud of their newfound superpowers that they couldn't stop obsessing about it. Nod your head in agreement and raise your hand if you're a sword swallower who got thoroughly obsessed with sword swallowing and sideshow stunts . . . Yep. There are a quite a few who follow this pattern.) During this time with Brooks and Dunn, I also began doing research on pride. As I was pridefully boasting about doing the impossible, a friend asked if I knew the proverbs about "pride." I thought pride was a good thing, something you got when your child was an honor student or got straight A's or served in the military. Instead, I learned that "pride goes before destruction, a haughty spirit comes before a fall," and "humility comes before honor" (Proverbs 16:18 and 18:12). It was a tough lesson to learn, but over three years of intensive study, I tried to deliberately change my attitude from one of pride to "get humble before you stumble." It's not easy, and I still struggle with it and constantly remind myself of this attitude every day. During this time on tour with Brooks and Dunn, my friend, hypnotist C. J. Johnson, wore red leather Puma driving shoes. I decided that I, too, wanted to wear red leather Puma shoes, but as a constant reminder that every time I looked down and saw my shoes, I would remind myself to try to be humble, to remember my humble childhood, and to swallow my pride before I swallowed any swords. The red shoes stuck and became my signature look as "The Sword Swallower with the Red Shoes" and as a constant personal reminder to swallow my pride. Twenty-five years later, I still wear the red shoes when I perform as a reminder to swallow my pride. I'm still working on it.

Later, in 2005, I was contacted by British radiologist Dr. Brian Witcombe of the Gloucester Royal Hospital in Gloucestershire, England, who had a fascination with unusual x-rays. He was especially fascinated with x-rays of sword swallowers. In 2005, Dr. Witcombe and I began working together on the first-ever comprehensive medical research study on sword-swallowing injuries in the four-thousand-year history of the art. I reached out to all the sword swallowers in my database and set out to do a comprehensive study on their training methods, who they'd learned from, age they'd learned, time to learn, height, weight, length of sword, number of swords swallowed, injuries, diagnosis, treatment, and how they had healed. Dr. Witcombe and I compressed every tidbit of data we could find about sword swallowing and submitted our paper, "Sword Swallowing and Its Side Effects," to the

On March 28, 2015, Dan Meyer swallowed twenty-nine swords at once at Ripley's St. Augustine to break the previous world record of twenty-five swords. The blades were 24 inches long by half an inch wide. *Courtesy of Dan Meyer*

British Medical Journal. To our surprise, it was accepted and published in the December 23, 2006, end-of-the-year issue of the journal. What a rare honor to get published in one of the world's most prestigious medical journals, especially for me as a nonphysician. Even cooler, the article soon went viral.

About this time, I connected with Tim O'Brien, VP of Ripley's Communications in Nashville. Tim and I hit it off with our love of the weird, bizarre, and unusual. Tim was working on a publicity stunt for Bike Week in Myrtle Beach, South Carolina, in conjunction with moving the Pirates of the Caribbean display into the Ripley's Aquarium there. I told Tim that I had swum with sharks for several years in the Bahamas, and that I had swallowed swords for several years, and that I knew I could do both separately, but I wondered if I could put the two of them together into a Ripley's Believe It or Not! publicity stunt. After months of brainstorming with Tim, I began practicing sword swallowing in swimming pools, with my dad holding me down with his feet to keep me from bobbing up to the surface. Once I realized I could actually swallow a sword underwater, the next step was to attempt it in a tank of sharks.

Dan Meyer swallowing a sword underwater in a tank of 88 sharks and stingrays on May 18, 2007, at Ripley's Aquarium Myrtle Beach, South Carolina. *Courtesy of Tim O'Brien*

On the morning of May 18, 2007, after doing a few late-night rehearsals with local ambulance crews and EMTs, I climbed into a tank of eighty-eight sharks and stingrays at Ripley's Aquarium Myrtle Beach and, before a live audience, managed to swallow a few swords underwater . . . within twenty-nine minutes of eating a full meal (Mom had warned me about that!). A few months later, I received my first Ripley's Believe It or Not! cartoon and was published in the 2007 *Ripley's Believe It or Not!* book. A childhood dream come true!

A month later, I flew into New York City to do the ribbon cutting for the grand opening of Ripley's Odditorium in Times Square. When I climbed into the long black limo waiting for me at JFK Airport, I found myself in the most surreal limo ride with some other Ripley's performers: Jim Goldman, the armless man; Moses Lanham, the backward-feet man; Chuy the Wolf Boy; and Erik Sprague, the Lizardman. As I was marveling at the surreal situation I was in, my phone rang with an even more surreal call— from a man who said his name was Marc Abrahams with

Improbable Research in Cambridge, informing me that Dr. Witcombe and I had been nominated for the 2007 Ig Nobel Prize in Medicine at Harvard. What!? I'm thinking this must be a joke; I didn't apply for anything like this! But of the 20,000 scientific papers that are nominated each year in various categories, our research had been nominated for the field of medicine. Dr. Witcombe and I were invited to Harvard to accept the award, along with nine other recipients and about 2,500 Ignitaries and world media. It was such a surreal event. When we finally met and Dr. Witcombe and I gave our joint acceptance speech (me with a sword down my throat), we became the poster story for the Ig Nobel Prize that year and ended up in *Time*, *Newsweek*, *Scientific American*, *Nature*, and hundreds of other publications. Over the next several years, we lectured on sword swallowing at Harvard, MIT, Oxford, Cambridge, Imperial College, Portsmouth University in England, Erasmus University in the Netherlands, Aarhus and Aalborg Universities in Denmark, BITS Pilani in India, and other prestigious universities all around the world.

In 2006 and 2007, I was contacted by more than fifteen different producers to swallow swords on a brand-new NBC reality show called *America's Got Talent*. I sent them all the promo videos they requested, and finally agreed to audition on season 2 in Atlanta, but at the last minute they called and said my swords were considered weapons so they weren't permitted on the set in the Cobb Performing Arts Center in Atlanta. Finally, in 2008, I was invited to perform on *America's Got Talent* season 3 auditions in Nashville, then on to the regionals at the Cobb Center in Atlanta, and then as one of seventy who were sent on to the quarterfinals and semifinals in Las Vegas. During this time, other sword swallowers advised me against doing the show, since they claimed I would just be teased and made fun of, and "a sword swallower won't make it very far on the show at all." As it turned out, I made it on nine episodes to the Top 50 before getting eliminated in Vegas at number 42. But after I got eliminated, they kept me on the list as an alternate wild-card contestant. A few weeks later, I got a call and learned that one of the Top 40 acts,

A surprised audience of Nobel Prize laureates, dignitaries, and world media react as Dan Meyer punctuates his acceptance speech at the 2007 Ig Nobel Prize in Medicine at Harvard on October 4, 2007, with his coauthor, researcher Dr. Brian Witcombe (*far right*), looking on. *Alexey Eliseev / Improbable Research*

the girl with the Russian Barre Trio, had had an injury and broke her foot and was eliminated from the Top 40, so the producers invited me to come be on the finals as an alternate wild card. They flew me to Hollywood along with seven other wild cards to fill the open Top 40 slot. After a national vote, I was eliminated once again, but at least I made it on to the finals in Hollywood. I made so many great friends at the finals and got to hang out with my friend George "The Giant" McArthur who also made it to the finals. What an honor, one I will never forget.

It was a crisp fall morning in October 2008 when I met up with legendary TED speaker and fellow sword swallower Hans Rosling on the cobblestone entrance to the bustling Stockholm Centralen station in Stockholm, Sweden. It was a year after his first big TED talk, "New insights on poverty," had gone viral, and only a few months after I had won the 2007 Ig Nobel Prize in Medicine at Harvard. I had lived and worked in the music business in Stockholm in the '90s, so Sweden holds a special place in my heart, and I love Stockholm in the fall. But this time I was there on a different mission: as president of the Sword Swallowers Association International to welcome Hans into the Sword Swallowers Association International as our most well-known Swedish sword swallower, induct him into our Hall of Fame, and present him his SSAI patch and T-shirt.

After meeting Hans and exchanging greetings in Swedish, we compared notes on our common pasts—our love of sword swallowing, and how we had both lived and worked in India, where we both had witnessed sword swallowing firsthand in the place where it had originated.

Then Hans told me about how he had become fascinated with sword swallowing: During his studies at medical school in Uppsala, Sweden, Hans's best friend was a magician. When they were shown an x-ray of a sword swallower, both students were fascinated, and Hans was determined to try it. But no matter how hard he tried, he always failed and just could not manage to swallow a sword at that time. It wasn't until years later, when he had a patient who was a sword swallower, that Hans got some tips and eventually taught himself sword swallowing. As an afterthought and fun finale to his first major TED talk, Hans said he decided to swallow a small Swedish bayonet at the end of his talk, which sent his TED talk viral with millions of views. What a great story, I thought.

Hans paid me his SSAI dues, and I presented him with his official SSAI T-shirt and patch. He grinned from ear to ear with the childlike exuberance of a child getting ready to see the circus for the first time.

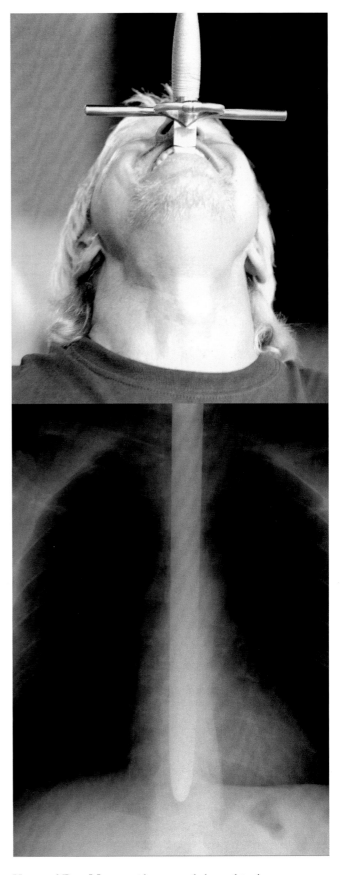

X-ray of Dan Meyer with a sword down his throat.
Courtesy of Dan Meyer

Then Hans said, "We need to celebrate this! Did you bring any swords with you today? Do you have a sword I could swallow?"

"Of course . . . ," I said hesitantly. "But right here, at Centralen? In public? With all these *polisen* around?"

"Ja!" he inhaled energetically in his soft Swedish accent. "They all know me!"

"Because of your TED talk?" I asked.

"Yes," he answered excitedly. "You wouldn't believe how much that helped spread my ideas! *You* should do a TED talk on sword swallowing."

I dug two of my favorite swords out of my sword bag and let Hans choose the one he wanted to swallow. He chose a nice little single-edged saber with a 22-inch-long blade, nicknamed "My Pride," one of the first swords I ever swallowed. I grabbed my favorite 24-inch-long double-edged sword and glanced around nervously at the police and security guards nearby. The authorities usually take a dim view of anyone brandishing shiny weapons around high-traffic areas such as train and subway stations.

Hans and I smiled at each other with mischievous grins. With a nod, we quickly raised our swords and swallowed them at the same time, right there in full view of the amazed public in front of Stockholm's Central Station. We leaned over and pulled the swords out of each other's throats. By the time we finished, people had stopped walking and were staring in stunned disbelief at the unusual sight they'd just witnessed.

But something more happened that day. Hans's challenge to do a TED talk was a turning point in my life.

That day, because of Hans Rosling's encouragement, I decided that I needed to tell my story about how swallowing swords helped me cut through social anxiety and fear—how something as abnormal as swallowing swords actually helped make me normal by building the courage to find my purpose and calling.

After rigorously studying TED talks for five years and working on developing my own TED talk, on September 4, 2013, I nervously told my story and did my first TED talk at TEDxMaastricht in the Netherlands, one of the largest TEDx events in Europe. Encouraged by Hans's inspiration, I infused some of his ideas into my talk and ended by swallowing a 24-inch-long blade. The response was overwhelming—a standing ovation, a viral buzz, and the talk has now been translated into over seventy-five languages—more than over 200,000 other TED talks.

In 2009 I was honored to be invited to perform with several Cirque du Soleil performers for two weeks at the Souq Waqif open-air market in Doha, Qatar. What an incredible experience that was. The Arab audiences really love swords, and my shows always attracted huge audiences.

Several things happened on that trip that I will never forget.

As I was finishing my very first show in Doha, just as I was in the middle of my final act, I heard a loud distortion being broadcast over the loudspeakers. At first, I thought it was an announcement of some sort, so I kept performing. But with the loud distorted sound coming through the speakers, it was really hard for me to concentrate on swallowing my swords, and I thought, "How rude for them to disrupt my act!" Then I realized it was their call to prayer. Nobody had warned me to let me know that the call to prayer was scheduled right in the middle of my finale. I didn't know what to do, so I just continued on, finished my show quickly, said my thanks, and exited the stage as quickly as I could. I later learned that was a very inconsiderate thing to do, and I was reprimanded severely and told that I should have stopped performing immediately during the call to prayer. After that, I made sure that all my shows were scheduled right after the call to prayer, so that it did not interrupt my shows.

One afternoon as I was doing the finale to my show, I chose a professor from Canada as a volunteer to whip a sword from my throat like Indiana Jones from 10 feet away. I was relieved that he spoke English because I knew he understood my instructions. I explained how he needed to hold his arm high as the audience counted backward in Arabic from ten to one, and then whip the sword from my throat when they got to one. Then I instructed the audience to move away from the tables and chairs in the section where the sword would go flying behind the professor. After several promptings and much waving of my arms, I managed to clear the audience away from where the sword would be landing behind the professor. But I had to repeat myself several times because people would walk up and sit down in the empty seats in the area where the sword was going to land.

After I finally got the area cleared, I proceeded with the trick. The *Indiana Jones* music played, the audience counted backward, the professor whipped the sword from my throat, and the sword went flying out of my throat and out into the area where the empty chairs and tables were. But during my setup, a man and his son had sat down at a table in the area. And, of course, the sword went flying right toward where the man and boy were sitting, and the hilt hit the boy in his shoulder. The man jumps up and starts yelling angrily in Arabic, and I see tables upturned and chairs flying. And I'm thinking to myself, "Uh-oh! I'm in big trouble now!" I can imagine myself in a Doha prison calling the US embassy for an attorney to get me out. A few days earlier on the flight over, I had just watched the movie *Midnight Express*, about an American tourist who ended up imprisoned in a Turkish prison for thirty years. So, I quickly finished my act by abruptly saying, "*Shukran jzylaan . . . Asmi Daniel!*" ("Thank you very much. I'm Daniel!"), grabbed my swords, and ran off the stage.

I ran back to my greenroom still shaking and trying calm down. But then I realized I had to go out and retrieve my sword, and in the process, I would need to face the situation and confront the man and the boy. So, I took a deep breath and slowly walked out to where the man and his son were sitting. I found my sword sitting on their table. The man was extremely agitated and upset, and the boy was in his lap still sniffling. I sat down next to the man and his son and apologized profusely. "I am so sorry!" I said. "What's your son's name?" "Yusuf," he answered curtly. I said, "Is Yusuf okay?," and the man angrily said, "No! He was really freaked out during your show thinking you were some sort of Superman. But then when the sword came flying and hit him, he was so scared that it *really* freaked him out!"

I apologized again to the man and his son. As I was trying to think of a way to change the subject, I asked, "Where are you from?" He said, "We live in Muncie, Indiana, in the USA." I said, "Muncie? That's where I live!" I said, "Would your son like an autographed card?" And the man and the boy said, "Yes, please," so I autographed a card for the boy. Then his father cooled down and offered to buy me a strawberry pineapple hookah. I was so relieved not to end up in jail in Qatar that night.

A few days later, I went to the Doha Airport to fly home. When I got to the airport, I checked my suitcase and my large sword case tube containing twenty-five swords and the props I used in my show. As the tube of swords went through the x-ray machine, the security guard, in his long white *bisht thawb* robe and *keffiyeh* headdress, stopped me and pointed toward my sword tube and yelled something at me excitedly in Arabic, apparently asking what was in the tube. I pointed toward the sword case and pointed toward myself, and I said in simple Arabic, "Swords . . . I swallow swords." He looked at me in disbelief, so I pointed toward the case, very carefully took the lid off the case, and very slowly pulled out a long sword. I realized at this point it was probably not a great idea for a blond-haired Westerner to be waving a weapon in a public airport in the Middle East. I held the sword in front of my body to show where it went, and then I carefully swallowed the sword very slowly. When I pulled the sword out, this man's eyes looked like they had almost popped out of his head. The other people that were standing in line behind me all got out their cameras and started taking photos and videos. I said to him, "OK, you understand?"

About this time, the man's supervisor showed up and started yelling at the man in Arabic, apparently asking why everybody had their cameras out and what the big commotion and holdup was. The security guard apparently explained back to the man in Arabic something like, "This guy just swallowed a sword!" So, the supervisor looks at me with a funny look and yells something angrily at me in Arabic. I pointed at the swords and explained in Arabic, "Swords . . . I swallow swords." Then I repeated the demonstration for the supervisor. This time, even more people got out their cameras and started taking pictures and videos. A few minutes later, another supervisor comes down and starts yelling at the other two guys loudly in Arabic because there's a big disturbance, with a large crowd of people making a commotion. Apparently, as far as I could guess, this higher supervisor asked the first two guys in Arabic, "What's the holdup and what's going on here?" And the security guard and supervisor apparently explained back to him in Arabic what had just happened. After some gesturing and even more pantomiming, I swallowed a sword a third time for this supervisor to prove what I did. This time, even more people took photos and videos. I was afraid I was going to be detained even later and miss my flight, since there were about fifty people taking photos and making a big commotion, so I pointed to my swords, then pointed to my watch and my ticket, and asked, "Can I please go catch my flight now . . . *inshallah*?" Reluctantly, they finally allowed me to pack up my swords in my sword case, and I ran on to my gate to catch my plane. I was sure glad when I finally made it on the plane, and even happier when my swords arrived at my final destination, but I sure wish I had a video of that whole turn of events. I thought I was never going to get out of Doha, Qatar.

In January 2010, I was honored to be featured on season 1 of *Stan Lee's Superhumans*. The producers were looking for a superhuman stunt. My blacksmith and I created a 38-inch-long sword that was heated to over 1,500 degrees red hot. Before the heat could be transferred down the blade, my blacksmith lowered the sword down my throat for one second before he removed it, and we branded wood with the red-hot hilt and then boiled water with the still-red-hot hilt. When the episode came out, I realized a childhood dream when Stan Lee called me a "Man of Steel."

Later in 2010, Guinness World Records invited me to fly to Rome, Italy, to set the Guinness World Record for swallowing swords underwater in a tank. I managed to swallow two swords underwater. But in the process, I ended up puncturing my esophagus, so they rushed me by ambulance to the Ospidale Humberto Policlinico in Rome, where I got to study Italian and enjoy Italian IV drips for a few weeks before I finally had to escape from the hospital to catch a flight home before the studio crew closed up for the season.

In 2012, I was honored to go back to India and perform at the prestigious Indian University BITS Pilani in Rajasthan, to BITS Pilani in Goa, and do CityFest Hyderabad and several other events around India. For me, it was so much fun to take sword swallowing back to India to the original place where it had begun about 2000 BCE. During this trip, another major coincidence was that I ended up at the exact location where I had almost died from malaria thirty-four years before, on my twenty-first birthday.

During my 2012 India tour, I was blessed to be invited to perform in Kathmandu, Nepal. One day, my driver took me on the back of his motorcycle up to the top of Nagarkot. The next morning, I was awakened at 4:00 for chai tea. While sipping our chai, we could make out the silhouette of the Himalaya Mountains in the dark. Surprisingly, there wasn't a cloud in the sky. As the sun rose, a bright-yellow sunbeam struck Mount Everest and lit the entire peak in bright-yellow golden rays of sunrise. It was amazing. Check. Another throme checked off my list.

In 2013, I worked on the idea of trying to pull a car a short distance by swallowed sword, just to see if I could do it. I worked on the logistics with my Toyota Corolla and with an 18-inch sword down my throat. In order to make it work, I needed a special bracket. I went to the local Toyota dealer in Muncie, Indiana, and had them turn a heavy piece of metal frame from the underbody of a car into a bracket. They drilled a hole in the center of the bracket, along with two holes at the ends for attaching towing straps. I put my 20-inch sword through the hole in the center, attached the other ends of the straps to the car, and swallowed the blade. From there, I leaned forward and attempted to take a step. But I couldn't. Finally, after fifteen seconds of not moving, the car finally gave way. With much grunting and groaning, I managed to tow the Corolla about 3 feet—using just the sword down my throat, with over 2,500 pounds of pressure on my teeth and stomach. It wasn't much, and it wasn't easy. As a matter of fact, it was practically 99 percent impossible to do. But I focused on that 1 percent that was plausible and did everything I could until I finally made it possible. It was only a few feet, but I had *done* it.

On World Sword Swallower's Day 2013, I took the stunt to another level—as a publicity stunt for Ripley's Odditorium Baltimore. It was a rainy Saturday, February 23, 2013, but the media and crowds of people showed up at the Ripley's museum, including Lady Diane Falk and several other sword swallowers. On February 23, 2013, at 2:23:13 p.m., we sword swallowers all downed our swords at once in the Big Swallow, along with other sword swallowers around the world. Then it was my turn. In spite of the rain, I mustered all my energy to pull a Mini Cooper car covered in a million Swarovski jewels (weighing an extra 300 pounds) out of the Ripley's showroom and into the rain of the Inner Harbor area by an 18-inch sword down my throat. I grunted and groaned, and at first the car didn't move. But I focused on that 1 percent that was possible, and finally got the car to move less than an inch, and I knew I could do it. I kept pulling, and by the time I had finished pulling the car out of the Ripley's museum and out into the rain, my mouth was numb and bleeding and my stomach was throbbing from over 3,000 pounds of pressure pushing on my teeth and my stomach, yet I was elated that I managed to do it.

On a Monday evening in March 2016, I got a voice message from Nigel, my old producer on *America's Got Talent*. In his message, Nigel said they had seen video of the car pull, and he asked if I wanted to be back on *AGT* again. They had heard about my Ripley's stunt and wanted me to swallow a sword and pull host Nick Cannon across the stage in a car. I immediately called him back to find out when . . . his answer: *tomorrow*, in Pasadena, California. I asked them what kind of car they wanted to use. "No idea," he said. "We haven't thought that far ahead yet. Just get here on the next red-eye flight, and we'll try to find a car by tomorrow!" Just a few days before that, I had been given a 1929 Model A car axle by Red Stuart that had been swallowed by Red and an old Ripley's sword swallower named Arthur Plumhoff. So, I decided that if I was going to be back on national TV again, I wanted to be the first to swallow a car axle on *AGT*.

The next night, after scrambling to make the red-eye flight to Pasadena and being awake for over twenty-four hours, I managed to swallow the car axle and then pulled Nick Cannon across the stage in a blue 1974 Triumph Spitfire by swallowed sword, which ended up getting a standing ovation and four yes votes. After the video hit over five hundred million views, I got invitations to compete on several other *Got Talent* shows around the world, including Italy, France, Israel, Australia, Sweden, Croatia, Spain, Germany, and Canada, some more than once, for a total of fifteen Got Talent appearances so far.

Among the highlights of my travels was becoming friends with one of the *Israel's Got Talent* judges, psychic mentalist, and legendary spoon bender Uri Geller. We hit it off so well that Uri brought along a surprise for me—an old bayonet he had just been presented for his collection that had been owned by Napoleon Bonaparte. Uri asked if I could swallow it. I wasn't sure that I could, but I quickly set a new throme to swallow Napoleon's bayonet and focused on making it possible! Very carefully, I maneuvered the sword into my body. It was extremely risky and stupid to attempt to swallow Napoleon's sharp, dirty antique bayonet, but I took the opportunity while I had it, and it was a magical moment I will never forget!

Among the lowlights of the past few years was returning home from my second tour of Australia and having a colonoscopy at age sixty-five. This was much less exciting than putting steel down my esophagus. Some people hate the test preparation, but for me, the results were the worst part. They showed that I had five colon cancer tumors in my abdomen—adenocarcinoma. I decided to look at the challenge of cancer like I look at the challenge of sword swallowing—to not focus on the 99 percent that is the negative, the cancer, but instead focus on the 1 percent of what's possible to overcome the cancer. Another hurdle to overcome, another way of defying death to do the impossible. Weeks after the diagnosis, I swallowed a car axle and pulled another car on *Sweden's Got Talent* and was surprised to be awarded the Golden Buzzer and sent on to the finals. In your face and down your throat, cancer!

That's just a bit of my story so far. Now I'm excited to be writing this book. This is the kind of resource I was looking for in 1997 when I was researching sword swallowing. Back then, there was very little information available on sword swallowing, and it was scarce and hard to find. Over the past twenty-five years, I've done as much research as I could to find the stories of the sword swallowers you'll see in the following pages. But as you're reading, please realize that this is not a how-to book on learning sword swallowing. Sword swallowing is an extremely dangerous art that requires years of practice, razor-sharp focus, and pinpoint accuracy. A lapse in concentration could mean a puncture, internal bleeding, or even death. As a sword swallower, I have to treat each time as if it were my first time, or it might be my last. Do not try it at home . . . or anywhere!

This is a book on the history of the sword swallowers who have come before us, so you can learn their stories and know what they've done and what colorful lives they lived. They're also an inspiration to those of us who just love circus and sideshow history. When I set out to put it all together, I asked author, sideshow historian, and long-time friend Marc Hartzman to help. In addition to the research I'd accumulated, we've researched the stories further, polished details, connected the dots, and reached out to modern sword swallowers to include their personal anecdotes. If it weren't for all these amazing sword swallowers who risked their lives to entertain the audience, we wouldn't have stories at all. They need to be told. I hope you find them as fascinating as I do.

—Dan Meyer
President, Sword Swallowers Association International
Phoenix, Arizona, 2024

Sword swallowers often honor the memory of past performers by downing a blade at their grave. Franz Huber (page 137) and Dan Meyer swallow swords at the grave of Joe Jagger (page 111) at Garching an der Alz, Bavaria, Germany. *Collection of Dan Meyer*

Dan Meyer with sword swallower Jim Ball (page 95), son of sword swallowers John "Lucky" Ball (page 74) and Estelline Pike (page 89), holding one of Estelline's swords. *Collection of Dan Meyer*

A NON SWORD
SWALLOWER'S
INTRODUCTION

I have no intention of ever putting a sword down my throat. I don't even like the tongue depressor at the doctor's office. But I *am* fascinated by the art of sword swallowing. In fact, I've always been fascinated by what the body is capable of doing. I suppose that's where my interest in sideshow is rooted. Ever since childhood, when I first discovered the world's tallest man, Robert Wadlow, in the pages of the *Guinness Book of World Records*, I've been amazed by the different shapes and sizes the body could achieve. Sword swallowing falls into that same category. It defies belief. It shatters preconceptions of our own physical nature, no matter the shape or size, and showcases the abilities of sheer mental willpower. Sword swallowers do the impossible. They remind us that fear can be overcome and that we're all capable of more. And along the way, they entertain us in ways that have surprised, horrified, and delighted audiences for thousands of years.

It was a sword swallower who first got me writing about sideshow performers. His name was Johnny Fox. I met him at a small but wondrous museum he owned called the Freakatorium on New York City's Lower East Side. This place was packed with sideshow memorabilia: cabinet cards of nineteenth-century freaks, colorful posters portraying remarkable performers, armless wonder Charles Tripp's carving tools, a mummified cat, a two-headed calf, and so much more. I started asking Johnny questions about his collection, and as he shared stories with me, he pulled out a sword and swallowed it. Right there behind the counter. At the time, I was publishing a zine called *Backwash* and decided I wanted to interview Johnny for the next issue. I ended up selling a version of that interview to *Bizarre* magazine. After that, I started connecting with other members of the sideshow community, such as Melvin Burkhart, the Lizardman, Keith Nelson and Stephanie Monseau of the Bindlestiff Family Cirkus, and James Taylor from *Shocked and Amazed*. Between *Backwash* and *Bizarre*, I found myself getting to know the kinds of extraordinary people I'd always been so interested in. And I wanted to do something bigger. It all led to my second book, *American Sideshow: An Encyclopedia of History's Most Wondrous and Curiously Strange Performers*, in 2005.

My goal with that project was to create the kind of sideshow book I wanted to read—one with stories about the unique lives that sideshow performers lived and the triumphs they overcame, with plenty of photos. Many other works on the subject approached it from a sociological point of view. They were like textbooks. Sideshows were fun and exciting. The book should be too.

Several years after *American Sideshow*'s publication, I was hired by AOL Weird News to write sideshow-related articles. This was an opportunity to continue writing about people I'd met while working on my book, cover new and interesting feats they'd accomplished, and share stories about others within the sideshow community. Over the course of about two years, I wrote more than eighty articles. Among them was a story about a group building a new home for Ronnie and Donnie Galyon (the world's oldest conjoined twins), which helped raise money to complete the project. In another article, I covered the reunion of bearded lady Vivian Wheeler with her son who'd disappeared thirty-three years earlier. George McArthur (George the Giant) and I had helped bring them together. And of course, I had a chance to write about sword swallowing.

"Man Swallows Rocket-Powered Sword," published on April 4, 2010, featured Scott Nelson's daring feat that did exactly what the headline promised: he attached a rocket motor to the hilt of his sword and shot it straight down his throat, stopping it with his teeth and throat before it could go too far. "It's completely insane, I must admit," he told me during my interview for AOL. Sadly, Scott passed away during the writing of this book. Though he lived on the edge, it wasn't a sword that bested him. It was cancer. Writing about him on several occasions and eventually meeting him in person in Los Angeles was a thrill and an honor. Nelson, best known as Murrugun the Mystic, is undoubtedly swallowing steel and pushing skewers painlessly through his arms to find out if people in heaven get squeamish too.

Writing about World Sword Swallower's Day in February 2010 was another adventure. I had met Dan Meyer, who created the event, years earlier at the Sideshow Gathering in Wilkes-Barre, Pennsylvania, and reached out for an interview.[1] This guy wasn't just a sword swallower. He was an enthusiastic promoter and a true supporter of the art. Dan had organized the event with Ripley's Believe It or Not! museums around the world. I ventured into New York City, where I knew several of the participants at the Times Square location, including Johnny Fox, Todd Robbins, and Harley Newman. That year's event featured twenty-two sword swallowers.

By November 2010 I had a chance to write about Dan once again to cover a lecture he was giving at the Bruce Museum in Greenwich, Connecticut—about twenty minutes away from my home. An exhibit called *Circus! Art and Science under the Big Top* included swords and other pointy objects once swallowed by Edith Clifford—all on loan from Dan's personal collection. As part of his lecture, which, of course, was also a demonstration, he swallowed Clifford's hundred-year-old serrated saw. My headline: "Man Swallows 100-Year-Old Museum Exhibit." Not only was it a joy to cover the story, but I was able to bring my two young daughters and meet with Dan afterward. Once the audience cleared and we had time to talk, Dan even let my older daughter, who was all of six years old, pull a sword from his mouth. To this day, my younger daughter, who was nearing her third birthday, still wants her turn.

Months later, I flew out to Ball State University in Muncie, Indiana, to write another story for AOL Weird News about a show that Dan organized to raise money for ten local women planning to do mission work in Kigoma, Tanzania, in the summer of 2011. He called it "Swords for Africa," and in addition to his own sword-swallowing performance, he included acts from an armless man, Jim Goldman, and a legless man, Danny Frasier.

Goldman demonstrated his remarkable dexterity with his feet onstage by doing everything from brushing his teeth and using a circular saw to throwing knives and shooting a basketball (he made the shot). Again, all with his *feet*.

Frasier, who was born with fetal alcohol syndrome, had his malformed (and useless) legs amputated at age

three. "I'm not missing nothing," he told me. "I don't let nothing stop me or slow me down. I just keep a positive attitude." Frasier performed as the "World's Smallest Elvis," dressed in flashy garb as he sang and danced, mimicking Presley's moves. Both he and Goldman donated their time to the cause.

As with any sideshow performer who was born different, those differences disappear after about a minute of talking to them. Even while eating dinner across from Goldman, with his bare foot handling the cutlery.

That same year, I wrote about sword swallowers once again for *Bizarre*. This time the theme was extreme sword swallowing—as if the art wasn't extreme enough already. The article included Thrill Kill Jill gulping blades while pregnant (more on that on page 148), Aerial Manx of Australia performing cartwheels and other acrobatics with steel down his throat, and Murrugun's rocket-powered sword.

More recently, I had the incredible opportunity to pull a sword from Dan's throat at the Ripley's Believe It or Not! museum in Scottsdale, Arizona. It's something I now have in common with Chubby Checker, Elvira, Uri Geller, Sharon Osbourne, Danny Glover, and Carmen Elektra.

Any time I've met up with Dan or spoken to him, it's been an amazing and educational experience. What else would you expect from someone who's constantly hopping around the globe swallowing swords in seemingly every country for every TV show? In fact, as I'm writing this, he's in Germany preparing for an appearance on *Das SuperTalent*. Dan is an automatic conversation starter, and aside from his amazing feats and adventures, he's a truly nice guy. So, when he reached out to me more than six years ago about writing *To The Hilt* together, I was thrilled. We got started but quickly found ourselves wrapped up in other projects. For me, it was writing *The Big Book of Mars*, not to mention my day job. Several books followed that one. And Dan, well, he was busy globetrotting with a throatful of steel. Early in 2023, we reconnected about this project and kicked it into high gear. It's a book we both believe needed to be written. Dan had already been collecting information for more than twenty years on his website, swordswallow.com. Together, we've pulled additional details from countless old newspaper articles, magazines, books, ephemera, and, when possible, conversations with living sword swallowers, surviving family members, and other historians. This resulting volume is intended to serve as a resource for the sword-swallowing community's past, present, and future. Not to mention a book that anyone interested in the sideshow world or just mind-boggling human stories would enjoy.

---

1 I began this introduction by saying I would never swallow a sword, but at the 2010 Sideshow Gathering, I learned to perform the human blockhead act, thanks to Harley Newman. He gave me a plastic cocktail sword and carefully and succinctly explained what to do. And I did it. Then I did it again onstage with thirty-five others as part of a world record display of human blockheads. My headline for AOL Weird News? "Human Blockheads Nail World Record."

After writing books about Oliver Cromwell's embalmed head, Mars, ghosts, and UFOs since *American Sideshow*, working on *To the Hilt* has been like coming home. So, thank you for joining us. This book offers brief biographies of history's greatest and strangest sword swallowers dating back to the early nineteenth century and culminating in the late twentieth century. Though we've tried to cover all of them, such a feat is more difficult than swallowing steel (well, Dan may disagree). We've also included a section of stories—jackpots, to use the lingo—from many modern-day sword swallowers keeping the art alive. Now turn the page and meet these death-defying performers. They're all here on the inside, preserved for our continued entertainment and endless fascination.

—Marc Hartzman,
New Rochelle, New York, 2024

Above: Lela and Scarlett Hartzman with Dan Meyer at the Bruce Museum in Greenwich, Connecticut, November 2010

Right: Marc Hartzman with Dan Meyer at Ripley's Believe It Or Not! in Scottsdale, Arizona, February 2024

A DOCTOR'S WARNING
BY DR. BRIAN WITCOMBE, RADIOLOGIST

In the event that the only sentence you read is this one, I'd like to begin by saying do not flip through this book and try to swallow a sword. If you read on, do not take any of the anatomical descriptions below as an instruction guide. The phrase "Do not try this at home" has never been more serious. With that said, sword swallowing is unquestionably a medical marvel.

My initial interest in sword swallowing was provoked when a colleague sent me a copy of a chest x-ray showing a sword extending down from the mouth of a performer to the diaphragm. As a radiologist I noted that the upper part of the sword lay well forward of the spine, and it seemed as though the sword passed through the tongue. Clearly the tongue and tissues of the neck were shifted well forward in the neck. I was curious and wondered how often sword swallowers injured themselves, how often they were able to pass the sword down into the stomach, and how they learned the technique. A search of the English-language medical literature in 2005 revealed only three medical papers relating to sword swallowing.

One paper described a Texan who had injured himself and had his esophagus removed but survived. The other two papers were studies of a single sword swallower each, by an ear, nose, and throat surgeon. Computer search engines were not well developed at that time, so I was surprised to find an extraordinarily large number of relevant papers on Google even though several included obviously fabricated images.

Other stories described a Canadian who had died trying to swallow an umbrella, and another described a performer who had fallen off the stage with the sword in situ but survived unscathed. Following my research, I wrote a short article for the *British Medical Journal* titled "Sword Swallowing Uncertainties," which concluded, "There are at least two uncertainties. What is the incidence of complications and how often do they stomach it?"

While researching this article, I came into email contact with sword swallower Dan Meyer, who was very helpful and with whom I corresponded for some months. We ultimately worked together to produce the 2007 Ig Nobel Prize–winning paper "Sword Swallowing and Its Side Effects." Despite our research and the mainstream press coverage we received, there remains much doubt among the public that sword swallowing is possible. As a doctor, not a performer, I assure you it is. What follows is a medical explanation of how 2 feet of steel can find its way down the throat safely—and on occasion does not.

A sword swallower must meet both physiological and anatomical challenges. He or she must remain relaxed, so normal secretions of mucus and saliva, essential for lubricating the sword, do not dry up. Retching, sometimes provoked when the esophagus is probed, must be suppressed, as must the gag reflex, which we all have experienced in dental surgery when the palate is irritated. These reflexes cannot be eradicated but can be diminished through repeated practice and the development of a mind-over-matter approach. Protracted practice is also needed to deal with the anatomical difficulties.

Most swords are straight, but the 18 inches of bowel extending from the mouth to the stomach are certainly not. Upon being swallowed, food passes around a right angle from the horizontal surface of the tongue into the funnel-shaped, almost vertical pharynx. The pharynx tapers down to the entrance of the esophagus or swallow tube, where a ring of muscle, the upper esophageal sphincter (UES) or crico-pharyngeus muscle, must relax before food can pass on. The esophagus then sweeps around the back of the heart and down to the bottom of the chest, where it passes through the diaphragm and bends to the left before entering the stomach. A rigid implement can pass through these structures only because biological tissues are not fixed. The esophagus is movable and distensible although constrained by surrounding structures. When dissected free of these structures at surgery, it can accommodate a small orange, so the esophagus is like the expandable inner tube of a bicycle tire—albeit a delicate inner tube. Even so, the mucosa or lining membrane of the bowel is fragile, and bleeding is easily provoked, while a solid implement can readily perforate the bowel, particularly at certain critical sites. Deaths from sword swallowing are now rare, but they are well recorded before the development of antibiotics. This suggests that the main cause of death is infection as a complication of perforation of the bowel.

The first step for the would-be sword swallower is to learn to suppress the gag reflex by repeatedly passing a finger down the throat. This step can take many weeks or months of practice and is best not done in public, to avoid unwanted attention and misinterpretations. The next step is to learn to push a blunt instrument, such as a drumstick, paintbrush handle, or the blunt end of a knitting needle into the top of the pharynx. That blunt instrument must be aligned with the entrance to the esophagus. This entrance is kept shut by the UES when swallowing is not taking place, and it lies exactly in the midline. If a swallowed implement is not absolutely in the midline, it will impinge on the wall of the pharynx as it tapers to the entrance to the esophagus. In addition, the implement will certainly impinge on the back of the pharynx just above the UES unless the neck is fully extended, with the head thrust right back. The muscles of the pharynx, the so-called constrictor muscles, run obliquely downward from the midline at the back of the pharynx. Where these muscles meet the horizontal UES, there is a potential triangular muscular deficiency called Killian's dehiscence. Studies involving postmortem dissections indicate that this defect is present in over a third of the population and is more common in men than women. Some medical patients suffer from a pharyngeal or Zenker's diverticulum, where the mucosa billows through this defect and forms a pouch. Small food items such as peas or tablets can lodge here, to be regurgitated later, and a pharyngeal diverticulum can slowly enlarge with time, sometimes up to the size of a tennis ball if surgical treatment is not undertaken. It is unfortunate that this potential muscular defect lies at the exact site where a straight implement will impinge if not inserted in the correct vertical fashion with the neck maximally extended. Unsurprisingly, there is an increased propensity for perforation at Killian's dehiscence.

The movement of the sword from the back of the tongue to the upper esophagus needs to be carried out as one smooth, coordinated action. The sword is introduced to the back of the tongue, the head is thrust back with the neck extended, and the hilt of the sword is elevated at the same time. The tip of the sword then acts like a tongue depressor pushing the tongue, the glottis, and adjacent tissues downward and forward. The sword is then vertical and can be advanced past the entrance to the trachea (windpipe) and its covering epiglottis to the esophagus. A swallow initiated at this moment will relax the UES so the sword can enter the upper esophagus. Movement down the esophagus is then more straightforward, even though the sword is passing down between the lungs and through the ring of major blood vessels formed by the aorta and its branches and the pulmonary veins. Some swallowers perform "the drop," where they just let the sword fall under its own weight. After nudging the heart slightly forward, the sword then falls to the lower esophageal sphincter, where the esophagus bends to the left just before the blade reaches the entrance to the stomach. The angle of this bend varies from one individual to another. Particularly in slim individuals, the angle is gradual, and the sword can displace the right esophageal wall farther to the right so it can pass on into the stomach. The angle is more acute in others, particularly in shorter stocky people. Indeed, in some individuals there is even a frank chicane here, and in many people the angle is too great for the sword to pass farther. Although in many sword swallowers the sword will go no farther than the lower esophagus, in others it can pass through the lower esophageal sphincter, behind the liver. It then passes down to finally lie against the lower wall of the stomach.

All of the above is well and good, but things don't always go well or good. Injuries are far too common and vary from the trivial to the life threatening. Friction between the sword and the lining of the throat commonly causes "sword throats." Friction can also occasionally lead to mucosal damage when there is difficulty in withdrawing the sword if secretions dry up because of nervous apprehension, particularly in a hot, dry environment. If more than one sword is swallowed at the same time, scissoring injuries can occur where the swords nip the mucosa, and this has led to severe hemorrhage. The point of the sword can impinge at certain sites, causing ulceration or even perforation. Common sites for these injuries are, first, the sidewall of the pharynx if the sword is not inserted absolutely in the midline, and, second, if the neck is not extended sufficiently, the sword will impinge on the posterior wall of the pharynx at the site of Killian's dehiscence. There may be an absence of a muscle layer here, so the mucosa is easily punctured at this site.

A sword will inevitably come into contact with the right side of the lower esophagus where the esophagus bends to the left at the level of the diaphragm. This is a known site of trauma and perforation. For those who can get the sword past this bend and farther down into the stomach, the sword will easily impinge on the lower gastric wall, and this is a reported site of ulceration secondary to sword swallowing.

I have been told that there are two sword swallowers in the hospital at the time of this writing. I believe that one woman was admitted to the hospital with a collapsed lung, and the other swallower punctured his lung last year. It is said that part of his lung had to be removed following the injury, and that his injury was associated with a protracted period of coma.

In short, a slight mishap in sword swallowing can send you to the emergency room and potentially kill you. Which brings me back to my first comment: Do not attempt to swallow a sword. Leave it to the professionals and offer them the praise and admiration their skill deserves.

As for me, almost two decades later I am still asked about my paper with Dan and get invited every few months to speak to local groups about sword swallowing. I'm now in my ninth decade, and it continues to provide me with a lot of entertaining social contact. At its core, isn't that exactly the point of sword swallowing?

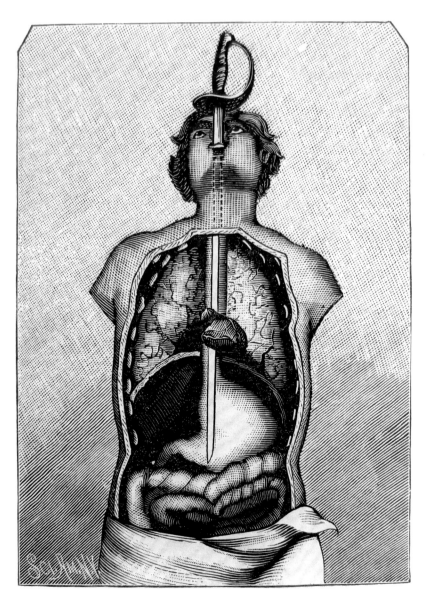

Position of the sword in the body. This image has been in use since the late 1800s. *Collection of Marc Hartzman*

A BRIEF
HISTORY OF
SWORD
SWALLOWING

Sword swallowing is absolutely real. Of that, there is no question. As for its history, well, that is a little less certain. No one knows who first decided it would be a good idea to put a long piece of steel down their throat. Or how many people tried it before one of them succeeded.

It's often said that sword swallowing dates back four thousand years to ancient India. Generations of sword swallowers have talked about fakirs and shaman priests swallowing blades as a demonstration of their invulnerability, power, and connection with their gods. But is the art of sword swallowing that old? It made an appealing story to late-nineteenth-century Americans who were aware of India but knew little of it. To them, it was a far-off exotic place where perhaps wondrous things were quite possible. Evidence indeed points to Indian fakirs swallowing swords for at least a few hundred years.

"If we look at some places like developing America, with circuses traveling around, and the only exposure you got to the farther reaches of the world was when the sideshow in the circus came to town once a year," says sideshow performer and historian Harley Newman, "you might travel 10 miles just to see the show. Those dreams of faraway places became the reality of your greater world."

Let's look back through time and trace steel's journey from being forged to being swallowed. Metallurgy goes back about five thousand years to the Bronze Age, and swords as we know them evolved from daggers by around 1600 BCE. So, it's possible that India's fakirs and shamans were showcasing their seemingly superhuman skills since then, along with snake handling and walking on hot coals to win respect and the subservience of others. But this cannot be confirmed.

Over the centuries, as metallurgy developed across continents, so did sword swallowing. Swords were, in a manner of speaking, being swallowed at least a couple of thousand years ago by Roman gladiators. But these types of performers did it only once. If a gladiator had fought valiantly but had received what were considered deadly wounds, it was an honor to use their sword to shove it down their throat for a clean, quick death. So, it wasn't exactly the type of performance we think of with modern-day sword swallowing, but technically, a sword was indeed swallowed.

An ancient reference to sword swallowing as less morbid entertainment was made by Roman writer and philosopher Apuleius in *Metamorphoses*. The novel, also known as *The Golden Ass*, was written in Latin in the late second century and first translated to English in 1566. No other ancient Roman novel in Latin is known to have survived in its entirety. In Book 1, the narrator shares a story of a sword swallower with two travelers on his way to Thessaly. "At Athens, not long ago, in front of the Painted Porch, I saw a juggler swallow a sharp-edged cavalry sword with its lethal blade, and later I saw the same fellow, after a little donation, ingest a spear, death-dealing end downwards, right to the depth of his guts: and all of a sudden a beautiful boy swarmed up the wooden bit of the upside-down weapon, where it rose from throat to brow, and danced a dance, all twists and turns, as if he'd no muscle or spine, astounding everyone there."

A Chinese sword swallower and a fellow entertainer swinging a rope with cast-metal weights attached to it. Painting by a Chinese artist, ca. 1850. *Wellcome Collection*

As early as the eighth century, sword swallowing was popular in the Japanese acrobatic form of street theater entertainment known as Sangaku. It also featured juggling, tightrope walking, contortion, and more.

Elsewhere around the world, sword swallowing was being performed as a cultural practice. A southwestern Native American medicine dance of the Pueblo's Beer-ahn tribe involved the swallowing of 18-inch swords to the hilt by nearly naked performers. With sharp-edged, pointy blades, successful swallows must have given people confidence in the medicine men's abilities.

A Navajo medicine dance known as Dsil-yíd-je Quacal during the "Nine Days' Dance" involved the swallowing of "great plumed arrows"—also by mostly nude performers. Once withdrawn, the arrows would be pressed to the knees, hands, stomach, or other ailing body parts of patients in need.

A South American tribe in the Orinoco River area, called the Warao, have shamans who have traditionally swallowed hollow reeds. One of their rituals involves hallucinogens, which are induced by pouring concentrated tobacco down the tube into the stomach. Of course, they had to use just enough to hallucinate, and not too much to become fatal.

By the Middle Ages, when gentlemen started carrying swords, the art began spreading as entertainment in parts of Europe. In seventeenth-century Turkey, for example, sword swallowers performed alongside fire eaters, acrobats, and other skilled entertainers for the sultan. However, not all places were welcoming of such physical feats. Jugglers who performed magic in England were often persecuted as witches—which may have prevented the spread of sword swallowing into western Europe. In the early 1800s, however, an Indian performer named Ramo Samee brought his daring and dangerous skills to England and fascinated all-new audiences. He received much applause—and no accusations of witchcraft.

That brings us to where this book begins. The short biographies and stories that follow start with Samee's steel and lead straight to today's new generation of sword swallowers, who are keeping the art alive and well. *Alive*, of course, being the key word.

A sword swallower as depicted in the 1901 edition of *Magic: Stage Illusions and Scientific Diversions Including Trick Photography*, by Albert A. Hopkins. *Collection of Marc Hartzman*

THE SWORD
SWALLOWERS

"Now, ladies and gentlemen, you are about to see something truly amazing, something you'll find incredible and hard to believe. Something you've probably never seen before in person. Something you may never again see in your lifetime. Something you'll want to tell your friends, neighbors, and grandchildren about for years to come. Yes, something you will never, ever forget. Yes, ladies and gentlemen, the show you're about to see is so strange, so extreme, so dangerous, so shocking, and so bizarre, that there are very few people left in the world performing this deadly feat today. And you may never see anything like this again. One of the last few remaining sword swallowers left in the world today. Yes, ladies and gentlemen, he really does swallow solid-steel swords, blades, sabers, bayonets, and other long, sharp, and pointed objects for your entertainment pleasure."

This bally was given by legendary sideshow impresario Ward Hall as he introduced Dan Meyer early in his sword-swallowing career. Hall's own career began as a teenager in the 1940s, when he left home to join the circus. He never turned back. Hall stayed in the sideshow world until his death in 2018 and exhibited many sword swallowers along the way. His words above ring true for every sword swallower who follows. So, step inside and let the show begin.

RAMO SAMEE
1791–1850

In the early 1810s, Ramo Samee performed a trick he called "Stringing Beads with the Mouth," in which he allegedly swallowed a handful of beads and a length of horsehair, then did exactly what the stunt's name claimed: he pulled the beads from his mouth, one at a time, tied to the hair.

Samee was born in 1791 in India and as a young man quickly became a skilled entertainer capable of various extraordinary acts. In 1814, he and other similarly talented Indian magicians were brought to England to showcase their talents. One of Samee's was the ability to swallow a sword. England had never seen anything like it. As one London advertisement announced, "The sword is then put down the throat, with as much ease as though it were being sheathed in its scabbard; the sword is afterwards drawn up and presented to the Company."

The troupe performed acrobatics, juggling, conjuring, yogic poses, sleight of hand, and more. Samee was known to close his act by swallowing a flaming sword. As magician John Mulholland wrote in 1932's *Quicker Than the Eye*, "It took almost as much courage to watch tricks in those days as to do them."

Adding even more audacity into the mix, one of Samee's partners, Kia Khan Khruse, expanded on the bead trick with a more dangerous version by replacing the beads with

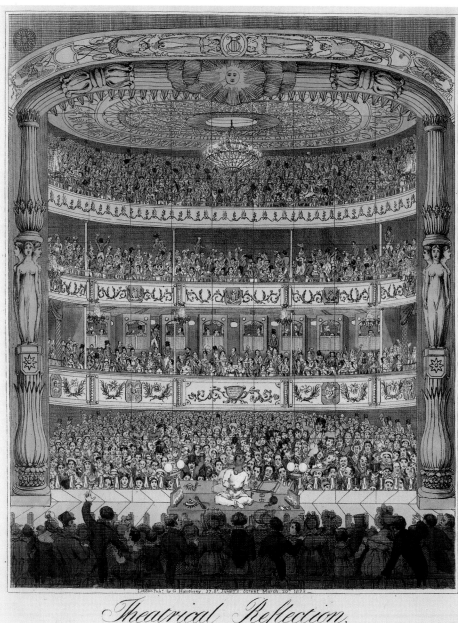

Theatrical Reflection.
or a Peep at the Looking Glass Curtain at the Royal Coburg Theatre.

Hand-colored etching of Ramo Samee at the Royal Coburg Theatre in London, 1822. *Public domain, via Wikimedia Commons*

needles. He first introduced the "Needle Swallowing Trick" to European audiences in 1818. Samee, not one to be outdone, mastered the same stunt with a hundred needles.

His performances in London, throughout England, and before numerous crowned heads of Europe earned him many fans. Perhaps the most famous was a young Charles Dickens, who mentioned his name in an 1854 issue of *Household Words*. Dickens's article, "An Unsettled Neighborhood," mentions a character who was "always lurking in the coal department, practising Ramo Samee with three potatoes." Perhaps Dickens had seen his act at London's Victoria Theatre, but in 1838 the two were actually on the same playbill in Hull, an English city about 200 miles north of London. That winter, the Hull Theatre Royal staged Dickens's novel *Nicholas Nickleby*. Samee's troupe followed the play. Dickens, perhaps inspired by his performance, began practicing magic and started performing in the early 1840s. By 1849, the renowned author was calling himself "The Unparalleled Necromancer, Rhia Rhama Rhoos." The name is clearly reminiscent of Samee's fellow performer, Kia Khan Khruse.

Samee's success onstage was eventually met with tragedy when his son, George, attempted to follow in his footsteps. In 1849, after spending months practicing sword swallowing, George attempted to demonstrate his new skill to friends at a tavern in London. When he met resistance in his esophagus, he pushed the blade through and penetrated himself. He was taken to a hospital, but the resulting inflammation proved fatal.

A year later, Samee passed away in poverty at age fifty-nine. According to an obituary, "His health had received a severe shock at the death of his only son."

SENA SAMA
DATES UNKNOWN

Sena Sama, from Madras, Tamil Nadu, India, was reported to be the first known sword swallower in America. The historic event took place at St. John's Hall in New York City in November 1817. Newspaper accounts claim that he swallowed "a sword manufactured by Mr. William Pyle of New York as a substitute for the one lately stolen from him by some villain." Fortunately, that villain didn't prevent the introduction of sword swallowing to an awestruck nation.

In addition to New York, Sama performed in Philadelphia, Baltimore, Washington, DC, and other cities along the East Coast and in the South. He was known to perform various other "feats of dexterity" as well, including magic, the swinging of a stone suspended

> **For a few Nights only!**
> AT THE COURT HOUSE, BATON-ROUGE.
> ## SENA SAMA,
> From Madras, (East Indies) late from London, and lately from New-York, Philadelphia, Baltimore and city of Washington, generally called
> *The Wonder of the World!*
> Respectfully informs the Ladies and Gentlemen of Baton-Rouge and its vicinity, that he will
> **This Evening, Saturday the 17th inst.**
> give an exhibition of his truly astonishing experiments : viz :
> ### MR. SENA SAMA,
> Will introduce the Cups and Balls, —The Top,—Brass Rings,—Chinese Castle,—a 12 lb. Stone, which he will raise by his feet and throw backwards, then make it alight on any part of his body,—and a 25 lb. Stone which he will suspend by a hook fastened in his nose and mouth, and swing it in the air to the utter astonishment of the spectators.
> *AND MANY OTHER TRICKS TOO TEDIOUS TO BE ENUMERATED.*
> The whole to be concluded by the experiment of the
> ### NEW SWORD,
> 22 inches in length, which will be introduced for the inspection of the audience ; after which, Mr. Sena Sama pledges himself to thrust it down his throat the whole length.
> N. B. Tickets, One Dollar—Children under 12 years of age, Half-price. Doors open at Six, Performance to commence at Seven.
> april 17.

Advertisement for Sena Sama's show in Baton Rouge, Louisiana, April 17, 1819. *Public domain*

by a hook fastened to his nose, and an ability to walk on water "without sinking his feet three inches below the surface of the water."

A March 1819 performance in Mississippi featured Sama alongside a magician named Mr. Humbert. According to a promotional ad, the prestidigitator made a volunteer's ring appear inside an orange, presented "enchanted seeds," and performed "many other tricks too tedious to be enumerated." The entire show was capped by Sama's grand finale:

The experiment of the SWORD,
22 inches in length, which will be introduced for
the inspection of the audience;
after which Mr. Sena Sama, pledges himself
to thrust it down his throat the whole length.

Through his American travels, Sama's remarkable skill caused a sensation primarily through word of mouth. As one Alexandria, Virginia, reporter commented, he wasn't well versed in the art of puffery and promotion and "had yet to learn that, *in this country*, a bladder of wind outweighs a globe of gold," since "no pompous bills were posted at the corners of our streets." As a result, his initial audiences didn't have high expectations for what they were about to see, but they soon fell in love with his "wonderful talents, astonishing muscular powers, and unparalleled activity."

Having built his reputation and having earned the respect of audiences and colleagues, Sama and a fellow entertainer, Hamed Ben-Alla, published a seventy-one-page booklet on magic in 1833, titled *The Whole Art of Legerdemain or Hocus Pocus Laid Open and Explained.*

JACQUES DE FALAISE
1754–1825

Jacques de Falaise swallowed swords, but he didn't consider himself a sword swallower. He was more of an everything swallower. Born in 1754, Falaise didn't develop his talent until he was sixty-two, after more than thirty years of working in a Parisian quarry. During dinner one evening at a local inn, his coworkers witnessed him down large volumes of a beverage at an unusually fast rate. One of them jokingly challenged him to swallow a live canary perched in a cage nearby.

JACQUES DE FALAISE.

Jacques de Falaise swallows a sword while clutching a mouse in one hand, an eel in the other, a bird watching from his shoulder—and hoping it's not next. Wood engraving, ca. 1816. *Public domain, via Wikimedia Commons*

Despite the protestations of the bird's owner, Falaise gulped it down— feathers and all—and surprised himself with the ease in which he managed it. His astonished pals spread the word of his exploits, and a truly unusual career was born.

Falaise seized opportunity in 1816 when Louis Comte, famed magician and manager of a Parisian theater, got word of Falaise's unique ability and signed him to a five-year deal for four hundred francs a year. A trio of Indian jugglers had just finished a run at the venue and amazed crowds with their sword-swallowing routine. Falaise would one-up their act and then some. All he had to do was "swallow in public everything that was given to him." That included birds, whole potatoes, walnuts, hard-boiled eggs, flowers, money, frogs, crabs, eels, snakes, and, of course, swords.

Falaise was known to swallow 13 to 14 inches of an 18-inch polished-steel blade, 1 inch in width. According to a witness account, he did this "without showing the slightest sign of suffering."

Since the blades were immediately extracted, they were an anomaly in his swallowing repertoire. However, an eel once tried to emulate the sword and immediately extract itself. As the *London Medical Repository and Review* in 1826 described, the eel "disapproved exceedingly of the unceremonious disposal of him" and "found his way back up the esophagus, whilst poor Jacques was on the stage." Falaise reportedly crushed it with his teeth and swallowed it again.

He surely preferred earning his money by swallowing other people's money. Any coins that hit the bottom of his stomach were his to keep. He just had to pass them through his system and wipe them off (one would hope).

After several years of polyphagia, he developed gastroenteritis and was hospitalized for three months. Upon his release, he promptly returned to the stage and soon was stricken with an even-worse infection. Heeding the advice of his doctors, he quit the swallowing-anything business. Though he had recovered his strength, he grew depressed. After a night of drinking in 1825, Jacques de Falaise hanged himself.

An autopsy showed nothing particularly notable about his physical condition, although the opening to his small intestine, the pyloric orifice, was of an unusual size. According to the *London Medical* article, however, "the colon and rectum presented nothing remarkable."

Advertisement for a Moses Berg performance. *Leavenworth Times*, September 28, 1878. *Public domain*

MOSES BERG
1829–84

Many sword swallowers throughout history mastered other stunts to bolster their repertoire, such as fire eating and the human blockhead (which allowed them to shove pointy objects into another orifice). In the case of Moses Berg, his most prominent additional skill was rope walking. And he did it with one leg.

Berg, who was reportedly born in Prussia in 1829, performed in a German circus for thirteen years. It was here that he learned his acrobatic skills before immigrating to the United States and settling in Texas, where he married and fathered six children.

By 1862, Berg found himself in the middle of the Civil War. Having joined the cavalry, he soon suffered his first wound when a saber sliced open his face and knocked out several teeth. But he fought on, until he was stabbed by a bayonet. Berg received medical treatment and soon after rejoined the military and battled in Middleburgh, Tennessee. On December 24 of that year, a gunshot struck his leg, and the limb had to be amputated. One newspaper claimed he'd suffered a total of thirty-four injuries and retained eleven bullets in his body. Whether this was an exaggeration or not, after losing his leg his fighting days were over.

Berg returned home to his family in Texas, whom he'd now have to support with one leg. According to an April 21, 1873, article in New York's *Evening Telegram,* Berg went back to his roots as a means to earn money. "It occurred to him that he might utilize his gymnastic knowledge, and he adopted the tight rope—a slender means by which to support himself and family," the paper wrote.

Armed with a wooden leg, Berg walked tightropes and slack ropes across the country. A notch at the bottom of the prosthesis helped him achieve his remarkable feats as the world's only one-legged rope walker.

"He has been eminently successful," the *Evening Telegram* added, "and it is said by those who have seen his performance that notwithstanding he is encumbered by an awkward wooden leg he is as agile as a cat and has no superior in his line."

Berg, who became known as "The Great Professor Berg," "Joseph Berg," and, at other times, "Professor DeHoune," began his shows with a variety of stunts. He swallowed swords, performed sleight-of-hand magic, and even showcased feats of strength, such as waltzing with a table clutched in his teeth. At times, his wife joined the act as a singer.

When it came time to walk the rope, the Professor raised the stakes by strapping an oven to his back as he began his high-stakes march. The oven, of course, was for cooking. High atop the middle of the rope, he stopped, placed the oven in front of him, and made pancakes to serve the crowd.

It would seem that sword swallowing was one of the safest parts of the act. Indeed, the risks of walking the rope eventually caught up with him. In 1869, he suffered a serious fall in Indiana, though no specific details were reported. Just two years later, Berg dropped again after the rope broke during an exhibition. His nearly 100-foot fall to the ground snapped his one leg in two places and badly injured his one and only head. According to a local report, he refused payment for the show, "saying he had not walked the rope yet."

Not one to let a few little injuries get him down, Berg recovered and continued his daredevil career. An article within a year and a half of the accident demonstrates that he made another triumphant return with a performance in New Orleans, where he crossed a rope between Carondolet and Baronne Streets.

However, peril would catch up with him one last time in March 1883, in the small town of Corsicana, Texas. There, a large crowd gathered on the dusty streets to gaze at the stuntman perched 20 feet up on a rope stretching across two rooftops. As usual, his stove was strapped to his back. He was ready to feed his audience a steady diet of danger and flapjacks. But the seemingly indestructible Berg finally met his match when, once again, the rope broke. This time he didn't get away with just another broken limb. The stove crushed his back.

Berg didn't die instantly though. He was too tough for that. He hung on just long enough to have his remaining leg amputated. And to let hospital officials know he was Jewish and needed a rabbi to offer a final prayer.

Oddly, the dying daredevil wouldn't answer any questions about his name or surviving family. Clearly, his wife had not accompanied him on this particular tour. Berg was laid to rest in the Corsicana Hebrew Cemetery with a headstone that merely read "Rope Walker."

For more than a century the enigmatic "Rope Walker" puzzled local residents, including Babbette Samuels. Samuels, who was ninety years old when we interviewed her in 2018, served as the curator of the cemetery and claimed that people had inquired about the performer since she and her husband moved to town in 1951.

In 2004, after vandals knocked the original headstone over, Samuels replaced it with a new one. "I did it for the preservation of history," she said. "Everybody should have a place, and it should be marked to show they lived in this world."

Just over a decade later, the story of just how the Rope Walker lived in this world came to light, thanks to new clues found in digitized newspapers and a curious genealogist, Jim Yarin, who dug into them. He unraveled the mystery in a series of articles in the *Corsicana Daily Sun* that connects the stories of Berg/DeHoune reported in various papers to the tragedy in 1883. His efforts restored the Professor's legacy and finally gave his headstone an identity.

Somewhere high above, Berg is smiling down on an amazed audience, just as he did for so many years.

JAMES ERWIN
1848–85

James Erwin was born in Dublin, Ireland, on May 15, 1848, and his life took a quick turn when he immigrated to America as an infant. Around the age of seventeen, he ventured into the world of the circus and learned the art of sword swallowing. After fighting in the Civil War (clearly underage), he was fortunate to still have a throat to push swords into.

During his time on the battlefield, Erwin had been sentenced to be shot for desertion on two occasions. The first time, being a mere boy, he was granted a pardon by President Lincoln himself. The second time, he displayed incredible courage and managed to escape, defying the grim fate that awaited him.

Erwin continued his career in show business by becoming an operator and manager of his own sideshow. As the years went on, he added sharpshooting to his arsenal of skills and gained a reputation as one of the finest marksmen in Indiana.

Tragically, at the age of thirty-seven on January 3, 1885, James Erwin succumbed to pneumonia in Indianapolis.

WILLIAM HENRY TURNER
1845–1941

Little is known about William Henry Turner's sword-swallowing exploits, though it's safe to assume the one-armed Civil War veteran lost his limb in battle, not during a performance gone awry.

Born on February 20, 1845, in upstate New York, Turner served in the Union army with the 2nd Connecticut Heavy Artillery. Sometime along the way, he learned sword swallowing, which he parlayed into a brief career as a circus performer. He later purchased the rights to a medical treatment and worked as a medicine man (though not to soothe sore throats). Turner's miraculous remedy contained a mix of dry herbs and water and allegedly cured sciatica, rheumatism, kidney problems, and cancer.

The sword-swallowing snake-oil salesman eventually settled in Lebanon, Missouri, where he was an active member of the Grand Army of the Republic and was elected as a justice of the peace.

According to a newspaper article, he once swallowed a blade at a political meeting to entertain the crowd. Like many sword swallowers, he was challenged by someone in the audience who didn't believe the stunt was real. Angered, Turner proceeded to offer undeniable proof. "He gulped a cheese sandwich, swallowed it, and talked to the man for a few minutes, then again put the sword down his throat and brought forth a piece of the cheese sandwich," the journalist said. "This satisfied the person."

On July 1, 1938, Turner demonstrated his skills again at the seventy-fifth anniversary of the Battle of Gettysburg for a friendlier crowd of old friends. At ninety-three, he was surely among the oldest.

Not only was Turner still swallowing swords at such an advanced age, but he was still serving as a judge and claimed to have no plans to retire until reaching his one hundredth birthday. Sadly, he didn't quite make it. Turner passed away peacefully on June 8, 1941, at his home in Missouri.

In 1938, William Turner swallowed a sword among friends at an event commemorating the seventy-fifth anniversary of the Battle of Gettysburg. *Collection of Dan Meyer*

MEDICINE HAS SWORD SWALLOWERS TO THANK

Dr. Adolf Kussmaul of Germany was a leading physician and surgeon in the mid-nineteenth century. One of his great achievements is owed to the help of a sword swallower.

It began with a German sword swallower known as *Der eiserne Heinrich*—the "Iron Henry"—and a Dr. Keller who happened to be watching his performance in 1868 in the town of Freiburg. Fascinated by the physical feat, Keller approached the sword swallower afterward and convinced him to visit his clinic for a throat examination. Keller's colleague, Dr. Julius Müller, suggested that Iron Henry might make an ideal subject for his professor's esophagoscopy studies. Again, the sword swallower agreed to help.

Müller's professor was Dr. Kussmaul, who was looking to develop a device that could help observe the upper gastrointestinal tract. A few years earlier, a French doctor created the world's first endoscope used to diagnose urethral and bladder ailments. That device had no chance of reaching the esophagus—nor would anyone want it to. Kussmaul welcomed the sword swallower's visit and enthusiastically observed his technique closely. He then had a local musical-instrument maker craft rigid tubes 18.5 inches in length and 0.5 inch wide. A gas lamp light source reflected visuals through mirrors to give him a view of the esophagus and stomach. The event marked the first successful esophagoscopy on a sword swallower.

Kussmaul then took the show on the road with a demonstration at the Society of Naturalists in Freiburg. The Iron Henry calmly sat with the tube down his throat, but the lighting was lacking and inhibited the visibility.

The surgeon's work was soon improved upon and has evolved today into endoscopes using thin, flexible fiber optic technology.

While Kussmaul was officially the first to succeed in experimenting with a sword swallower, twenty years earlier a Scottish doctor had the same idea. Unfortunately for him, his local sword swallower was less cooperative and refused to work with the doctor's rudimentary instrument.

In recent years, German sword swallower Franz Huber has attended medical conventions to pay homage to the Iron Henry by gulping new endoscopes from the same Freiburg company that produced them in Kussmaul's era.

LING LOOK
1841?–1878?

Like those of any performer today, acts in the nineteenth century always looked for a way to stand out. Some found their competitive edge by portraying themselves as exotic—as in someone from the mysterious Far East, where amazing things seemed possible because little was known about it. Chung Ling Soo the great magician, for example, was actually William Ellsworth Robinson from New York. Che-Mah, the celebrated Chinese dwarf, was said to be Jewish and from London. And Ling Look, the Chinese sword swallower, was born in Budapest as David Gueter (or Guder).

To create his look, Ling Look shaved the front of his head and wore the rest of his hair in a long braid to emulate Chinese stylings. The earliest records of his performances

come from Marseilles in 1868, when he daringly attached a rifle to his sword and pulled the trigger with the blade down his throat. It proved as dangerous as it sounds.

"Having failed to seize the sword between his teeth, to guard against the recoil of the rifle, the latter kicked and forced the sword into the coat of his convenient stomach," one newspaper reported. "He fell down a prey to dreadful internal sufferings, when some doctors who were present rushed upon the stage and drew the Celestial's sword from its lugubrious sheath."

Look survived and continued to gulp swords and eat fire. Though, as is the case with all sword swallowers, many doubted the stunt's authenticity—despite having had a rifle shoot a blade down his throat. So, in 1869, he allowed a French physician to examine the process. The physician, Dr. Fournie, witnessed Look swallow a 3-foot-long saber and traced the point down to his pelvic region.

Look followed the blade with an egg—swallowing it whole, puffing a cigarette, and bringing the egg back up. Dr. Fournie, though "thoroughly satisfied with the honesty" of the sword swallowing, questioned the egg regurgitation. So, he had him swallow it again so he could take a closer look. The doctor "produced a larynscope, and directed a powerful beam of magnesium light down the patient's throat, when sure enough, the egg was discovered in a cavity or nest, which Ling Look had habituated himself by long practice to form below the tongue, in the laryngean region."

Back onstage, Ling Look continued to both dazzle and disgust audiences. After an 1872 performance, one reporter described the act as such: "He gorged his blade, last night, with such an appetite as might have smitten the African ostrich with envy, and with such ensuing satisfaction as quite shook our faith in the scriptural announcement that whoso taketh the sword shall perish by the sword. How much sword he took we are not prepared to state; but he did not perish."

A year later, another reporter was less enamored with the daredevil's skills: "He produced a nasty, long sword, that looked longer than he was; measured it on the outside of him; proceeded to grease it and then deliberately opened his mouth, threw back his head, and jammed it down his gullet. He hammered it down with a stone, past his aesophagus, past his larynx, past his throat, through his diaphragm filter, and the horrid wretch never flinched. Report and the programme say a pistol was fired from the handle. I never lived to see it. I arose, a deathly parlor [sic] seated on my brow. I made a motion as if to embrace the big riddle and I don't remember any more. I was got out some way, and if any sword swallower is ever going to be hung [sic], Judge Dowling and I are going to witness the spectacle with thanksgiving and praise."

Love him or hate him, Ling Look was becoming a star. He was soon joined by his brother, Louis, who also adopted

This beautiful 1883 poster appears to be promoting an imposter, since Ling Look had died several years earlier. *Public domain, via Wikimedia Commons*

an Asian persona with a memorable name, Yamadeva. His escapist and contortion acts earned him the moniker the Man Serpent. In May 1876, the duo joined forces with young magicians Harry Kellar and J. H. Cunard to form a group called the Royal Illusionists.

The troupe embarked on a world tour, starting in America before heading overseas. In addition to Look's sword swallowing and Yamadeva's rubbery ways, Kellar dazzled audiences with a trick called "The Flying Cage" in which a bird cage and the canary inside disappeared right before the audience. He

and Cunard also mystified crowds with manifestations in a stunt called "The Spirit Cabinet," which capitalized on the popular Spiritualism movement at the time.

Their world travels, however, were cut short after tragedy struck just as they were about to leave Shanghai for Hong Kong. In a game of bowling, Yamadeva grabbed a ball heavier than he could handle and bowled it as hard as he was able. An account from Harry Houdini says, "He had misjudged his own strength, and he paid for the foolhardy act with his life, for he had no sooner delivered the

ball than he grasped his side and moaned with pain." Yamadeva had ruptured an artery and died shortly after the game. The Royal Illusionists took the body to Hong Kong. Look was distraught at his brother's passing and told Kellar, "I shall never leave Hong Kong alive. My brother has called me to join him." Sure enough, Look was right. Just a few months later, the sword swallower suffered complications in his liver and had to undergo a surgical procedure. It was not successful.

According to Kellar's 1886 book, *A Magician's Tour*, Look died in December 1877. His headstone in Hong Kong, however, gives April 1878 as his date of death. History leaves his passing in confusion. But then, people were confused right afterward too. Shortly after his death, another Ling Look surfaced in England. Fans and friends were greatly relieved to learn the performer was alive. His likeness and act were so similar that he fooled everyone who saw his show. He nearly fooled Kellar, who had buried the sword swallower himself.

The magician recalled the story in a letter:

I came all the way from Scotland to see the man calling himself Ling Look, now performing in this city, *only to find him an impostor*. I had corresponded with this man for some days, and his letters deceived me and led me to believe that he was actually my old companion. He certainly knows all of Ling Look's past life, and must have been in constant correspondence with him while we were making our tour through China and Australia. I introduced myself to this man as a friend of Kellar, and questioned him on our route, etc., and he gave me satisfactory answers, until I asked him about what month we arrived at Hong Kong, when he told me April. Now, we were there in October. He also stated that the name of the hotel at which we stayed was the Victoria, whereas it was the Hong Kong Hotel at which we stayed (there being no Victoria Hotel). I asked him if he would know Kellar, and he replied, "Do you think I am an impostor?" I said, "Yes." I then told him, "I am Kellar," when he immediately took his hat and left the room.

The impostor eventually confessed he was a younger brother of the real Look but continued performing under his brother's stage name. In 1882, during a show at the Oxford Music Hall in England, he damaged that respected name

while swallowing a blade with a gun attached to it. His wife fired the weapon, and a young boy was hit and killed. According to an article, "The wadding in the gun struck [George] Smythe, who was sitting in the gallery, in the head, and shattered his skull." The wannabe Look was charged with manslaughter but was acquitted.

Skilled as the impostor was, he proved he was no Ling Look.

JOE RILEY
1866–?

Joe Riley was born as Joseph R. Fleming around 1866 in Hillburn, New York, where he lived most of his life except for when he was on the road performing with his own show or in vaudeville. Riley's first career with a pointy object was as a pencil artist. He added the sword to his repertoire by 1898, when he swallowed onstage for the first time.

According to his pitch card, he was known as the "Sensational Sword Swallower," and his act was described as "presenting a realistic and thrilling scientific exhibition in the art of 'Swallowing of the Swords,' also carving-knives, daggers, shears, saws, cimeters [*sic*], curved swords, bayonets and other allied props and various other articles of steel without any deception at all."

The May 20, 1905, *New York Clipper* "Directory of Show People" states that "Joe Riley is with the Andrew Downie Circus, doing his sword swallowing act in the side show, also his Irish specialty and rapid picture drawing act in the concert. He reports success, also that the show is doing a very nice business, despite the past recent cold and rainy weather."

At the end of 1906, *Billboard* reported that Riley would be performing comedy and sword swallowing in a vaudeville show that also featured singers, a trapeze artist, an equilibrist, and a conjurer.

Riley's performing career ended in 1914 during World War I, when his eyesight began to fail. A 1929 article reported he, at age sixty-three, was living in Ramapo, New York, where he had gone totally blind, but had learned Braille and learned how to walk with a white cane. Presumably, he made no attempts to swallow it. It is not known exactly when he died.

Late-nineteenth-century sword swallowers displaying a range of skills, including adding danger by holding a large snake during the act. *Collection of Karla L. Raymond*

CONFESSIONS OF A SWORD SWALLOWER FROM THE *LONDON MORNING CHRONICLE*, 1850

I have been connected with the conjuring and tumbling professions, and every branch of them, for forty-six years. I lost my mother when a child, and my father was a carpenter, and allowed me to go with the tumblers. I continued tumbling until my feet were knocked up. I tumbled twenty-three or twenty-four years. It was never what you call a good business, only a living. I got £3 a week certainly, at one time, and sometimes £4; but you had to live up to it, or you were nothing thought of; that is to say, if you kept "good company." Now there is not a living to be made at the trade.

Six and twenty years ago I began to practise sword swallowing against the celebrated Ramo Samee. who was then getting £25 or £30 a week. I first practised with a cane, and found it difficult to get the cane down. When I first did it with the cane, I thought I was a dead man. There's an aperture in the chest which opens and shuts; and it keeps opening and shutting, as I understand it; but I know nothing about what they call anatomy, and never thought about such things. Well, if the cane or sword goes down upon this aperture when it is shut, it can go no further, and the pain is dreadful. If it's open, the weapon can go through, the aperture closing on the weapon.

The first time I put down the cane I got it back easily, but put my head on the table and was very sick, vomiting dreadfully. I tried again the same afternoon, however, three or four hours afterwards, and did it without pain. I did it two or three times more, and the next day boldly tried it with a sword, and succeeded. The sword was blunt, and was thirty-six inches long, an inch wide, and perhaps a sixth of an inch thick. I felt frightened with the cane, but not with the sword. Before the sword was used it was rubbed with a handkerchief, and made warm by friction.

I swallowed swords for fourteen years. At one time I used to swallow three swords, a knife, and two forks, of course keeping the handles in my mouth, and having all the blades in my stomach together. I felt no pain. No doubt many of the audience felt more pain in seeing it than I in doing it. I wore a Turkish dress both in the streets and the theatres. I never saw ladies faint at my performance—no, there was no nonsense of that kind.

Gentlemen often pulled the sword and knives by their handles out of my mouth, to convince themselves it was real, and they found it was real, though the people to this day generally believe it is not. I've sometimes seen people shudder at my performance, but I generally had loud applause. I used to hold my head back with the swords in my stomach for two or three minutes.

I've had a guinea a day for sword swallowing. This guinea a day was only for a few days at fair times. I was with old "salt-box" Brown, too, and swallowed swords and conjured with him. I swallowed swords with him thirty times a day—more than one each time, sometimes three or four. I had a third of the profits; Brown had two-thirds. We divided after all the expenses were paid. My third might have been 30s. a week, but it wouldn't be half as much now if I could swallow swords still. Sometimes—indeed, a great many times—say twenty—I have brought up oysters out of my stomach after eating them, just as I swallowed them, on the end of the sword. At other times there was blood on the end of the blade. I always felt faint after the blood, and used to take gin or anything I could get at hand to relieve me, which it did for a time.

At last I injured my health so much that I was obliged to go to the doctor's. I used to eat well, and drink too. When I felt myself injured by the swallowing, I had lost my appetite, and the doctor advised me take honey and liquids, tea, beer, and sometimes a drop of grog. At three months' end he told me if I swallowed swords, it would be my death; but for all that I was forced to swallow swords to get a meal to swallow.

I kept swallowing swords three or four years after this, not feeling any great suffering. I then thought I would swallow a live snake. I'd never heard of any one, Indian, or anybody, swallowing a live snake. It came into my head once by catching a grass-snake in the fields in Norfolk. I said to myself, as I held it by the neck, "There seems no harm in this fellow; I'll try if I can swallow him." I tried then and there, and I did swallow him. It felt cold and slimy as it went down. I didn't feel afraid, for I kept tight hold of him by the tail; and no one has any right to be afraid of a grass-snake. When I brought the snake up again, in about three minutes, it seemed dead.

After that I introduced snake swallowing into my public performances, and did so for about four years. I catch all my own snakes a few miles from London, and killed very few through swallowing on 'em. Six snakes, properly fed on milk, lasted a year. The snakes never injured me; and I shouldn't have given it up, but the performance grew stale, and the people wouldn't give me anything for it.

I have swallowed swords in the streets thirty to forty times a day, and snakes as often, both in town and country. I thought once I couldn't have followed any other sort of life; you see I'd been so long accustomed to public life; besides, I may have liked it far better than labor, as most young men do, but no labor can be harder than mine has been.

If my father had been what he ought, he might have checked my childish doings and wishes. I have tried other things though, in the hope of bettering myself. I have tried shoemaking for five or six years, but couldn't get a living at it. I wasn't competent for it—that's two years ago—so now I'm musician to a school of acrobats. Very many like me remain in the street business, because they can't get out of it; that's the fact.

Whilst I swallowed swords and snakes I played the fire eater. I did it once or twice last week. I eat red-hot cinders from the grate, at least I put them in my mouth, really hot cinders, I have had melted lead in my mouth. I only use a bit of chalk. I chalk my palate, tongue, and fingers; it hardens the skin of the tongue and palate, but that's all. Fire-eating affects the taste for a time, or rather it prevents one tasting anything particularly. I've eaten fire for twenty years in the streets and in public places. It hasn't brought any money of late years. I wasn't afraid when I first tried it by eating a lighted link—a small flambeau. I felt no inconvenience. The chalk did everything that was right. You may stroke a red-hot poker with chalked hands, and not be burnt.

I make the same as the acrobats; perhaps I average 12s. a week, and have a wife and six children, the oldest under eleven, to maintain out of that. Sometimes we're obliged to live upon nothing. There's one thing coming from sword swallowing that I ought to mention. I'm satisfied that Ramo Samee and I gave the doctors their notions about a stomach-pump.

SALLEMENTRO
DATES UNKNOWN

All that is known of Sallementro comes from 1861's *London Labour and the London Poor*, in which the sword swallower claims to have learned the art at the age of seventeen or eighteen from his friend Clarke. Sallementro also describes his affinity for swallowing snakes—in glorious, slimy, detail:

"I swallow snakes, swords, and knives. . . . It was a mate of mine that I was with that first put me up to sword and snake swallowing. I copied off him, and it took me about three months to learn it. I began with a sword first—of course not a sharp sword, but a blunt-pointed—and I didn't exactly know how to do it, for there's a trick to it. At first it turned me, putting it down my throat past my swallow, right down, about 18 inches. It made my swallow sore, very sore, and I used lemon and sugar to cure it. It was tight at first, and I kept pushing it down further and further. There's one thing—you mustn't cough, and until you're used to it, you want to very bad, and then you must pull it up again. My sword was about three-quarters of an inch wide.

"At first I didn't know the trick of doing it, but I found it out this way. You see, the trick is you must oil the sword—the best sweet oil, worth 14 pence a pint—and you put it on with a sponge. Then, you understand, if the sword scratches the swallow, it don't make it sore, 'cos the oil heals it up again. When first I put the sword down, before I oiled it, it used to come up quite slimy, but after the oil it slips down quite easy, and is as clean when it comes up as before it went down.

"The knives are easier to do than the sword because they are shorter. We put them right down till the handle rests on the mouth. The sword is about 18 inches long, and the knives about 8 inches in the blade. People run away with the idea that you slip the blades down your breast, but I always hold mine right up with the neck bare, and they see it go into the mouth 'tween the teeth. They also fancy it hurts you, but it don't, or what a fool I should be to do it. I don't mean to say it don't hurt you at first, 'cos it do, for my swallow was very bad, and I couldn't eat anything but liquids for two months whilst I was learning. I cured my swallow whilst I was stretching it with lemon and sugar. I was the second one that ever swallowed a snake. I was about 17 or 18 years old when I learnt it. The first was Clarke as did it. He done very well with it, but he wasn't out no more than two years before me, so he wasn't known much.

"In the country there is some places where, when you do it, they swear you are the devil, and won't have it nohow. The snakes I use are about 18 inches long, and you must first cut the stingers out, 'cos it might hurt you. I always keep two or three by me for my performances. I keep them warm, and I give them nothing to eat but worms and gentles. I generally keep them in flannel or hay in a box. I've three at home now.

"When first I began swallowing snakes, they tasted queer like. They draw'd the roof of the mouth a bit. It's a roughish taste. The scales rough you a bit when you draw them up. You see, a snake will go into ever such a little hole, and they are smooth one way. The head of the snake goes about an inch and a half down the throat, and the rest of it continues in the mouth, curled 'round like. I hold him by the tail, and when I pinch it, he goes right in. You must cut the stinger out or he'll injure you. The tail is slippery, but you nip it with the nails like pinchers. If you was to let go, he'd go right down, but most snakes will stop at two inches down the swallow, and then they bind like a ball in the mouth. I generally get my snakes by giving little boys ha'pence to go and catch 'em in the woods. I get them when I'm pitching in the country. I'll get as many as I can get, and bring 'em up to London for my engagements.

"When first caught, the snake is slimy, and I have to clean him by scraping him with a cloth, and then with another, until he's nice and clean. I have put 'em down slimy, on purpose to taste what it was like. It had a nasty taste, very nasty.

"When I exhibit, I first holds the snake up in the air and pinches the tail, to make it curl about and twist 'round my arm, to show that he is alive. Then I holds it above my mouth, and as soon as he sees the hole, in he goes. He goes wavy-like, as a ship goes, that's the comparison. I always hold my breath whilst his head is in my swallow. When he moves in the swallow, it tickles a little, but it don't make you want to retch. In my opinion, he is more glad to come up than to go down, for it seems to be too hot for him. I keep him down about two minutes. If I breathe or cough, he draws out and curls back again.

An ad for Vannuchi's Museum in New Orleans with "Signor Forrestle" featured among many others, from the *Times-Picayune*, February 24, 1859. *Public domain*

"I think there's artfulness in some of them big snakes, for they seem to know which is the master. I was at Wombwell's Menagerie of Wild Beasts for 3 months, and I had the care of a big snake, as thick 'round as my arm. I wouldn't attempt to put that one down my throat, for I think I might easier have done down his'n. It was a f'urren snake, all over spots, called a boa-constrictor."

SIGNOR FORESTELL
DATES UNKNOWN

Sword swallowers have historically performed in sideshows, carnivals, fairs, and dime museums, and occasionally before a medical audience. But on January 9, 1876, Signor Forestell added "courtroom" to the list.[1]

The lawsuit took place in Providence, Rhode Island, and involved a showman who failed to pay his board during a stay with his "traveling company of players." Among those players was Forestell, who brought his swords when he was put on the stand. The *Providence Press* described the scene:

> The lawyers wanted to see him swallow it, and so asked if he had any objections to showing his performance. He had none, and down went twenty-seven inches of steel, to the gratification of the lawyers. Signor handed his sword to the admiring legal gentlemen, asking them to examine and see that there was no fraud. He had a very business-like air, and when asked what other branches his business took in, he remarked that it was his habit to eat marbles. Everybody wanted to see him eat marbles, and down went four good-sized "allies." He remarked that the great trick was putting the sword down also and hearing it chink against the marbles, and down went the sword, and the chink was heard. Signor's performance was "immense," and had a jury witnessed this novel exposition of a legal point, his fortune would have been made.

Signor Forestell was also known to swallow canes and bayonets and to eat fire. Articles and advertisements indicate that he performed in cities across America from at least 1859 to 1888. In February 1859, for example, Forestell appeared at Vannuchi's Museum in New Orleans and was referred to as the "Great Fakir of Canada, swallowed the Enchanted Sword 2 feet in length."[2] In the 1880s, Forestell performed with John Robinson's Circus, and in 1887 he

---

1   Also referred to as Professor Forestell, Forestelle, Forrestelle, Forrestle, and other iterations.
2   Vannuchi's was a wax museum owned by renowned clown Dan Rice, who did just about everything, except for swallow swords.

swallowed swords and canes from members of the audience as an opening act for a boxing match in San Francisco.

A year later, Forestell appeared at the California Dime Museum & Theatre in Los Angeles. Those who witnessed his act were so enamored with his "marvelous feats" that they were "induced to make him a suitable recognition of his merits." Thus, on September 30, 1888, he was presented with a gold-and-silver badge inscribed "Professor Forestell, Champion Sword Swallower of the World," for which he thanked them with "a few neat remarks."

Though his origins are unknown, Signor Forestell may be of Swedish origin. The word "föreställning" translates to "show" or "performance."

SIGNOR WANDANA
?–1875

Signor Wandana was known as "The Wonderful Sabre, Bayonet, and Sword-Swallower" in the 1870s. Wonderful as he was, he suffered a fatal injury in May 1875 while performing in Calais, Maine, with Gibbs' Zoological Exhibition. According to a brief obituary, he cut himself internally and died from the ensuing inflammation on May 9.

CARLO BENEDETTI
1849–99

In the spring of 1874, Carlo Benedetti appeared at the Jefferson Medical Clinic in Philadelphia as a guest of Professor F. F. Maury. Filling the lecture hall were a host of eminent surgeons from across the city. There, in front of the distinguished medical crowd, Benedetti swallowed a sword 23 inches in length, then bowed, and bent the steel with his movement.

Next, he swallowed a 29-inch blade to the hilt and held it there for about one minute while several of the surgeons approached him for a closer examination. They confirmed among themselves that the sword indeed passed through the esophagus and into the stomach.

Beneditti wasn't done yet. According to a newspaper report, he "took a musket weighing about sixteen pounds, with a bayonet attached. The bayonet he swallowed, and bending over, supported the musket in several positions by the strength of his jaws."

After that, he swallowed six swords at once and allowed six doctors to pull them from his throat, one by one.

The article confirmed that there "appeared to be no malformation whatever about the sword swallower," and explained that he first discovered his ability to perform such feats "by thrusting his finger down his throat once while sick, and finding that it would not make him vomit."

That vomitless experience occurred when he was fourteen, in 1863. Born in Norrköping, Sweden, to Italian immigrant parents, young Benedetti joined a circus at age thirteen as a horseback rider and toured Europe. Within several years he became proficient enough at sword swallowing to make it his main act. Standing about 5 feet, 8 inches, he was known to swallow a sword as long as 30¼ inches. After moving to America, he performed with the Schumann Company in the eastern United States and Cuba as "Signor Benedetti."

In 1874, several months after his show for the surgeons, Benedetti traveled with the Schumann troupe to Havana, Cuba, and performed to a packed theater. According to a newspaper report, "He swallowed His Excellency the Captain General's sword, a cane, and other articles, but could not stomach the umbrella."

Three years later, Benedetti crossed the Atlantic for a stretch of performances in England. His "marvellous performance" could be seen at London's Royal Aquarium, the Crystal Palace, and other venues. One of these shows took place in his room at the Westminster Aquarium. It was April 1878, and just as he did four years earlier, Benedetti gave a private show to a group of bewildered doctors.

As the physicians watched the steel descend into his body, they struggled to understand where it went. "Standing on tiptop, I looked into his mouth, and there could see plainly the sword in the pharynx; but where was the other end of it? It must be somewhere in the abdomen," wrote one doctor in *Land and Water*. "My friend, Dr. Priestly, who has, of all medical men in London, the most delicate power of touch, very quickly discovered the other end of the sword far away down in the body, a hard, metallic point plainly to be felt. Here, then, was no doubt a proof that the sword was actually swallowed."

Another doctor said he "distinctly felt the sword recede as it was withdrawn from the stomach lying quite in the groin," reported *London World*. "The M.D.s present found his throat a good deal inflamed, and gave him a gargle."

Having amazed his medical audience, Benedetti returned to the public stage in London. At Canterbury Hall, while swallowing a bayonet at the end of his musket and "swinging it around, as usual," he nearly found himself in need of one of his new physician friends.

"In the middle of his circumvolutions, the musket fell to the floor with a crash!" described *Land and Water*. "Terrible to think, the bayonet had just at that very moment snapped in half; the musket lay on the floor with the socket of the bayonet still attached to it; the bayonet itself was of course out of sight, sheathed in the living esophagus."

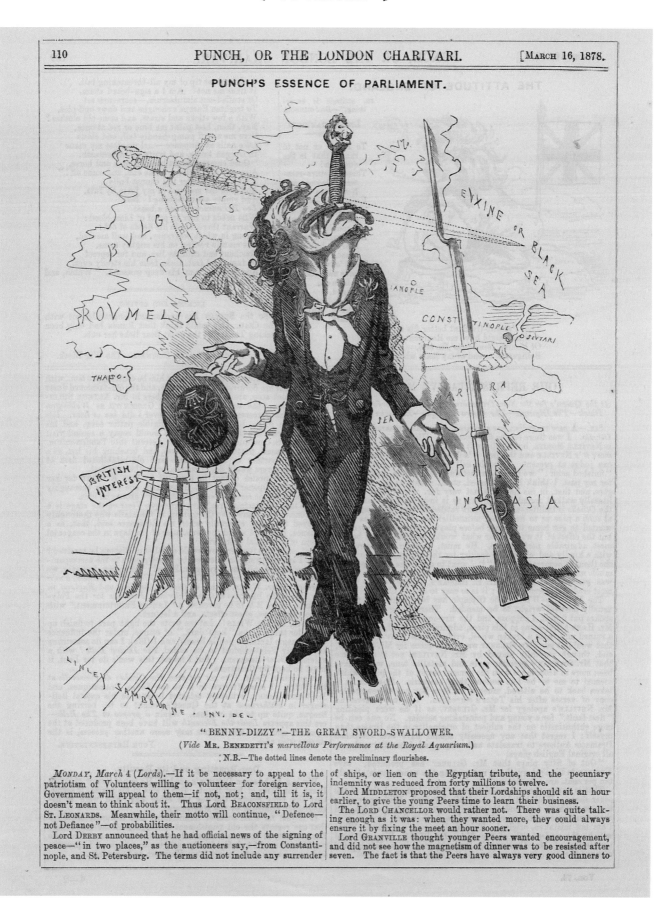

PUNCH'S ESSENCE OF PARLIAMENT.

"BENNY-DIZZY"—THE GREAT SWORD-SWALLOWER.
(*Vide* MR. BENEDETTI'S *marvellous Performance at the Royal Aquarium.*)
N.B.—The dotted lines denote the preliminary flourishes.

MONDAY, *March* 4 (*Lords*).—If it be necessary to appeal to the patriotism of Volunteers willing to volunteer for foreign service, Government will appeal to them—if not, not; and, till it is, it doesn't mean to think about it. Thus Lord BEACONSFIELD to Lord ST. LEONARDS. Meanwhile, their motto will continue, "Defence—not Defiance"—of probabilities.

Lord DERBY announced that he had official news of the signing of peace—"in two places," as the auctioneers say,—from Constantinople, and St. Petersburg. The terms did not include any surrender of ships, or lien on the Egyptian tribute, and the pecuniary indemnity was reduced from forty millions to twelve.

Lord MIDDLETON proposed that their Lordships should sit an hour earlier, to give the young Peers time to learn their business.

The LORD CHANCELLOR would rather not. There was quite talking enough as it was: when they wanted more, they could always ensure it by fixing the meet an hour sooner.

Lord GRANVILLE thought younger Peers wanted encouragement, and did not see how the magnetism of dinner was to be resisted after seven. The fact is that the Peers have always very good dinners to

Carlo Benedetti swallowed swords at London's Royal Aquarium in 1878. The March 16, 1878, issue of *Punch* magazine turned his performance into a political illustration. *Collection of Dan Meyer*

Benedetti quickly put his face and arms toward the floor as his attendants lifted his legs up in the air. With him turned upside down, the bayonet slid outward, harmlessly. Benedetti caught it with his fingers as the end of the blade reached his tongue.

He continued performing in Europe and America into the 1890s. At around that time, he was earning about $25 a week. Eventually, after a performance at Phillion's theater in Paterson, New Jersey, Benedetti decided he liked the town and settled there. He continued performing but also took ownership of a local café, which became a hangout for local Elks Club members.

Sadly, by 1898, he began to suffer from mental illness. "Of late Mr. Benedetti's mind has been much affected, and frequently he has wandered off without aim or object," the *Paterson Evening News* reported on November 7. "During the past few months his friends have had to watch him constantly." That day he was committed to the State Asylum for the Insane in Morris Plains, New Jersey.

The *Trenton Evening Times* noted that "he imagined he was a millionaire and threw his money away." Benedetti passed away on July 26, 1899, at the age of forty-nine in Morris Plains and is buried in Laurel Grove Memorial Park in Totowa, New Jersey.

PROFESSOR CHARLES E. GRIFFIN
1859–1914

When Charles Eldridge Griffin wasn't swallowing swords, he was entertaining as a magician, ventriloquist, yogi, contortionist, hypnotist, and fire eater. Offstage, he was writing and publishing books, lecturing, managing sideshows, and promoting circuses. Though he was known as "Professor" Griffin, the epithet was clearly an understatement.

Griffin's many adventures began in St. Joseph, Missouri, where was born on June 16, 1859. Young Charles's family moved to Iowa three years later. Eventually, he'd find himself the oldest of ten children. Together with several of his siblings, Griffin began dabbling in the performing arts. At age sixteen he started touring schoolhouses, town halls, and county fairs as a magician and ventriloquist. Within a few years he landed a gig as a conjuror with Hilliard & DeMott's Circus, until it folded in 1881. But despite being out of work, there was no turning back from show business. He had a whole world in front of him to entertain—starting with France.

At twenty-two, he crossed the Atlantic and became the general manager of the Paris Pavilion Shows. Though little is known about his experiences there, he returned to America two years later and began working with Pullman and Mack's Circus and Sells Brothers Circus as "The Comic Yankee Conjuror" and a sideshow lecturer and fire eater.

In 1886, he became a member of New York City's newly formed Hurlburt & Hunting Circus (which soon after became Bob Hunting's New York Circus). His repertoire was growing, as reflected by his latest moniker in 1889: "Professor Griffin, the Yankee Yogi, Magician, and Sword Swallower."

Griffin spent twelve years with the troupe. During this time, he eventually owned and operated the sideshow and established the New York Conjuring College to share his knowledge and teach others how to perform. Like any school, textbooks were needed, so Griffin wrote his own. His first instruction manual, *Griffin's Book of Wonders*, was self-published in 1887. It was followed by numerous others, including *How to Be a Contortionist! Bending Made Easy: A Practical Self-Instructor by a Well-Known Professional* in 1896 and *The Showman's Book of Wonders* a year later. The latter showcased his many skills, from magic and ventriloquism to fire eating and sword swallowing. While these may have been ideal for students at the Conjuring College, they were available to anyone who attended his circus for just ten cents.

Following his run with the Bob Hunting Circus, he managed Frank A. Robbin's Circus and became enchanted with a young snake charmer, Olivia. She was only about seventeen years old at the time and performed as "Octavia, the Serpentine Enchantress." The two were soon married and moved on to a bigger stage: the Ringling Brothers Circus Side Show. For four years, Griffin was the stage manager and a performer, billed as the "Lecturer and Sword Swallower," while Olivia continued as a snake charmer as well as "Octavia, the White Witch."

In 1902, after the end of the Ringling Brothers season, the Griffins were invited to join Buffalo Bill's Wild West Show and head east, all the way to Europe. They began in England and over the next four years toured the country, along with Wales and Scotland, and made their way to France, Italy, Hungary, Germany, Belgium, and Russia. Octavia continued her snake-charming act, while Griffin performed his many talents. His 1905 pitch card shows him swallowing three swords.

After returning home in October 1906, Griffin suffered a mild stroke. But it didn't slow him down for long. He was soon touring again with Buffalo Bill's Wild West Show and wrote a memoir of his European travels, *Four Years in Europe with Buffalo Bill*, published in 1908. In it, he described the many wondrous architectural sights and different cultures he encountered with each stop of the tour. Not to mention the venues they filled—some of which held up to 17,000 people.

Sadly, despite his energy and will to stay active, Griffin's health soon began to decline. In 1909 he suffered a second stroke. Three years later, he was stricken by a third. He battled through each, until succumbing to a more severe stroke at the beginning of 1914. Charles Griffin passed away on January 3 at age fifty-four.

CHEVALIER CLIQUOT (FRED MCLONE)
1862–1939

"You should get a doctor and pay him by the week," Chevalier Cliquot told a reporter in 1895. "He will cure your throat as fast as you make it raw and irritated, and he can give you a preparation to harden it." These words of wisdom came despite an incident with a doctor just a year earlier that nearly ended Cliquot's distinguished sword-swallowing career.

Cliquot, who was born as Frederick McLone in Chicago in 1862 (though he told everyone he was French Canadian), had visited a group of medical men at New York's Metropolitan Throat Hospital and exhibited his ability to swallow swords. According to a January 21, 1894, *New York Times* article recounting the event, the staff had been accustomed to what the throat could endure, and found the demonstration "startling, but not especially wonderful." Dr. Bowditch, a professor of physiology at Harvard who was in attendance, wondered if he could see more.

"Can you swallow anything?" he asked.

"Yes," replied McLone.

"Then swallow my cane."

"I will if you'll wipe the ferrule."

"This was done," the article stated, "and the cane was pushed 22 inches down the Chevalier's throat, and the spectators marveled."

Cliquot followed the act by swallowing four blades, then attached 14-pound weights to them. Next, he swallowed fourteen swords—all designed to fit together next to each other in a tightly nested stack. He told his audience of physicians that if they wanted to withdraw the swords, they should do it one at a time. But as he was in the process of pushing the blades down his throat, he "appeared to be suffering and turned pale." One of the doctors cried, "My God, this is going too far," and he grabbed the handles of the swords and pulled them out all at once. "McLone gave a groan and leaned forward," the article said. "He appeared to be in great agony, and could not speak for several moments. He then complained of severe pain in the stomach and throat." The doctors gave him a hypodermic injection of morphine and sent him home. Fortunately, his throat hadn't been lacerated and his stomach hadn't been punctured. It took months to fully recover and resume his act for less panicked people.

McLone's adventures in sword swallowing began at the early age of sixteen, after he'd run away to join the circus. He quickly learned acrobatics and feats of strength, but according to an 1896 issue of the *Strand Magazine*, his path in the circus shifted after "seeing an arrant old humbug swallow a small machete in Buenos Aires." He allegedly asked the performer to teach him but was refused because he couldn't pay for lessons. Instead, he trained himself with a 6-inch piece of silver wire. Clearly, he taught himself well and eventually took on at least one pupil, Delno Fritz, who would become his most skilled peer in the 1890s and early 1900s.

According to the *Times* article, McLone gained his pseudonym in a Paris café, "after a bottle of 'The Widow's' had been splashed over him." The bottle referred to a champagne house run by a visionary matriarch and widow, Madame Clicquot Ponsardin. McLone adopted the "Cliquot" name and designated himself "Chevalier," the French term for "knight."

By 1902, Chevalier Cliquot—who was also known as the Human Scabbard—had swallowed swords of up to 22 inches nearly every day for over twenty-three years and possibly longer. Cliquot's act also included swallowing an electric lightbulb connected to an 8-volt battery, gulping down chained pocket watches and smoking a cigarette while the watch ticked in his stomach, and, as shown to the doctors, up to fourteen 19-inch bayonet swords at one time. But his biggest stunt was to partially swallow a bayonet sword, weighted with a crossbar and two 18-pound dumbbells. He'd allow the rest of the blade to be "kicked" by the recoil of a rifle that was fixed to a spike in the center of the bar and then fired.

Cliquot was known to have performed with the Forepaugh Circus, at various dime museums and theaters across America, and at the Westminster Royal Aquarium in London. According to Houdini's book *Miracle Mongers and Their Methods*, Cliquot eventually sheathed his swords to become a music hall agent in England.

In early March 1939, at the age of seventy-six or seventy-seven, Fred McLone died following an operation at the Royal Infirmary in Oldham, England. After a demonstration years earlier before the Chicago College of Surgeons, he was offered a life pension if he would agree to leave his body for research purposes. He refused, but according to newspaper reports covering his death, a few days before his last operation he bequeathed his body to the Oldham infirmary.

"They have treated me so well when I have been in Oldham Infirmary that as a mark of my gratitude, I intend to bequeath them my body," the ailing sword swallower had said. "It may have some interests for science."

Chevalier Cliquot with his magnificent sword board.
Collection of Dan Meyer

THE WORLD'S FIRST AND LAST VIOLIN BOW SWALLOWER: PATRICK MULRANEY

For as long as sword swallowing has been around, people have believed that the swords are fake. This has driven many performers to find creative ways to prove their skills are real. Over the centuries, that's meant gulping down items that could not possibly disappear into a handle: bayonets, neon tubes, giant shears, pool cues, and long screwdrivers, to name a few.

But in 1891, a performer named Patrick Mulraney proved the art is as dangerous as it looks by swallowing a violin bow. As the *New York Times* reported on June 30, "Twice he essayed to swallow this, but failed each time, desisting on account of the intense pain caused by inserting the bow in his throat. He immediately commenced vomiting blood, and continued to have these paroxysms until this morning, when he died."

No accounts of violin-bow swallowing have surfaced since.

AUGUST REICKE
1844–?

Every swallowed sword is accompanied by an element of danger. But when the sword swallower is suffering from depression, the blade poses a much-greater threat. In the case of August Reicke, it led to an attempted suicide in October 1894.

According to the *New York Herald*, Reicke, a fifty-year-old professional sword swallower, had not had any recent work. He had a family to support and was growing despondent. As the article reported, "Monday night he took an old cavalry sabre blade twenty-three inches long and started to plunge it down his throat. His hand was not steady and the sword cut his throat. The pain made him cry out, and, whirling it around his head, lunged about the room. The screams of his wife and children startled one of the tenants in the house, who peeped in the door. Seeing Reicke with the sword in his hands and the wife and children in fear, he slammed the door and ran yelling to the street for a policeman."

When the officer arrived, he saw Reicke in his room and swinging the sword. "What are you trying to do?" asked the policeman. "I've killed seven people and have buried their bodies, and I'm ready for more," Reicke replied.

He was sent to Bellevue Hospital in New York for psychiatric treatment.

In 1889, Zulu Zingara was billed as the "only female sword swallower in the world" for her appearance at the Nickelodeon in Boston. A month later she was featured at the Westminster Museé in Providence, Rhode Island. It's unknown if she swallowed the fly swatter seen in Charles Eisenmann cabinet card. Perhaps she simply didn't have her swords at the photo shoot and made do with what was available. Zulu, also listed as Zula, was a Circassian performer, who were known for their Afro hairstyles and were hailed as the ideal picture of feminine beauty. Swallowing swords surely offered a little extra excitement. *Collection of Warren A. Raymond*

WILLIAM GRIFFIN
DATES UNKNOWN

William Griffin dueled with danger for more than thirty years, until he finally lost. In 1903, while swallowing swords in Sawtelle's circus in Bridgewater, Maine, Griffin did what you never want to do with a long blade down your throat. He lost his footing. The slip caused the steel to pierce his windpipe.

"He was unable to be moved and was left by the show, and steadily grew worse and died after intense suffering," newspapers reported. Griffin's family could not be located, so he was buried in town, at the town's expense.

The fatal accident wasn't the first time the sword swallower flirted with death. In 1889, Griffin, who had been described as having an "abnormal breadth of throat, combined with an exceedingly elongated person," swallowed a 3-foot-long blade in front of a San Francisco crowd. If the audience was impressed, their delight was short lived. The lengthy blade cut an internal organ, which started to hemorrhage.

According to newspaper reports, "The amount of blood which was discharged from his stomach so weakened him that when taken to the hospital he fainted away, and was with great difficulty revived."

A year later, Griffin headed south to Los Angeles and found trouble without having to swallow it. While passing through town, he ventured into a dime museum, looking for work. The manager, eager to add a sword swallower to his roster of talent, hired him on the spot. There was just one problem: Griffin didn't have any swords with him.

He explained that he'd been hit by hard times and had to sell off his equipment, leaving him unable to perform his act. His new boss kindly took him shopping and purchased a Japanese sword for him so he could get to work. But Griffin had other ideas. Instead of taking the stage, he ran from it—taking the weapon with him. A week later he was caught and charged with petit larceny. He had reportedly pulled the same stunt at least once before.

MLLE AMY MURPHY
DATES UNKNOWN

In the early 1900s, a beautiful young European woman known only as "Mlle Amy" and "Amy the sword swallower" worked with a variety of shows, including Barnum & Bailey's 1900 tour in Germany, Forepaugh-Sells, John Robinson's Circus, and Hagenback-Wallace. Between circuses she also performed at the Ninth and Arch Dime Museum in Philadelphia and Huber's 14th Street Museum in New York City. While at the latter, she appeared with numerous curious acts, such as Miss Welch, Ireland's long-haired beauty; Ferrari's troupe of trained rats; and Mme Schell's performing lions.

There are no reports describing her specific act, but she did sustain an injury in 1908. However, it wasn't from a steel blade, but rather a steel pole. While performing with the John Robinson Ten Big Shows in Mt. Carmel, Illinois, heavy rains and winds blew the sideshow down into what was described as "a tangled mess." Several performers were injured by the falling poles. A fortune-teller, who didn't see the storm coming, suffered a bruised arm; the show's announcer was knocked unconscious; and Mlle Amy was badly bruised and forced to walk with a cane for several weeks.

By 1913, Mlle Amy appeared to have either added snake handling to her act or simply transitioned from swords to fangs after marrying Frank J. Murphy.

PROFESSOR A. J. PIERCE
1868–1913

In 1905, a sword swallower named Professor Albert J. Pierce, a.k.a. "Prince Yellow Boy, the Sword-Swallowing Wonder," was the star of a show in Bangor, Maine, that also featured LaCrosse the Human Stone Crusher and Madame LaMonte, the Hindoo rope juggler.

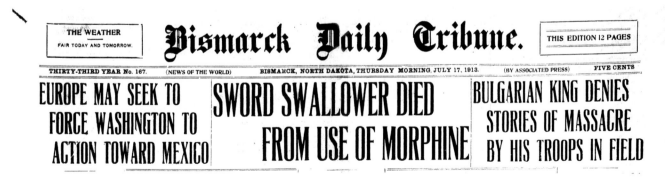

| THE WEATHER | | | | | |
| FAIR TODAY AND TOMORROW. | | | | | |

Bismarck Daily Tribune.

THIS EDITION 12 PAGES

THIRTY-THIRD YEAR No. 167.   (NEWS OF THE WORLD)   BISMARCK, NORTH DAKOTA, THURSDAY MORNING, JULY 17, 1913.   (BY ASSOCIATED PRESS)   FIVE CENTS

EUROPE MAY SEEK TO FORCE WASHINGTON TO ACTION TOWARD MEXICO

SWORD SWALLOWER DIED FROM USE OF MORPHINE

BULGARIAN KING DENIES STORIES OF MASSACRE BY HIS TROOPS IN FIELD

Professor Pierce's death made the front page of the *Bismarck Tribune* on July 17, 1913. *Public domain*

An astonished reporter witnessing Pierce proclaimed, "There's no 'fake' about him," while colorfully describing his show. "He runs swords and small saws and scissors and bayonets down his throat until it seems that it must slash his vitals; but he gets through all right and smiles at the frightened spectators. He chews and swallows glass, eats hot pitch and rosin and sealing wax, swallows tacks and does other stunts that cause the observer to wonder what his 'insides' are composed of. . . . He finishes his stunt by swallowing about 16 inches of a snake."

Several physicians attended his performance, hoping to gain an understanding of how Pierce achieved such marvelous feats. "They keep right on going, trying to solve the mystery," the reporter added. "He doesn't know how he is made, and he says he doesn't care." What Pierce did explain was that there was a "small fortune" in swallowing sharp objects and snakes, and he was happy to earn it.

These stunts eventually took their toll on his body. In 1907 he was admitted to New York's Bellevue Hospital due to pains in his stomach from the "bric-a-brac" he reportedly had ingested. As an article stated, "He believes he has engulfed a cavalry sabre and the physician thinks a sane man would not get such a queer idea."

Pierce kept swallowing swords and other hardware and subsequently kept making appearances in hospitals. In 1908 he was treated by doctors in Connecticut after a blade punctured his stomach. A year later it happened again in Harlem. Doctors claimed he suffered from a gastric hemorrhage.

In July 1913, a day after receiving a brand-new shipment of snakes and six weeks into a stint with the Allman Carnival in Bismarck, North Dakota, Pierce succumbed to an overdose of morphine. He had taken enough to kill six men. Morphine had allegedly been a habit for the previous twenty-four years of his life. It's unknown whether he'd been attempting to manage the pain from his performances all that time, or if he'd gotten addicted before filling his body with unnatural things. According to an article, "He had contracted with a large hospital in New York to have his body delivered there after his death, as that institution desired to make an examination of what effects these strong drugs have had." Pierce was forty-five years old and was survived by a wife and three sons in New York City.

THE GREAT MILSE
1881–1918

In 1910, a sword swallower and fire eater known as the Great Milse boasted a standing offer of $500 to anyone who could eat more fire and swallow more swords and saws. It's unknown if he had any daring takers.

According to Milse's pitch card, he was born in Russia on March 6, 1881, and began his act at the alarmingly early age of nine. "I have traveled around the world 3 times and have mystified about 50,000,000 people," it claimed, just before adding, "I am doing my act yet clean and honest, and I am feeling happy all the time." The act may have been honest, but the truth of who exactly Milse was is unclear. He's also been called a Spanish sword swallower and appeared as both Milo and Yale Milse. Were they one and the same or brothers?

If he was one person, he may have performed as two. A 1908 *Chicago Tribune* article on the "Freak Appetites of Curious People" mentions "Miles, the sword swallower and fire eater," followed directly by an academic anagram, "Prof. Milse, the owner of a cast iron stomach." He or they were joined by Prof. Harrison, who took bites out of knife blades, but one hopes not Miles's.

A year later, Prof. Y. Milse billed himself as "Champion Sword Swallower and King of Fire Eaters" and promised audiences they'd witness him gulp down twelve 16-to-20-inch swords at once. All for just a dime admission.

As for the Great Milse, whether Milo or Yates, one of his featured acts was swallowing a bayonet attached to a twelve-gauge shot gun, then shooting it with the blade down his throat. "It is a hair-raising stunt worth seeing," a newspaper said.

By 1914, the Great Milse worked at Coney Island with Samuel Gumpertz's show. Between shows he exhibited other skills by rolling his own cigarettes and making clothing. "Give him a few yards of cloth in the morning, come back at four in the afternoon and he will have made himself a pair of trousers, coat, and vest," a reporter observed.

Yale Milse died four years later after suffering from heart failure while performing in Chicago. Did a Milo or Miles Milse live on?

DELNO FRITZ
1871–1925

On an October night in 1894, sword swallower Delno Fritz suffered a frightening accident while performing at Austin & Stone's Dime Museum in Boston. Not from swallowing a sword or a dozen swords or even a bayonet attached to a musket that he'd fired down his throat on many occasions. Instead, Fritz had swallowed a silver watch attached to a slender chain.

Audience members had stepped toward him, put their ears beside his thorax, and listened to the timepiece tick. He'd done it hundreds of times, but on this night the chain broke away when he began to retrieve the watch from his

Delno Fritz with
a mouthful of
swords and
more filling his
board. *Courtesy
of Robert Way
and Scott
Bellinger*

esophagus. He couldn't reach the swallowed object or utter a cry for help. Fortunately, his young assistant shrieked with fright, and a physician in the crowd rushed forward, pulled a set of forceps from his pocket, and quickly dislodged the watch before Fritz's time ran out.

According to a newspaper report, "Restoratives were applied, and Fritz was soon apparently as well as ever, but he did not swallow any more watches last evening." He was twenty-three years old then and had already been swallowing swords for about thirteen years.

William "Delno" Sherman Fritz was born on February 16, 1871, in Ashley, Pennsylvania—a borough in Luzerne County, just a mile from Wilkes-Barre. He was one of seventeen children of Martha Stevens Fritz and Nathan Delong Fritz.[3] As for Delno, he claimed to have learned the art at the age of ten or eleven. Fritz told a reporter that his father was also a sword swallower, adding, "I suppose to a certain extent it's hereditary." At that age, he'd also crawled under the tent of a visiting circus and became enamored with a Mexican sword swallower's performance. Inspired by his act, Fritz went home and started swallowing lead pencils and handles of spoons with ease. He may have also had a lot of time to practice. At around the same time, young Delno lost a leg while hopping a freight train in Wilkes-Barre. For the rest of his life, he wore a wooden leg and walked with a cane. But like sword swallowing and even eating fire, he had quickly learned to get around with his wooden leg. In fact, Fritz had enough dexterity to run away and join a dime museum in Philadelphia. His father quickly brought the young boy back home, but at age sixteen, after three more escapes from home, he was finally allowed to pursue his dream.

By the early 1890s, Fritz claimed to have added to his sword-swallowing studies under the tutelage of Chevalier Cliquot when they both worked together at the Wonderland Museum in Scranton, Pennsylvania. The two sword swallowers were constantly competing and performing within days or weeks of each other at theaters, medical centers, and dime museums throughout their careers. For a time in the mid-1890s he even adopted Cliquot's "Chevalier" title to market himself as an exotic Frenchman. Fritz's reputation was growing quickly, as evidenced by the *Philadelphia Times*, which crowned him "the most daring and versatile of living sword-swallowers," whose performances "will raise a big crop of goose flesh upon everybody with sufficient hardihood to gaze upon his blood-curdling performances."

In the late 1890s, Fritz added to his act with the addition of a sword-swallowing wife. He had met Maud D'Auldin in 1897 in Scotland and successfully taught her the art. It was just a year after divorcing his first wife, a young New York City actress named Maud Churchill.[4] Together, Fritz and D'Auldin toured the United Kingdom with the Barnum & Bailey Circus and even performed for Queen Victoria. During a stint at the Olympia in London (December 1897 to April 1898), Fritz's performance caught the attention of the medical community. His abilities were reviewed in an 1898 volume of *Gaillard's Medical Journal*:

> One of the entertainers, whose name is Delno Fritz, is a sword swallower, and asserts that he can swallow longer swords than have ever been swallowed before. . . . To those who know the surface markings of the abdomen and the situation of the stomach it is a little short of appalling to see this man pass a sword down his gullet until the hilt impinges upon his teeth and then withdraw the weapon and demonstrate by outside measurement that in the erect posture the point falls some inches below the usual line of the curvature of the stomach. What really happens, of course, is that Delno Fritz has learnt, consciously or unconsciously, to stretch the somewhat loose and elastic tissues between the lips and the cardiac orifice of the stomach, so that these tissues will lie along his blunted sword in a condition of extension, while a protruded chin assists in the prolongation of the pharynx. It should be added that the solidity of the weapon with which the feat is performed is beyond question.

Upon returning to America, he and D'Auldin toured the country for decades with the Al G. Barnes Circus, Buffalo Bill's Wild West Show, the Greater Norris & Rowe Circus, John Robinson's Circus Sideshow, and eventually the Ringling Bros. and Barnum & Bailey Circus. Among his many fans was Harry Houdini, who called Fritz a "master in his manner of indulging his appetite for the cold steel."

Aside from risking his life for the entertainment of others, sword swallowing also saved Fritz's life—and others—according to anecdotes he shared with reporters. On one occasion, while performing in the unruly West, he stood on the platform awaiting his turn, when a drunken cowboy shouted at him to "swaller some swords, quick!" Fritz said he'd swallow according to the show's schedule.

---

3   One of Delno's younger sisters, Ada, married Robert Price in 1893 and birthed another family sword swallower, Edna Price.

4   According to an article in the February 4, 1896, *Scranton Republican*, Fritz had treated Maud cruelly, causing her to seek a separation. "The father and mother of the petitioner allege that on one occasion Fritz and his wife started to quarrel before them and then retreated to another room," the article stated. "They heard her scream, and rushing in, found Fritz choking her. When he was reprimanded, he said he could do as he pleased with her, kill her if he wanted to. The father swore that he heard Maud say in the presence of her husband that she was locked in a room in Boston without food for three days and three nights and had to pawn her watch and opera glasses to keep from starving. Fritz explained this by saying that he went out with the boys and got drunk, played poker and lost all his money."

The cowboy, not being one to care about schedules, pulled out a gun, pointed it at Fritz, and said, "Swaller, ye son of a gun, or I'll let daylight into ye." So, Fritz swallowed and lived to tell about it. At another show out west, a group of cowboys threatened the entire show. Fritz was working with the John Robinson Circus when the gang said they were going to "shoot up" all the performers. Robinson, in a desperate attempt, told them that if anyone in their group could do what Fritz could, they could do whatever they wanted. Fritz swallowed swords, and the cowboys kept their bullets to themselves.

In 1920, however, after thousands of performances, a sword proved tragic. While Fritz and D'Auldin performed on board a ship before the king and queen of England, Maud died from an accident caused by a nicked blade. Fritz then taught sword swallowing to his twenty-one-year-old niece, Edna Price. The two performed together with the Al G. Barnes Circus during the 1920 and 1923 seasons, and with Ringling Bros. and Barnum & Bailey Circus in 1923 and 1924.

In May 1925, Delno Fritz returned home to Wilkes-Barre from a Ringling Bros. and Barnum & Bailey show in Philadelphia to rest after suffering from a case of pneumonia and pleurisy. He received medical treatment at home for weeks and appeared to improve, but when his condition suddenly worsened, he was hospitalized and succumbed to his illness on July 14, 1925, at age fifty-four. According to his death certificate, the official cause of death was a cerebral hemorrhage. Some reports indicate that Fritz's illness had developed after a screw came loose and lodged in his lung while he tested a bronchoscope for doctors in Philadelphia.

In addition to his travels across Europe and America, Fritz also left his mark on film. Tod Browning cast him as the sword swallower in his 1925 film *The Unholy Three* with Lon Chaney. Chaney, who was no stranger to performing unusual stunts in his movies, grew fascinated with sword swallowing and took lessons from Fritz, apparently just before his passing. Chaney later swallowed swords in the 1928 film *West of Zanzibar*.

Delno Fritz is also believed to have swallowed swords in the 1928 film *The Man Who Laughs* and is credited in 1932's *Freaks*. However, since he passed away in 1925, both roles seem quite unlikely. Perhaps the credits were simply in tribute to one of the art's most celebrated performers.

DEMETRIUS LONGO
1872–?

Of all those who've swallowed swords, Demetrius Longo may have been the longest living. According to a United Press International article from January 25, 1972, Longo was celebrating his one hundredth birthday the next week.

"Longo spent most of his life swallowing swords, walking on nails, drinking molten tin, and pulling out his eyeballs," it stated, stressing that the dangerous stunts clearly "did him no harm."

Longo claimed to have begun his career at the age of eleven in the Russian town of Nizhegorodsk, where he joined a carnival as a roustabout, ticket taker, and part-time magician. In a memoir he was writing, he said that he learned to swallow swords from an Italian performer named Augusto Leonelli.

A Soviet magazine, *Yunost* ("Youth"), which published excerpts of his memoir, shared a few of his sword-swallowing secrets. "At first, you must tickle your throat many times with long goose feathers," he said. "Then you cautiously introduce into the esophagus a narrow wooden tube which has been lubricated with goose fat. Later on, I started swallowing a broader tube made from wax and paraffin, and only after perfecting that did I introduce a polished sword with a dull blade." That blade was 2 feet long and ¾ inch wide. He warmed the steel by briskly rubbing it with wool before his act. "It was easier to swallow a warm sword," Longo claimed.

In the 1890s, Longo teamed up with—as he stated with true sideshow ballyhoo—a 9-foot-tall giant and a 20-inch-tall woman. At about this time he also acquired a French-speaking parrot named Ara. "Ara was five years older than me at the time," he wrote. "He still lives so that makes him 105 years old now." Longo, the parrot, the giant, and the little person took their act to cities in Russia. Their show expanded with what Longo described as a "family of acrobatic cockroaches that performed tricks in a miniature playground."

According to the UPI article, the "famous fakir and dervish" also "thrilled audiences in Kharkov by conjuring a human fetus in a chemist's glass beaker, causing it to grow immediately to full term, and then smashing the beaker to produce a fully formed live baby."

He didn't share his secret for growing babies before live audiences, but he did offer the secret of his longevity. Longo said he became a centenarian because he never feared death. Quoting his favorite poet, Omar Khayyam, he added, "You will die but once so it is not worth worrying about it."

CHARLES RAYMOND
DATES UNKNOWN

Canadian sword swallower Charles Raymond was a multitasker. While dazzling audiences by swallowing a 30-inch blade, he also drank water and smoked a cigarette. If they doubted its veracity, he had x-rays ready for skeptics' inspection.

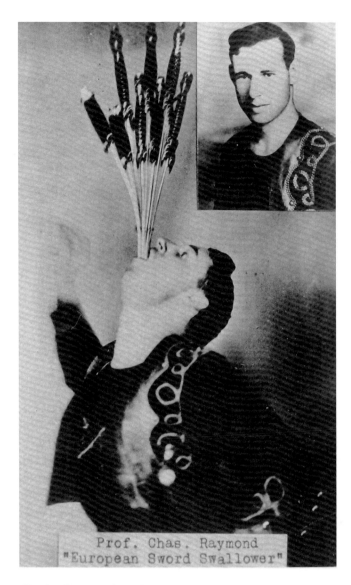

Prof. Chas. Raymond
"European Sword Swallower"

Charles Raymond swallows multiple swords. He was
Canadian but is referred to as European in this image.
Collection of Warren A. Raymond

Raymond appeared at a variety of venues during the
1920s and '30s. In the late twenties he worked fairs with
Boyd & Linderman Shows and was part of a ten-in-one
with Ralph R. Miller Shows. By the early thirties he performed at the Miracle Museum in Pittsburgh, where he
was joined by Victor-Victoria, the half man, half woman;
Schrado the human skeleton; Jolly Kitty, a 620-pound fat
lady; and Rico, the one-man band. By 1932, Raymond was
swallowing swords alongside his wife, a magician known
as Mlle Maria, with Billy Bozzell's Side Show. His act also
merged with vaudeville performers—namely, at Orlando's
Winter Visitor's club in 1933, when he shared the stage
with an impersonator, a pianist, and a comedian—but
surely stole the show from all of them.

BOB ROBERTS
1875–1936

Bob Roberts swallowed swords for thirty years, from 1906
to 1936. For the last thirteen, however, he flirted with
danger more than most. Not only did he swallow blades,
but as a grand finale he also dropped a twenty-gauge
shotgun barrel down his gullet and ignited a fuse that
caused an explosion audible throughout the sideshow tent.
It was a clear crowd-pleaser. But then, on June 2, 1936,
something went horribly wrong.

According to *Billboard* from June 20, 1936, it was
believed that "the gun was too heavily charged, causing
him to lose control of the barrel" and badly burn his stomach. The accident proved fatal two days later and made
headlines across the nation. Roberts was sixty-one.

The daring sword swallower had spent his career working
with numerous sideshows, appearing at Al G. Barnes's Big
4 Ring Wild Animal Circus, Beckmann & Gerety Shows,
Snapp Greater Shows, and various dime museums.

ALEXANDER JOSEPH DOUROF
1881–1949

Alexander Joseph Dourof was born into a circus family in
St. Petersburg, Russia, in 1881. The Dourofs were known
as skilled animal trainers, and young Alexander followed
in the family trade—then went above and beyond. As a
child (no exact age is known), he allegedly learned to
swallow swords and gave his first public performance
before the czar in Moscow. The Dourofs joined the Russian
Royal Circus until the Russian Revolution in 1917, at which
point they fled to Europe.

Within a year, Alexander got back to business and is
believed to have run a circus in the United Kingdom and
in Belgium with his wife, Sophia, who performed as a
tightrope walker. But Dourof soon found himself pulled
into the war. As a soldier, he served as an animal trainer
and handled horses in the cavalry with great skill. Afterward,
he settled in the UK and made a drastic career change by
becoming a carpet salesman in London. Perhaps it was a
safer line of work for Dourof's growing family—he and
Sophia eventually had ten children.

During his sword-swallowing days, Dourof, like many
performers, fell victim to injuries. On at least one occasion,
he cut himself with the blade down his throat, then treated
the wound by putting a piece of cotton on the tip of his sword,

dipping it in iodine, and swallowing it. He withdrew the steel once he felt confident that he'd disinfected the laceration.

In the early 1940s, a UK casting director was asked to find a sword swallower for a new film, *The Man in Grey*. He searched the entire country but had no luck until he got a tip about Dourof, who was then in his sixties. Dourof effortlessly swallowed a 27-inch sword in the background of a carnival scene in the movie. A 1943 article covering the filming said he "gave a remarkable demonstration of the almost dead art of swordswallowing [*sic*] at Shepherd's Bush Studios."

Prior to debuting on the silver screen, Dourof had made his final public appearance at St. Thomas' Hospital fifteen years earlier, where he spent two weeks swallowing swords for doctors and students. He swiftly put all their doubts and suspicions of trickery to rest.

The authenticity and mastery of the performer's art were sources of pride, as it's forever indicated at his gravesite. Dourof's headstone reads: "A Great Showman and the Last of the Sword Swallowers."

EDITH CLIFFORD
1884–1962

Swallowing a bayonet might not sound unusual for a sword swallower. Shooting it down your throat, however, is another story. Edith Clifford began performing the stunt as early as 1903 at Walker's Museum in Boston. The *Boston Post* referred to her as "the only lady who swallows a bayonet, having attached it to a loaded cannon, and while the cannon is supported by the bayonet that is down the throat the piece is discharged." Years later, Harry Houdini called it "the sensation of her act." He described her bayonet as being 23½ inches long.

Mlle CLIFFORD
Champion Sword Swallower of the World

Edith Clifford swallows a bayonet fastened to the breech of a cannon. The bayonet seen here is now owned by Dan Meyer. *Collection of Dan Meyer*

Edith W. Clifford was born in London, England, in 1884 to Captain John Clifford and Emily Rivers-Clifford, who later immigrated to Boston. According to Clifford, her father was a captain in the British army, and she used his military sword to teach herself sword swallowing at the age of thirteen in 1897.

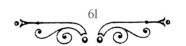

"First I wanted to tame lions, but I was only thirteen and they wouldn't let me," Clifford told the *Washington Herald* in 1918. Perhaps all the swords around her house inspired her to attempt an equally dangerous line of work instead. "I practiced with Father's sword the first day, and the family was surprised when I could swallow it after only three hours."

She failed to clarify why she was forbidden to tame lions but was given free access to swords. Fortunately, she also received guidance from experienced sword swallower Delno Fritz, who performed with the Barnum & Bailey Circus in London in 1897–99. Clifford soon joined the same circus and performed throughout Europe.

The young performer was said to be "generously endowed" and "possessed of more than ordinary personal charms, a refined taste for dressing both herself and her stage, and an unswerving devotion to her art." Under the name "Mlle Edith Clifford, Champion Sword Swallower of the World," she was known to swallow 18-to-20-inch blades without a problem. Her daring act also extended to longer blades of up to 26 inches long, and at times included ten, sixteen, and up to twenty-four swords at one time. Razor blades, scissors, saw blades and, of course, bayonets all found their way down her throat as well.

In 1901, at the age of fifteen, Clifford married thirty-three-year-old Thomas Holmes, who worked under the stage name "James Morris" or "James Maurice" as the "Elastic Skin Man." They adopted the stage name "The Cliffords," and the couple joined Barnum & Bailey Circus for five years from 1901 through 1906. During this time, they had two daughters, Margaret Emily Holmes (1903–2003) and Edith Holmes (1906–?).

While Clifford never suffered any accidents, she described one occasion that left her flirting with death. "In Maysville, Kentucky, I was playing in a theater built in the center of an old graveyard. That nearly proved my undoing," she recounted in 1923. "While I had the bayonet down my throat the cannon was fired but something happened and the cannon blew into pieces. It was only the timely action of my husband that saved me from serious injury. He helped me draw the bayonet from my throat."

Despite their success as an act, and the Elastic Skin Man's earnings as a solo performer, his popularity dwindled due to a slight drinking and gambling problem. Within a few years his health began to suffer. After a six-month battle with paralysis of the bladder and kidney trouble, he passed away on February 22, 1910, at the Carney Hospital in Boston.

Edith continued swallowing a collection of sharp and dangerous items and soon fell in love with a German circus trapeze artist named Karl Andrew Bauer, who performed under the name Signor Zanton. Bauer also served as Edith's assistant, and the couple performed together under a new version of "The Cliffords." Their spectacular promotional posters feature multiple Ediths swallowing an array of blades. As Ricky Jay noted in *Learned Pigs and Fireproof Women*, "Her husband, whose sole function appears to be handing his wife the objects she will devour, is generously given equal billing."

In 1911, the Cliffords expanded into the Great Clifford Show: a one-ring show including acrobats, contortionists, and clowns. Edith and Karl married soon after, on April 18, 1912.

Apparently, the Great Clifford Show never materialized as Edith had planned. Shortly after their wedding, the Cliffords spent the next ten years working for Gollmar Bros. Circus, Barnum & Bailey Circus, and, by 1919, the newly combined Ringling Bros. and Barnum & Bailey Circus.

During this time, Edith's two daughters, Edith and Margaret, grew up with an aunt in Pawtucket, Rhode Island. It wasn't until she retired from performing in 1922 at the age of thirty-six that she and Karl took her daughters home to live with them in Canton, Ohio. There, Clifford went by her married name, Edith Bauer. She and Karl ran a corner grocery store under the name "Bauer Grocery."

For the most part, Clifford remained anonymous and did not mention her circus history to most of her neighbors, but she received numerous visitors whenever Ringling Bros. and Barnum & Bailey Circus came to Canton in the 1930s. Circus performers and sideshow acts would roam in and out of their home.

Edith died at Aultman Hospital on September 3, 1942, at the age of fifty-five of a "cancerous right ovary" that she had battled for four months. She was buried on September 7, 1942, in West Lawn Cemetery in Canton. According to her obituary, Edith Clifford was active in the Women's Republican Club and other interest groups, but the obituary mentions nothing about her circus background. Karl remained in Canton for nearly twenty more years until his passing on January 2, 1962.

Clifford's grandson, Karl Spinden, from Massillon, Ohio, told Dan Meyer that he doesn't remember his grandmother ever talking about her past in show business, and that he never saw her swallow a sword. He worked in his grandparents' grocery store as a child and knew her mostly as a "typical nice, sweet grandma." He keeps one of her swords in a closet at his home.

The full collection of Clifford's swords, bayonet, saw, photos, and death certificate is owned by Meyer and is preserved in the archival collection of the Sword Swallowers Association International Museum and Hall of Fame. Meyer bought the various blades and a ragged photo in 2002 from a couple in Canton who claimed to have purchased the collection at a garage sale in the 1950s. At the time, Meyer knew only that they belonged to Edith Bauer, but he soon realized she was, in fact, Edith Clifford. He has since used her swords, giant serrated handsaw, and straight razor in his performances as a tribute—including at a November 2010 lecture at Bruce Museum in Greenwich, Connecticut.

"It's a privilege for me," Meyer told AOL News after swallowing her saw at the event. "This creates a connection for me to Edith Clifford, now that I've swallowed the same prop she's swallowed. It's like doing a straitjacket escape using Houdini's straitjacket." His collection of Edith's swords and other artifacts was featured on display in the museum's exhibit titled *Science and the Circus* from September 25, 2010, to January 9, 2011.

Clifford was also immortalized in a 1999 Discovery Channel documentary called *Mysteries of Magic: The Impossible Made Possible*, featuring modern sword swallower Amy Saunders as Edith.

MAUD D'AULDIN
1878–1920

"That her sword swallowing is very extraordinary and marvellous is undoubted, and that there shall be no doubt of the genuineness of the show, as many of the audience as like to accept the invitation are invited on to the stage to clearly watch her proceedings." So stated an article from March 24, 1900, about Maud D'Auldin, who not only swallowed swords but also downed a "16 candle power electric light, which is seen clearly descending through her flesh." [5]

D'Auldin was born around 1878 in Paisley, Scotland. In 1897, she met sword swallower Delno Fritz while he was touring the United Kingdom with the Barnum & Bailey Circus. She learned the art of sword swallowing, and by 1899 the two were wed. The couple lived in the UK another eight years, where Fritz bought and operated a few theaters, before they moved to Ashley, Pennsylvania, in June 1907.

D'Auldin swallowed 18- and 22-inch swords, each an inch in width. Along with her electric light, she and Fritz began performing an act known as "Sword and Gun Manipulation" with the Hagenbeck Wallace Sideshow in 1912. Presumably, this act included a bayonet shot down the throat at the firing of a gun.

On December 9, 1914, during a show in Los Angeles, D'Auldin suffered a near-fatal injury. According to *Variety*, she "miscalculated the length of her esophagus and subsequently lacerated her throat" while swallowing a blade. At the hospital, doctors had trouble locating the cut. They decided to retrace the incident by having her swallow a 29-inch sword on the operating table.

---

5   Sometimes spelled Maud D'Aulin, Maud D'Auldin, Maude D'Auldin, Maud D.Auldin, Maud DeAuldin, Mlle de Aldine, Maud DeAulden, Maud D'Aulden, Maude D'Lean, or Mrs. Maude Fritz.

GRAND CIRCUS OF VARIETIES,
AUCKLAND-ROAD, CAMBRIDGE.

TO-NIGHT (Saturday).

Maud D'Auldin,
The only Lady Sword Swallower in the World,
assisted by
Delno Fritz,
The Great Continental Sword Swallower, five years with the Barnum and Bailey's Greatest Show on Earth.
Jenny Lynn,
Character Comedian, from the leading London Music Halls.
Four Musical Japs,
(Violet Fred, Florence, and Sylvia), in their grand Japanese Illuminated Bazaar, and others.

SPECIAL NOTICE.

This Attractive Place of Amusement finishes a successful season to-night. Due notice will shortly be given by advertisement of a Grand Re-opening.

Advertisement for one of Maud D'Auldin's performances with Delno Fritz in England. *Cambridge Daily News*, November 3, 1900.

Once the steel was in place, they took a radiograph and discovered the precise points of contact and the places where the injury occurred. Proper treatment put her on a quick road to recovery.

After the demonstration, D'Auldin was thrilled with the results. "Of course I am glad to know that my injury is to be healed but the picture shows conclusively that I really do swallow the sword," she said. "Many have claimed that the business of sword swallowing is a fake. All sword swallowers will welcome this demonstration."

By 1916, D'Auldin and Fritz were performing again as featured sword swallowers on the John Robinson Circus Side Show, while their seventeen-year-old niece, Edna Price, worked as the "floating lady." Over the years, the sword-swallowing couple also performed with the Al G. Barnes Circus, Buffalo Bill's Wild West Show, the Greater Norris & Rowe Circus, and various dime museums.

In 1920, having escaped death once already, D'Auldin suffered a more severe injury that proved fatal. She and Delno Fritz had just given a command performance on board a ship before King George V and Queen Mary of England. It was her practice to pass out her sword to the crowd for examination so they could see that it was real. Apparently, someone in the crowd nicked the blade, which resulted in an injury that led to her death.

Their niece Edna soon after followed in her aunt's footsteps by learning sword swallowing from Uncle Delno and carving out her own successful career (see page 71).

MARIE DEVERE
1874–1941

In the early twentieth century, Marie DeVere was known to swallow up to fifteen swords at once and performed with circuses and sideshows from 1905 to 1929. Born Marie Ellmore in 1874, she immigrated to the United States from either England or Ireland. An article referring to her as Edith Clifford's pupil indicates that she learned the art of sword swallowing from one of the legendary practitioners of the craft.

Clifford, however, wasn't the only star whom DeVere was connected to. It's believed her cousin was famed actress Mae West. In West's 1959 autobiography, *Goodness Had Nothing to Do with It*, she mentions that Ellmore, who performed under the stage name "DeVere," was "already in show business, having ignored her family and done what she wanted." West described her cousin as a showgirl and actress, even recounting her appearance in hair tonic advertisements with the Seven Sutherland Sisters, known for their luxurious locks that reached down to their ankles.

Stories suggest that DeVere's fascination with sword swallowing began at a very young age, leading her to practice with silverware to master her gag reflex. Despite her presumed training under Clifford, DeVere faced an unfortunate accident early in her career.

In 1905, a newspaper reported that the young performer attempted to swallow a 16-inch glass sword with an incandescent light at its end. While she successfully swallowed the illuminated sword, trouble arose when she attempted to withdraw it. The sword bent forward and broke, causing severe injuries in her mouth.

"She became excited, and in her hurry to get the remainder of the sword from her throat, she cut two very deep and ragged gashes in [her] mouth, one in the roof of her mouth and a deep gash in her tongue," the article stated. This created a shock beyond what the audience had paid for—especially when, as the newspaper described, "blood spurted out of her mouth." It caused two women in the audience to faint. DeVere retreated to her dressing room, took the time to grab her coat, then rushed to a doctor. Fortunately, she recovered and continued her career for more than two decades.

In 1907, DeVere performed as "World Champion Lady Sword Swallower" with the Barnum & Bailey Circus, following in the footsteps of her mentor. A few years later, she, along with two fellow female performers, strongwoman Betty Rose and sharpshooter Helen Engelhart, pooled their savings to invest in an escape from circus life. The three women purchased 40 acres of fields and woodland in Rhode Island, where they raised poultry and ran a dairy

Marie Devere appeared as the "Queen of Sword Swallowers" at Austin & Stone's Museum in Boston in March 1908. She performed with other acts employing sharp blades, including a knife thrower and a vegetable sculptor. That and more for only ten cents. *Public domain*

farm. Rose took on the outdoor work, Engelhart managed the business, and, as described in a 1911 newspaper report, DeVere "found congenial employment as goddess of the poultry yards and between caring for the hens, ducks, rabbits and a kennel of French poodles, finds little time when at home to indulge in the luxury of somber soliloquies on the passing of time."

Yet, farm life never fully supplanted show life. In the years that followed, DeVere continued swallowing swords for Frank A. Robbins Shows, John Robinson's Shows, at Huber's Museum, and at numerous other establishments. By 1925, her shows typically began by gulping a 10-inch sword, followed by three swords at once, and eventually shocking audiences by downing a 2-foot blade.

Records indicate that she continued performing as late as 1929 at Coney Island, where she appeared alongside Albert-Alberta, the half man, half woman; Paul Harold, the Belgian giant; Henry Bulson, the spider boy; and the 640-pound fat lady Sweet Marie.

DeVere's personal life remains shrouded in mystery, since she reportedly had three husbands, none of whom were frequently seen by those around her. After a long illness, she passed away at the age of sixty-seven on April 9, 1941, at the Cranston State Infirmary in Rhode Island. It's unknown when she had been admitted to the mental illness facility, or what type of specific illness she suffered from. Following her death, her prized swords were sold off, closing a final curtain on her career.

THE ART OF SWORD SWALLOWING

SWORD SWALLOWING

THE SECOND WAY

SWORD SWALLOWING

HOW IT IS DONE

SIXTEEN DIFFERENT WAYS

THE FIRST WAY

The Victorinas sold tips on sword swallowing, which were not to be taken seriously. *Collection of Dan Meyer*

THE VICTORINAS

JOSEPH BRYANT HALLWORTH: 1872–1958
KITTY FISHER: 1880–1953

The Victorinas were a sword-swallowing husband-and-wife team in the 1890s and early 1900s. Joe Van Victorina (better known as Kar-Mi, the "Prince of India," and a "high priest of conjurors and spirit workers") would swallow a loaded gun barrel and, while it was down his throat, shoot a cracker off a man's head. Miss Victorina was said to have swallowed a record sixteen swords at once around the turn of the century.

Kar-Mi / Joe Van Victorina was a Native American born as Joseph Bryant Hallworth in Chelsea, Massachusetts, on April 30, 1872. He claimed to have been a child prodigy who learned to read at three, finished the Bible by four, and consumed most of the English classics by age six. At fourteen he ran away from home and soon found himself in British Columbia learning to hunt, camp, shoot, and ride horses from a Cherokee Indian trapper. A year later he entered the world of entertainment by joining a small circus in Kansas as a sharpshooting cowboy. The circus eventually folded, and Hallworth moved on to a medicine show before getting work with Pawnee Bill's Wild West Show and later with Buffalo Bill's Wild West Show.

In 1891, his act expanded with his marriage to Kitty Fisher, a sword swallower who started at age twelve and became known as the Viennese Venus. As one article described, "Her astonishing feats are executed gracefully and rapidly, and cannot give the slightest offense to the most sensitive beholder."

Soon after, the young couple began their act as the Victorinas. Aside from swallowing swords, they added song-and-dance routines, snake charming, fire eating, fortune-telling, and acts of magic, illusion, and mind reading.

The *Boston Herald* once said this of Victorina's sword-swallowing ability: "Her throat and food passages have become so expansive that she can swallow three long swords almost up to the hilts, and can accommodate a dozen shorter blades."

Skilled as she was, Miss Victorina had a few accidents that nearly put an end to her career. In 1894, while

Victorina, a.k.a. the Viennese Venus. Ca. late 1890s. *Collection of Karla L. Raymond*

performing at Kohl & Middleton's Dime Museum in Chicago (alongside a young Harry Houdini), she swallowed a long, thin dagger that snapped in two upon its withdrawal. She dropped the hilt and immediately reached her finger and thumb down her esophagus to catch the blade and extract it. On another occasion in Boston, a sword pierced a vein in her throat. The blade was halfway down, but instead of immediately pulling it out, she pushed it farther in. She was hospitalized for three months.

Despite these near disasters, the Victorinas penned a pamphlet in 1899 outlining methods of sword swallowing for anyone curious. They titled it *Sword Swallowing—How to Do It Sixteen Different Ways*. However, the "sixteen different ways" were just another piece of entertainment, for example:

> The Fourth Way: Get a piece of rubber tubing of the same diameter as the inside of your esophagus and of sufficient length to reach from your palate to the pit of your stomach. . . . You will find that you can place an article down the throat (inside the tube) and not feel it in the slightest and as the tube is out of sight and very pliable it may be kept there indefinitely provided you can breathe, which by the way is sometimes impossible.

> The Ninth Way: Have a sword made with a detachable handle and when performing let the blade slide down your sleeve and hold the handle in your teeth.

> The Fifteenth Way: Hire somebody to do it for you as it may save you much annoyance and though more expensive is very satisfying in the long run.

One wonders if any readers took the pamphlet seriously and reinforced the common notion that genuine sword swallowing was similarly nonsensical.

Offstage, Joseph and Kitty began a family in 1898 with the birth of a daughter. Two sons followed soon after and were eventually brought in the acts. One dressed as a female assistant to aid Kar-Mi's illusions, and the other was made to levitate.

Though the Victorinas began performing in vaudeville and Kar-Mi expanded his showmanship by being buried alive (for thirty-two days, according to his colorful poster), they put an end to their career when their two sons were drafted into World War I. The Hallworths retired near Boston, Massachusetts, where Joe found less daring work as a printer and engraver.

They remained there for the next forty years. Kitty passed away in 1953, leaving Joe a widower until his passing in 1958 at the age of eighty-six.

VSEVOLOD IVANOV
1895–1963

Vsevolod Ivanov may be the only great Russian writer of the early twentieth century who was also a sword swallower.

Born on February 24, 1895, in a remote village near the border of Siberia and Turkestan, Ivanov ran away from home at the age of fourteen to escape peasant life. Yearning for exploration, he spent the next seven years thriving on adventure. Ivanov apprenticed as a printer, entertained as a clown, recited couplets in a circus, swallowed swords in county fairs, jumped through hoops of knives, and stuck pins in his flesh as a human pincushion. At times his metamorphosis even led to occasional billings as a wrestler.

By 1915, Ivanov added "author" to his unique resume with the publication of his first story. His new career took a brief pause in 1917, when he joined the Red Army and fought in Siberia during the brutal civil war.

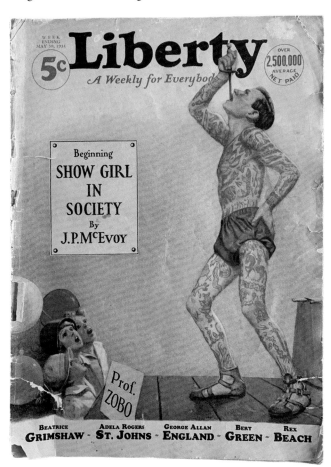

Liberty magazine, May 30, 1931. The cover story has little if anything to do with sword swallowing, but the image reflects the popularity of the art during this era. *Collection of Dan Meyer*

Ivanov's military experiences inspired several of his short stories, including one of his greatest literary achievements, the novella *Armored Train 14-69* (1922). This narrative masterfully portrays a band of Red partisans as they besiege a White Guard locomotive in the vast expanses of Mongolia. The story's impact was so profound that it was adapted into a highly successful play, a mainstay in the repertoire of the Moscow Art Theatre for an impressive span of seventy years.

Ivanov later published *The Adventures of a Fakir* in 1935. The autobiographical nature of the story returned him to his circus roots.

LAWRENCE BOWDEN'S GET-OUT-OF-JAIL-FREE BLADE

There are a lot of crimes that could be committed with swords. Swallowing them shouldn't be one of them. Yet, on December 27, 1913, Lawrence Bowden of LaSalle, Illinois, was arrested in Kenosha, Wisconsin, for doing just that in a downtown saloon.

The incident made the front page of the *Kenosha Evening News*. According to the article, that night Bowden had dropped into the bar and began "making propositions to eat up pretty nearly everything in a metallic line that could be found about the place." The other guests watched in awe, and Bowden decided to pass the hat around so his impromptu audience could show their proper appreciation.

Unfortunately, it was about this time that a police officer walked in and witnessed the event. He determined that Bowden had broken an ordinance by performing a free show without a license. As a result, the by-the-book officer hauled Bowden to jail. The offending showman had money in his pocket to pay a fine, but he argued that swallowing a sword was not a crime.

"He declared in words profoundly deep that the officer was interfering with a right granted to him under the constitution and that to the best of his knowledge and belief he had a right to eat as many swords and bayonets as he saw fit," the article reported.

The night sergeant at the desk convinced Bowden to sleep it off in lockup. Tired, the angry sword swallower complied. Early Sunday morning, Police Chief Owen O'Hare came to the station and saw there was an inmate booked on a charge of "sword swallowing." He immediately asked the desk sergeant to bring Bowden from his cell.

"Well, get busy and let's see you swallow some swords," the chief yelled. Without hesitation, Bowden gulped down an old-fashioned broad sword and an

EATS EIGHT SWORDS

Lawrence Bowden "of the Profession" Meets Hard Luck in Kenosha.

GIVES POLICE DEMONSTRATION

Offers to Swallow His Whole Equipment, in Order to Secure His Liberty and Is Taken at His Word—Gets Out of Town With Blessing of the Chief.

Headline from the *Kenosha Evening News*, December 29, 1913. *Public domain*

army bayonet. The police couldn't believe their eyes, but Bowden assured them that he had only begun.

"He continued to crowd away in his esophagus any number of things metallic, and finally he made the proposition to the chief that he would swallow eight swords at once, if liberty was guaranteed to him," the article said.

"Get right to swallowing!" replied the chief.

Bowden picked up eight swords and swallowed them all. The chief honored their agreement and set the sword swallower free.

CAPT. FRITZ LECARDO

1876–1959

Fritz Lecardo was born in 1876 and began swallowing swords as early as 1919. Over the decades that followed, he performed as "Capt. Fritz Lecardo," "Professor Fritz Lecardo," and "The Great LaCardo."

Lecardo was known for swallowing a sword and hanging a chair over its hilt. Fortunately, there's no evidence of anyone trying to one-up him with a volunteer sitting on a hilt-hanging chair (yet). Later he added a neon tube to his arsenal and, based on one of his sideshow banners, a large pair of shears.

In 1920 he swallowed swords with Bobby Fountain's sideshow in the Al G. Barnes Circus. Joining him at the time was the legendary Al Flosso, then known only as the "boy magician."

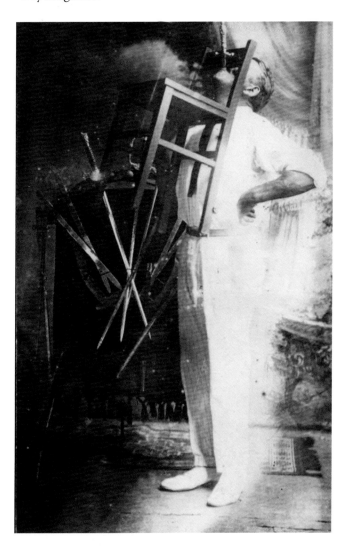

Fritz Lecardo holds a chair hanging from the hilt of a swallowed steel. *Collection of Dan Meyer*

By the late twenties, Lecardo was also working as a tattoo artist, and while performing with Christy Bros. Side Show in 1929, he swallowed swords and also threw knives in an impalement act with Madame Ada.

In the early thirties he joined Cash Miller's winter show, Miller's Modern Museum, and performed alongside John the Elephant-Skin Boy, Agnes Schwarzenbacher (a.k.a. Schmidt) the Rubber Skin Lady, Prince Tiny Mite, Madam Leona the mentalist, and others.

During a stint at a carnival sideshow in 1933, a local newspaper article hailed Lecardo as "the sword swallower who 'eats' five sabres at one time." This, however, was only after hyping the "star performers" of the show, which it stated were "a group of educated Pekingese dogs."

In 1940, his repertoire expanded even further with a listing as "the man with iron eyelids." Eventually the title of "weightlifter" was added as well.

Three years later, at least one of Lecardo's unique talents appeared to have caused an unknown injury in San Francisco. A September 1943 blurb in *Billboard* states that he was released from a hospital and promptly joined the Frank Forest Museum as a ticket taker.

According to Lecardo's brief obituary on April 13, 1959, he passed away in San Francisco. It adds that he "made the trip to Europe with the Ringling Show and was with Sells-Floto, Mighty Haag, and other shows." Lecardo was also a charter member of Showfolks of America.

THE MIGHTY AJAX

1884–1959

Sword swallowers find their way into the entertainment world through different paths, but only the Mighty Ajax started as a pigeon trainer in a dime museum.

Born of Italian descent as Joseph Milana on December 6, 1884, in Washington, DC, just as his mother became a US citizen, he began finding any type of work at an early age. According to 1900 US Census records, Joseph received only a fourth-grade education, and by age fifteen he was working as a jeweler in Brooklyn to help support his mother as the oldest of four children. His father, unlisted in the records, was apparently absent. Shortly after his jeweler gig, Joseph found his way into the dime museum and eventually added puppeteering with Punch and Judy shows to his pigeon-training skills. By around 1903 or early 1904, he claimed to have taught himself sword swallowing. Milana is first listed as a sword swallower in the *New York Clipper* on March 5, 1904, with the Miles Orton Big Southern Railroad Shows. Later that year, having adopted the name the Mighty Ajax, he toured Europe with Buffalo Bill's Wild West Show and by the end of 1905 had returned to America and toured twelve states.

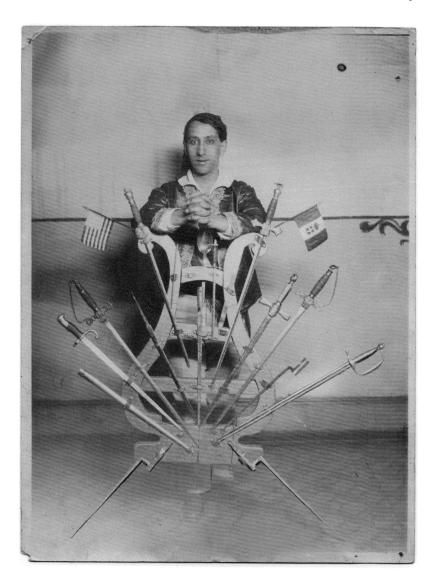

The Mighty Ajax and his swords, circa 1920s. *Collection of Warren A. Raymond*

The Mighty Ajax seen with his swords in this promotional piece for a performance at Coney Island.
Collection of Warren A. Raymond

During his act, Ajax would stand on the bally, swallow a sword, and put it back in its scabbard. When audience members would inevitably doubt its authenticity and shout that it was fake, Ajax would offer them a simple challenge: "If anyone doubts that I'm really swallowing a sword, bring me your own sword, and I'll swallow it, with the provision that if I swallow it, I get to keep it!" On at least one occasion, the challenge was accepted. Ajax was performing for King George V of England, and His Royal Highness did not believe that Ajax actually swallowed the sword. So, Ajax issued the challenge, and the king produced a sword. Ajax carefully swallowed the sword, convinced the king, and was allowed to keep George's blade.

Over the course of several decades, Ajax worked at Coney Island's Dreamland Circus Side-Show, the Ringling Bros. and Barnum & Bailey Circus, and Hubert's Museum. While performing at Hubert's in 1928, legendary circus photographer Edward Kelty captured an x-ray image of Ajax with a sword down his throat.

Outside the Dreamland stage, Ajax's sideshow banner read as follows: "Robert Ripley says, 'The only man in the world who can swallow a red-hot sword!'" Ajax had upped the danger ante by heating up a sword in a charcoal fire until the steel was red hot, then put the blade in its scabbard and swallowed both at the same time. He had to remove the sword quickly before it transferred the heat to the sheath. According to reports, other sword swallowers later died while trying to imitate Ajax's feat.

In 1944, *Billboard* reported that Ajax had "shelved sword swallowing" at Coney Island *and* changed sideshows to replace a departed performer as "a Frankenstein impersonator." Four years later, he picked a blade again to teach a teenager named Jerry Pickard—who would later perform as Slim Price—how to swallow swords in a doorway between shows. By the 1950s, Ajax returned to sword swallowing for Ripley's Believe It or Not!

Shortly after, following fifty-four years of performing, the Mighty Ajax passed away in Brooklyn, New York, on April 27, 1959. According to his son, Richard Milana, Ajax was always cautious and never suffered any serious injuries during his performances. As Slim Price said in 2004 while recalling his experience as a teen, "Ajax was a pretty good sword swallower."

EDNA PRICE
1899–1987

When Edna Price's aunt died from a sword-swallowing accident, she mourned her loss as any loved one would. And then she learned to swallow swords from her uncle. Her aunt, Maud D'Auldin, and uncle, Delno Fritz, were among the most notable sword swallowers of the early

Edna Price with her good friend, Major Mite. *Courtesy of Robert Way and Scott Bellinger*

twentieth century. Edna, born on September 12, 1899, in Ashley, Pennsylvania, near Wilkes-Barre, had already worked as a "floating lady" in the John Robinson Circus Side Show by the age of sixteen. At twenty, Uncle Delno taught her the family business.

In 1920, Price and Fritz performed with the Ringling Bros. and Barnum & Bailey Circus and the Al G. Barnes Circus. As the June 5, 1920, issue of *Billboard* noted, "Her youth and beauty has played an important part in her success." That youth and beauty, not surprisingly, attracted attention. Uncle Delno looked after her, but when Edna wanted to go out on a date with someone that he didn't approve of, she would hide his wooden leg to ease her escape.

Price spent more than ten seasons with the Ringling show. There, she found a best friend in Major Mite (Clarence Chesterfield Howerton), a 28-inch-tall fellow performer. Price often came to his defense—possibly with a sword in hand—when others picked on him. She also fell in love

Edna Price made many friends in the circus, including this orangutan. *Courtesy of Robert Way and Scott Bellinger*

Thousands See Ripley Oddities

Thrill at Exhibition of 'Believe It or Not.'

The Temple of Gasps, Ripley's Believe It Or Not Odditorium, went into its third day today at the old Higbee store building, Euclid ave. and E. 13th st., leaving behind it a wake of "Oh's" and "Ah's" very much like those that greet the famous cartoon which runs daily in The News.

Here for a nine-day appearance in the interest of The News Toy-

Edna Price and the sword she swallows.

Edna Price, as seen in the 1930s scrapbook of Agnes Schwarzenbacher, the Rubber Skin Lady. *Courtesy of Dori Ann Bischmann*

with elephants during her years with the circus. They became a lifelong passion.

By 1933, Price joined Ripley's Believe It Not for a twenty-week tour that included the Chicago World's Fair. Throngs of crowds watched her swallow swords alongside a host of Ripley's human oddities, including Grace McDaniels, the mule-faced woman; Frieda Pushnik, the armless and legless girl; Betty Lou Williams and her parasitic twin; Paul Desmuke, the armless knife thrower; Agnes Schwarzenbacher, the rubber-skin lady (a.k.a. Agnes Schmidt); Martin Laurello, who rotated his head 180 degrees; John Williams, the alligator-skin man; and others.

Ripley dubbed Price the "Queen of Sword Swallowers"—a deserving title for her ability to gulp up to twelve swords at a time, and for becoming the first woman to swallow the white neon tube. During an act she performed at Coney Island, Price even attached the tube to a rifle, then fired it once the tube was in her throat.

Of course, she was especially careful, knowing that her aunt's accident involved a nicked sword. Price made it a practice to have her blades chromed each year to protect against similar imperfections and scratches. She did, however, have several tubes break, but fortunately it always happened after the act. On one occasion the light fractured due to the cold weather at Rye Beach in New York. The tube had been heated by the current running through it and Price's body temperature, but it cracked when it touched the cool air upon its removal.

Despite the danger, Price loved her job. As she told a reporter in 1937, she enjoyed "the glamor of it all, the pleasant associations," and, most of all, "the salary end." According to a 1923 article, she earned between $500 and $750 a week at the time. Considering that's roughly equivalent to $10,000 today, the article likely exaggerated, but she apparently was quite satisfied with her earnings.

Though the Queen of Sword Swallowers never performed in her hometown, she worked with a Wilkes-Barre director named Lyman Howe to create an early 1930s educational film called *Strange Occupations of Women*. In it, she swallowed a long rod with a flashlight bulb attached, which shined in her throat in a darkened room.

By 1939, following her performances at the New York World's Fair, Price hung up her swords in retirement. She had a young daughter to raise by then. The former circus star later worked with Ripley's Believe It or Not! in Atlantic City as a hostess and then took a series of jobs that were quite different from her previous gigs by working for railroads and the military. Eventually she and her husband, a former boxer named Jack Harris, settled in Florida.

In the late fifties, Price spent most of her time helping her daughter, a single mother, raise her four children. She didn't entertain them with swords, but she often spoke of her old performing days.

"If there was something on TV and it had a circus and there was a sword swallower, she'd say, 'That's what I did,'" her grandniece Cyndi Price, who was also raised by Edna, recalls. "I was grossed out. 'You stuck that down your throat?' She said, 'Yes, I used to do the lightbulbs too.'"

Price eventually was stricken with dementia in her early eighties. She battled it for five years before passing away at the age of eighty-eight in Melbourne, a coastal town southeast of Orlando, on October 17, 1987. Her swords and neon tube were kept by her sister, Catherine Evans, in Pennsylvania.

"[Edna] was the rock in this family," Cyndi Price says. "She's definitely one of those that believed if women could do it then, there's nothing that they can't do now."

NOT THE SHARPEST SWORD SWALLOWER

The art of sword swallowing is undoubtedly dangerous. Though it's rare, performers have died in the act of entertaining others by gulping down a couple of feet of steel.

In 1925, a twenty-four-year-old Ohio sword swallower, Jack Hill, risked his life for the entertainment of others by swallowing a 9-inch knife at a local theater. He bowed, the audience cheered, and he left the stage.

Now, normally the performer pulls the blade right back out for all to see. But Hill neglected this second half of the act because he literally swallowed his knife. It remained in his stomach until a surgeon could remove it hours later.

According to the newspaper account, "An x-ray revealed the knife, the blunt end down and the point piercing the esophagus. Through an abdominal incision the blade was removed and except for incidental shock had caused no harm. Hill will recover."

And yes, that unfortunate evening for the young performer was billed as "amateur night."

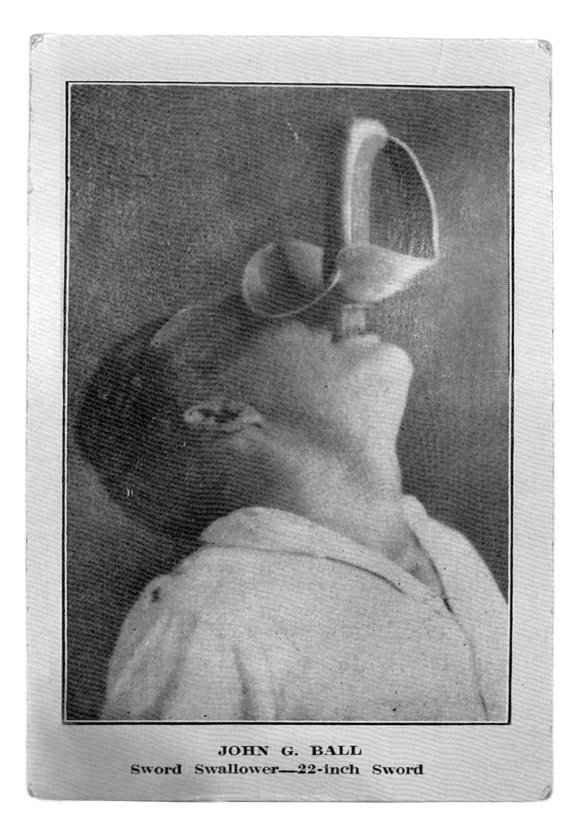

JOHN G. BALL
Sword Swallower—22-inch Sword

A pitch card of John "Lucky" Ball featuring a 22-inch sword fully swallowed. *Courtesy of Jim Ball*

JOHN "LUCKY" BALL
1898–1977

Lucky Ball's career in sword swallowing started after an incident that was anything but lucky. While working as a lion tamer, one of the great cats mauled him to the point where he decided that swallowing blades of steel would be a far safer way to make a living. According to one newspaper account, the lion slashed him across his left arm, "bashed" him in the head, and ripped his stomach open.

Lucky Ball was born into the circus life as John Gregory "Lucky" Ball in Claysville, New York, on December 29, 1898. Both his parents, James Ball and Alice Bonfoy, were performers. According to a newspaper interview with Ball in 1949, his mother was an "iron jaw artist" and his father was a lion tamer. Growing up under the tent, Ball found work as a clown for the Ringling Bros. circus before following in his father's footsteps and stepping into the ring with lions. After the attack caused his pivot to sword swallowing, he claimed to have taught himself in a full six weeks of practice in 1916.

From the 1920s to the late 1940s, Lucky Ball worked with a number of traveling sideshows and circuses, including the Clyde Beatty Circus and Royal American Shows. Aside from downing up to 28 inches of steel and neon tubes, and swallowing swords while sitting down, Ball also invented a crooked sword that he described as a "corkscrew-shaped iron rod." As the sword went down and came up, it put a ripple in his Adams apple. Robert Ripley illustrated Ball swallowing the unique sword for a Believe It or Not! cartoon. No one else had attempted such a swallow until Ball gave Alex Linton a corkscrew of his own.[6]

In 1927, while working in Hoxie, Kansas, Ball met Estelline Lovin and fell in love. The couple married in 1928, and Ball promptly taught her to swallow swords. Together, the newlyweds made for a unique husband-and-wife sword-swallowing act. By 1935, Estelline gave birth to Jim (see page 95); two other children followed shortly after.

Between raising kids and performing onstage, Ball found his way onto the big screen. In 1936 he appeared in the W. C. Fields film *Poppy* and in *Pennies from Heaven* with Bing Crosby and Louis Armstrong. The following year he swallowed swords alongside two other stars: Spencer Tracy in *They Gave Him a Gun* and Shirley Temple in *Wee Willie Winkie*.

"Shirley, like many other people, looked at me with astonished eyes and asked me if I really swallow that sword," he told a reporter. "Most people believe that the sword disappears into the handle or that it curls up in my mouth, and my answer is to let them feel the blade. People watching me almost invariably open their mouths when I open mine, and start to swallow when I place the sword on my lips."

Capping off his year of Hollywood hobnobbing in 1937, Ball was featured in *Look* magazine and swallowed a record sixteen swords.

Ball seemed to be impressing everyone except, as he explained to a reporter, doctors. "Medical people are never astonished, because they know that when you throw back your head, the passage from your mouth to your stomach is a straight line. The only 'trick' to sword swallowing is to acquire control over your throat muscles—merely a matter of practice."

Despite all his professional successes, his homelife was suffering. By 1940 he had separated from Estelline and left the kids behind. A divorce followed soon after. Ball remarried by 1944; Estelline remarried at around the same time and became Estelline Pike.

Though Ball's new wife wasn't a sword swallower, he wasn't done teaching women his trade. In the early 1940s, a Hawaiian dancer named Maxine Logsdon was performing in Indianapolis and saw Ball in attendance. She asked him to teach her to swallow swords and after being told, "Maybe," she persuaded him. Five days later, after much gagging, she succeeded.

Ball got out of show business in 1948 and settled in Akron, Ohio. His wife convinced him to go into the cleaning business, but he continued performing at local clubs and private parties. Ball eventually spent the last twenty years of his life working with Goodrich Tires. He passed away at age seventy-eight.

ALEX LINTON
1904–72

If you're reading a book about sword swallowers, chances are you've seen Tod Browning's classic 1932 film, *Freaks*.[7] And that means you—like thousands of sideshow-goers a century ago—have seen Alex Linton swallow swords.

Linton was born in Roscommon, Boyle County, Ireland, on October 25, 1904.[8] He moved with his family to the United States (possibly arriving in Washington, DC, in 1919). He had already learned to swallow swords at the tender age of twelve from his father, who was a sword swallower.

"The first time I tried it, I gagged and became ill," he recounted decades later. "Afterwards it started getting easier though. I got tired of telling other kids my old man was a sword swallower, and that's why I started. They thought I was lying."

---

6   Dan Meyer eventually gained possession of one of these rods and passed it on to Ball's sword-swallowing son, Jim Ball.

7   *Freaks* lists Delno Fritz as the sword swallower in its credits; however, Fritz died in 1925. Instead, it was Linton in the role.

8   Linton is sometimes referred to as "Alec Linton" or "Alex Lonton."

Early in his career, but well past the gagging stage, Linton adopted the stage name "The Young Ajax" to capitalize on the reputation of "The Mighty Ajax" (Joseph Milana), a sword swallower who'd gained popularity in the early 1900s. He also performed using his own name with a royal title, "Alex Linton, Prince of Swords," and armed himself with twenty different blades onstage. By 1930, he claimed to have sharpened his skills under the tutelage of longtime sword swallower Lucky Ball.

Over the years, Linton performed with various shows, including Ringling Bros. and Barnum & Bailey Circus, Cole Bros. Circus, Clyde Beatty Circus, and E. K. Fernandez Shows. Linton's signature stunt was called the "Shimmy-Shawabble," in which he swallowed a plated layout pin bent into a series of S curves that made his Adam's apple visibly wobble from side to side when he passed the pin up and down his throat. He liked to conclude his act by throwing his final sword into a block of wood on the stage. It was a simple demonstration that proved its authenticity.

Throughout his career, Linton performed alongside many notable sideshow performers, including the Doll Family, armless and legless girl Frieda Pushnik, Rasmus Nielsen, the Fischer giants, and Betty Broadbent, "the living art gallery" tattooed lady. Linton, who had been heavily tattooed by famed artist Charlie Wagner in the late 1920s, let Broadbent add a few of her own designs to his body.

During a stint at Hubert's Museum in New York City in the late 1930s, *Billboard* reported that in his ten-month stay as a knife thrower and sword swallower, he had "thrown an average of 300 bayonets a day or a total of 90,000 for the 10 months without hitting Stella, tattoo girl, his target" and had "swallowed approximately 260 feet of steel per day, or about 78,000 feet in all." Among that 78,000 feet of steel, Linton often swallowed four 27-inch swords at once, and two with a lit cigarette sandwiched between them. It's worth noting that those 27-inch swords were going into a 5-foot, 3-inch body. At the time, they also earned him a Guinness World Record.

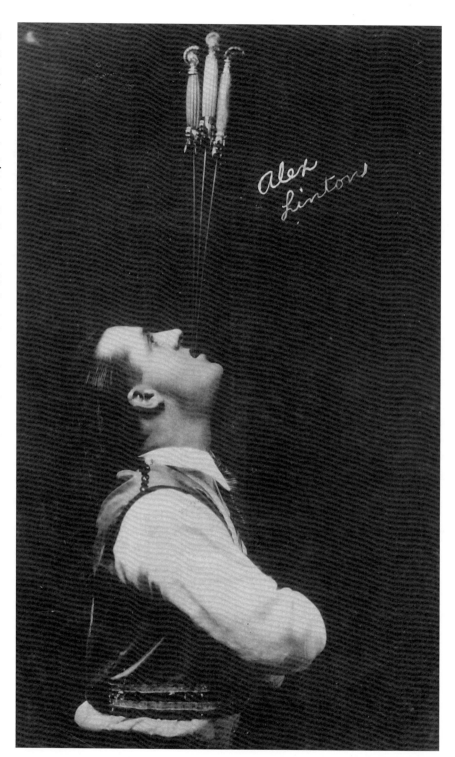

Alex Linton, Prince of Swords, swallows three blades. *Collection of Dan Meyer*

Along with his collection of steel, Linton swallowed neon tubes—both onstage and in medical rooms. He once downed the lights for a doctor at Bellevue Hospital. "All I did was to sit on a table and swallow tubes," he told a reporter. "Then he lit me up inside and explained to his medical students just what was taking place."

As for his knife-throwing act, he eventually gave it up. "On a job like that, a man can't afford to take a drink, and I didn't like that," he said. "I can take a snort any time I want to and still guzzle down my swords."

In 1941, Linton was drafted into World War II. While training at Camp Bowie in Brownwood, Texas, as "Pvt. Alex Linton," he swallowed three blades at once for his fellow soldiers of the 27th Signal Construction Battalion. One newspaper noted, "They were three more than the other selectees had swallowed, and each onlooker felt a tickling in his throat as the three swords went down."

Fortunately, Linton survived the war, though it's unknown how long he served. By 1946, however, he was once again appearing with Ringling Bros. and Barnum & Bailey. Around that same time, it's believed he played the role of a sword swallower in 1947's *Nightmare Alley*.

While performing at the Minnesota State Fair in 1948, the *Star Tribune* asked what Linton thought of the people who came to his show. "I prefer kids," Linton answered. "You've got to prove everything to them, and they're quick with the comeback. A kid got a whipping once because of me—tried my act at home with a bread knife. I gave him a picture autographed 'to a future sword swallower.' I don't mind the drunks and the wise guys. You get numb to them after 32 years in the business."

That bread-knife-swallowing kid might not have become a future sword swallower, but Linton did mentor two young apprentices who went on to have illustrious careers in the sideshow: Bobby Reynolds and Captain Don Leslie. Reynolds, a legendary showman, learned at around age sixteen in the boiler room of Hubert's Museum in the late '40s, and Leslie perfected the art with Linton's help while they were with the Clyde Beatty Cole Bros. Circus in 1954. Prior to working with Linton, Leslie claimed he'd been gagging and retching with every swallow. "He told me with some of the things I was doing, I was lucky to be alive," Leslie said to a reporter in 1987. Linton's star student went on to break his Guinness World Record by swallowing five 30-inch swords at once.

Linton officially retired in 1966 and resided in Sarasota, Florida, where many circus and sideshow performers lived. Despite leaving the stage, he kept swallowing swords until his death on September 2, 1972. Linton was sixty-seven. He had no surviving family, which meant there was no one to claim his body. And that meant it could've been sent to a medical school for anatomy studies. When this news became apparent, a local organization of retired performers called Show Folks of Sarasota pulled together enough expenses to ensure that after so many decades of swallowing blades, Linton's body would remain uncut and receive a proper burial.

HARRY LESTER: THE SWORD SWALLOWER WHO WASN'T KNOWN FOR SWALLOWING SWORDS

Many sword swallowers perform a variety of acts, but few become wildly famous for them. Maryan Czajkowski is an exception—even though you've likely never heard his name.

Czajkowski (sometimes spelled Tschaikovsky) was born on September 9, 1879, in Poland. And yes, that alternate spelling does mean he was related to the great Russian composer Pyotr Ilyich Tchaikovsky, though it's unclear if they had ever met.

As a young boy, Maryan's family immigrated to the United States. At the age of sixteen he dropped out of school and ran away to join the circus. Once there, he took on whatever job was needed. Eventually, that included entertainer. And within that role, he became a clown, a magician, a mind reader, and a fire eater and performed as Bosco the Snake Eater and, of course, a sword swallower. But at some point in the mid-1890s, he fell in love with the art of ventriloquism, and everything changed. After voraciously reading every book on the subject that he could get his hands on, he mastered the craft in around 1898 and started performing strictly as a ventriloquist. Not as Maryan Czajkowski, but as Harry Lester.

Lester would soon take the vaudeville circuit by storm with his dummy Frank Byron Jr. at his side. Performing as the Great Lester, he became a sensation, toured theaters across America and Europe, and became one of the highest-paid headliners of the vaudeville circuit. He reportedly earned thousands of dollars a week throughout the 1920s.

Today, Lester is known as the "Grandfather of Modern-Day Ventriloquism." He claimed to be the first ventriloquist to drink while his dummy continued to talk. According to one tale, stagehands decided to substitute whiskey for wine. As the master carried on his routine, it was said that "not a muscle on Lester's face moved, but the dummy almost choked to death."

The 1929 film *The Great Gabbo* was said to be based on Lester's life. The movie portrays a ventriloquist whose dummy, Otto, moves its body and talks apart from any control. Eventually, Gabbo becomes envious of Otto and quickly falls from stardom. Lester sued the filmmakers for $250,000.

A final legacy of Lester's came through his greatest pupil, Edgar Bergen. Bergen and his dummy, Charlie McCarthy, would go on to become arguably the most famous ventriloquist act of all time.

On July 14, 1956, at the age of seventy-six, Harry Lester died from complications of an appendicitis operation in Los Angeles, California. Today, Frank Byron Jr. and Lester's other ventriloquist dummies are on display at Vent Haven Museum in Fort Mitchell, Kentucky.

MIMI GARNEAU
1896–1986

Mimi Garneau has been billed as the "Dean of Women Sword Swallowers" and gained acclaim in the late 1920s as the first woman to swallow a neon tube. But for all the risks involved in swallowing swords, life away from the stage was far more difficult.

Garneau was born as Hazel Kirk Thomas in 1896 near Phillipsburg, Pennsylvania.[9] Her father died in 1899 due to complications from work as a miner, leaving Hazel to grow up with her widowed mother and four siblings. By age sixteen she married George J. Hamilton and within just a few years gave birth to her first son, Billee. Despite the child, her marriage was short lived, though for unknown reasons. She rebounded quickly, however, and married a steam plant engineer named Walter Hartshorne in 1916.

9   Some sources claim she was born in 1890 or 1894, but a 1940 census lists her as being forty-four years old—which puts her birth year at 1896 (although ages given in US censuses are notoriously inaccurate, in particular by women).

The couple had three sons, but sadly one of them, Edwin, died at age six from acute dilation of the heart on December 28, 1922.

A year later, Hazel's life took a dramatic turn when she learned to swallow swords and began performing under the name Jude. Toward the end of the decade, she divorced Walter, allegedly due to his troubles with alcohol, and met Fred Garneau. The couple lived in Detroit, where Fred worked in an automotive plant and Hazel took a job as a sales lady in a candy store.

But the budding sword swallower wanted more. By the early 1930s, she began calling herself "Mimi" and soon found herself working with Ripley's Believe It or Not! at the 1933 Chicago World's Fair. As the thirties rolled on, she also worked with the Al G. Barnes Circus, Sells-Floto Circus, and the Ringling Bros. and Barnum & Bailey Circus. Her husband joined the act as well, performing with her as a tattooed man. In addition to swords and neon tubes, Garneau also swallowed bayonets and saws.

After a decade of success, Garneau experienced several hardships in the early 1940s. The first saw the passing of Fred on April 11, 1941, from a subdural hemorrhage sustained just a few weeks prior. Months later, on August 18, her second ex, Walter, also passed away. But perhaps the most painstaking event came two years later. On August 23, 1943, her first son, Billee, while serving as a lieutenant in World War II, was killed in Sicily by a German bomber.

Garneau persevered through it all and continued performing for several decades alongside such attractions as Francesco Lentini the three-legged man, Grady Stiles the Lobster Boy, and Schlitzie the pinhead. By the mid-1950s, she trained Toni Del Rio, a sideshow hermaphrodite, to swallow swords.

A Mimi Garneau pitch card, showcasing her talents. *Collection of Warren A. Raymond*

Mimi Garneau displaying the tools of her trade. Mimi gave the uppermost sword in her left hand to Toni Del Rio (page 100), who passed it on to Red Stuart (page 118), who bequeathed it on to Dan Meyer. *Collection of Dan Meyer*

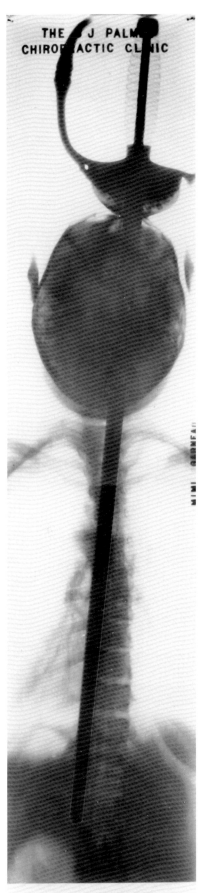

X-ray of Mimi Garneau with steel down her throat.
Collection of Warren A. Raymond

MIMI GARNEAU

With the lights dimmed, Garneau's neon sword glows bright onstage. *Collection of Warren A. Raymond*

Mimi Garneau kept meticulous records of each sword she swallowed. *Collection of Warren A. Raymond*

Outside of the sideshow, Garneau appeared on television at least twice. On March 14, 1951, she was featured on the DuMont Television Network's show *You Asked for It*, on which she swallowed four swords simultaneously and allowed viewers to peek into her throat through a fluoroscope. Twelve years later, she was a guest on *The Steve Allen Show*.

Toward the end of the sixties, Garneau finally hung up her swords, but she didn't give up show business. Instead, she joined an entirely new group of entertainers: a flea circus, complete with specially designed props and real fleas. These prodigious parasites included Captain "Zoom-Zoom," billed as "the world's fastest flea juggler performing unbelievable feats high on top of a flag-pole," and "The Cyclettes," a pair of "daring fleas riding bicycles on a tight wire." She traveled for several years with her tiny troupe before finally retiring in the late 1970s.

Garneau spent her final years in Tampa, Florida, where she passed away at the age of ninety-two on February 22, 1986. Per her wishes, her body was cremated and the ashes were spread along Highway 301 near her home. As Garneau explained when making the request, she had always been on the road all her life. Why should it be any different in death?

CHARLIE LUCAS
1909–91

In the late nineteenth and early twentieth centuries, the role of "African wild man" was not terribly uncommon in sideshows. Richard Charles Lucas was one such performer. In 1933, for example, he performed as WooFoo the Immune Man and the "African chief of the duck bill women" at the Chicago World's Fair "Century of Progress" exhibit. The Black entertainer from Chicago, however, also learned to amaze audiences with physical acts that didn't rely on cultural misrepresentation and ignorance. Such as sword swallowing. Having mastered the feat, Lucas holds the unique distinction of being history's only known Black sword swallower. The performer also added fire eating and walking on hot coals to his arsenal of talents, which he displayed on tour with Ringling Bros. and Barnum & Bailey, Hagenbach-Wallace, Forepaugh & Sells, and other circuses and sideshows around the US and Canada.

By the 1950s, Lucas and his wife, Virginia (a.k.a. Woogie the snake charmer), settled in New York City, where both of them performed at Hubert's Museum on 42nd Street. Lucas was soon elevated into a managerial role but also worked as an inside talker to hype a host of strange and unusual performers, including Mildred the Alligator Skin Girl; Eddie Carmel the Jewish Giant; Sealo the Seal Boy; William Durks, the man with two noses and three eyes; Professor Heckler's Flea Circus; and, of course, fellow sword swallower Estelline Pike.

Lucas eventually befriended Diane Arbus and helped her connect with the many wondrous sideshow people she famously photographed.

Charlie Lucas stands with Buck Nolan inside Hubert's Museum. Nolan was known as "The World's Tallest Clown" and was reportedly 7 feet, 4 inches tall. *Collection of Warren A. Raymond*

DANIEL MANNIX
1911–97

The life of a sword swallower has never exactly been Disney material. But a sword swallower writing a story that got animated by Disney? Daniel Mannix managed that feat when his 1967 children's story, *The Fox and the Hound*, was turned into a film in 1981. But before he had the opportunity to be published, he swallowed swords.

Mannix sold his first story at the age of eighteen but took ten years to sell another as he pursued his dream of being a writer. During that decade, he found his way into the world of sideshow, where he learned to swallow swords. It took him three difficult months to learn.

"Sometimes when my throat muscles were so tired from constant gagging that I couldn't eat, I'd wonder if learning to gulp steel was really worth it," he wrote in *True* magazine in 1951. "But I knew that once I became a

recognized sword swallower, I could walk into any side show in the country and get a job."

Mannix claimed to have bought his blades from the widow of an Italian sword swallower named Rafael who had recently killed himself with them (accidentally, that is). He'd been performing at a Philadelphia dime museum and, according to Mannix's telling, had "tried to swallow a sword with engraved work on the blade and the engraving caught on the lining of his stomach. Rafael had then tried to work it loose by wriggling the hilt around, but you can't breathe very well with a sword down your throat, so he finally had to jerk the blade out. This ripped his stomach and he died a few days later of peritonitis."

Undeterred, Mannix purchased the collection of eight swords differing in length, a sickle, two saws, a long steel rod, and a pair of giant shears. At 6 feet, 4 inches tall, he easily handled the longest of the blades at 26 inches. Once he'd mastered his new tools, he added a neon tube to his repertoire. Though Rafael's steel showed no signs of being haunted, the neon nearly led Mannix to the same fate.

A true story of carnival life. In which the author learns the tricks of the trade, meets some wonderful people (and some crooks) and lives an odd and interesting life.

STEP RIGHT UP!

DAN MANNIX

Daniel Mannix's adventures in sword swallowing led to his quintessential 1951 book, *Step Right Up!*
Collection of Marc Hartzman

"The closest escape I ever had came while I was swallowing neon tubes in a lodge hall," he described in *True*. "I swallowed the first tube and my assistant threw the switch on the transformer. Instead of giving off a steady, even glow, my body began to throw off flashes. Then my bones started to hum. The whole tube was vibrating so hard I could hardly hold it and I expected the thing to explode at any instant." The lodge hadn't been wired properly.

As Mannix jerked it out of his throat, it broke in two, leaving the lower half inside his body. He reached his fingers down his throat and managed to safely retrieve it.

In addition to learning how to swallow sharp or lighted things, Mannix also picked up skills in fire eating, magic, and mentalism. Perhaps best of all, his work introduced him to a host of other colorful characters, including Krinko the Human Pincushion, Jolly Daisy the fat lady, and Bronko the cowboy. They all gave him plenty of fodder for his writing.

In addition to the aforementioned *True* article, Mannix wrote a series for *Collier's* magazine on his sideshow adventures. Both eventually led to his 1951 chronicle of carnival life, *Step Right Up!* (later republished as *Memoirs of a Sword Swallower*). The book has fascinated readers and inspired many to follow in his footsteps for the past seventy-five years.

A 1939 article says that Mannix gave up sword swallowing for his bride, Jule Junker. Fortunately, she didn't make him give up another passion: animals. Mannix had maintained a menagerie of rabbits, snakes, skunks, porcupines, raccoons, falcons, goshawks, vultures, and more. They led to an early publication, *The Back Yard Zoo*, and surely gave rise to his beloved Disney movie.

Daniel and Jule Mannix and their animals settled in Pennsylvania, where they added two children to their otherwise furry and feathered family. He ultimately wrote more than twenty-five books and numerous articles for the *Saturday Evening Post*, *Life*, and *Playboy*.

Mannix's adventures through life came to an end on January 29, 1997, when he passed away at his home at the age of eighty-five.

JOSEPH GRENDOL
DATES UNKNOWN

Being a sword swallower was Joseph Grendol's childhood dream. At least, that's what he told a reporter in 1935. "Didn't want to be an engineer, or a policeman, cowboy, or sea captain," the journalist wrote. "He wanted to be the Great Grendol in the circus." Young Joseph, of Worcester, Massachusetts, pursued his goal by training his throat muscles with pencils, then swallowing dull table knives, and eventually daggers.

Before Photoshop, there was the Photo Art Shop in Dayton, Ohio, which created this image of Joseph Grendol's sword reaching the pit of his stomach. *Collection of Warren A. Raymond*

As early as 1928, his wish came true when he joined the Gentry Bros. Circus sideshow as its sword swallower and fire eater. A year later he jumped to the Ringling Bros. and Barnum & Bailey Circus for at least a season. Grendol swallowed sabers, curved knives, saws, and a neon tube.

His talents took him to Rosen's Wonderland Circus Side Show at Coney Island in 1930, then to Dick Best's sideshow with Royal American Shows, and in 1933 to the Chicago World's Fair at the Ripley's Odditorium.

By then, Grendol had expanded his repertoire by swallowing a bayonet attached to the butt of a rifle, which, when fired, would propel the blade down his throat.

Having found success at his dream job, in 1935 he was ready to retire and live on a farm with his wife, known only as Miss Virginia, the Iron-Tongued Girl. Or so he told the aforementioned reporter.

"There ain't any future in my kind of art; I won't ever be able to swallow anything really important, like an ax, or a ploughshare," he said in jest. "So I'm goin' to leave the profession. Besides, it'll be nice to get some good home cookin' again. The restaurant grub we live on while the show is in New York has got my stummick so touchy, I can't hardly swallow a bite."

Fortunately, he could still swallow his steel. Grendol held off retirement for at least a few more years. He was last known to perform with the Cole Bros. Circus in 1940.

JOHN AND VIVIAN DUNNING
JOHN: 1900–79
VIVIAN: 1908–98

When Vivian Parish visited a traveling carnival in her hometown of Princeton, Minnesota, she met John Dunning, fell in love, and found her ticket out of farm life. Dunning was a performer who swallowed swords and dragged heavy objects—such as a car—from hooks in his eyelids.

"He asked me to join the show," Vivian once explained to a reporter. "So, I joined the show, first as an illusion girl, and then I married him. I thought working on a carnival show would be a pleasant way to see the world."

Dunning soon taught her to swallow swords, but not to develop iron eyelids (perhaps that was her choice). Calling herself Lady Vivian, the young Mrs. Dunning soon began swallowing multiple swords, including one with a pistol mounted on the end of it, which, when shot, would ram the sword down her throat. Together, the Dunnings performed from the 1920s through the '50s for A. J. Budd's Show, Harry Lewiston's Big Circus Sideshow, Johnny J. Jones Carnival, Ripley's Believe It or Not!, and other shows.

In 1939, a reporter watched her act in awe, and described it as follows:

> She seemed omnivorous, with cold sharp steel. Fifteen, 20, 25 inches, the fierce weapons slipped down her graceful length, and as well as one may, with a mouthful of blade, Miss Dunning smiled. She swallowed two swords at once, bent over while they were still in her throat, and then I knew I was in the presence of genius; for the lecturer solemnly announced, "You are now beholding a feat that no other sword swallower alive dares attempt, say nothing of accomplishing." Miss Dunning withdrew the flexible blades, straightened her lithe form, and with a delicate gesture wiped them dry with a rag on the sword rack. After she had swallowed seven or eight swords, she swallowed a long neon tube, which pinkly tinted her bare throat, and came off the platform with a little moue of apology.

Lady Vivian had given a flawless performance but told her agent afterward that her tonsils were infected. Overhearing this, the reporter asked her why she hadn't cut them out. "Oh, gee, I couldn't stand to have a doctor put a knife in my throat," she responded. "It gives me the shudders to think about it."

During World War II, the couple performed apart for at least a brief period. According to the August 12, 1944, *Billboard*, "Corp. John W. Dunning" was in Italy "entertaining the boys and amazing Arabs in his spare time by swallowing swords, eating fire and performing his iron-eyelid act." Meanwhile, Lady Vivian was touring with Harry Lewiston's World's Fair Freaks along with Martin Laurello the Human Owl, Carlos Carpenter the indestructible man, Geraldine Shover the alligator girl, Michaelle the frog boy, and others.

By 1946, John was back in the United States and the couple were reunited on the stage. Together they had three children, though none are known to have followed in their parents' footsteps.

John Dunning died at the age of seventy-nine on July 22, 1979, in Charleston, South Carolina. Vivian remained a widow until her passing nineteen years later in Greensboro, North Carolina, on September 23, 1998, at the age of eighty-nine.

BETTY BANCROFT
1902–85

Most people who witnessed Alex Linton swallow swords gazed in awe, then moved on to the next attractions and went home to resume their lives. Not Betty Bancroft. After watching the master perform in the mid-1930s, she left inspired to be just like him.

"It took me three years to learn," Bancroft told a reporter in 1954. "Once you've mastered the knack of keeping the channel straight, and also mastered the tendency of the law of gravity to reverse itself—you know what goes down tends to come up—then you're okay."

Bancroft was born Elizabeth Jane Wrisley on January 15, 1902. Though little is known about her early life, aside from a short-lived marriage that produced a daughter, she eventually married Fred Bancroft, and the two embarked on a life of daring acts together.

By the 1940s, Fred and Betty were living in Forrest City, Arkansas, and performing as "Fred Bancroft's Circus Side Show." Over the years they traveled with several different circuses under the names "Colorado Fred, the Knife Thrower" and "Buckskin Betty," or under the combined name the "Shooting Stars." The highlight of their early act was when Colorado Fred threw knives at Buckskin Betty while she was spinning on the Wheel

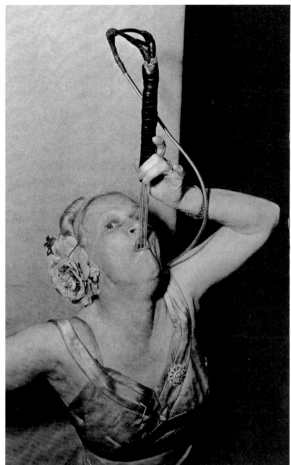

Betty Bancroft seen swallowing a sword and a neon tube and performing as a target girl for her husband's knife-throwing act. Circa mid-1900s. *Collection of Warren A. Raymond*

of Death. Besides being an impalement artist and target for Fred, Betty also performed as a trick rifle sharpshooter, a rope spinner, a whip artist, and, like Linton, a sword swallower.

At 5 feet, 2 inches tall, Bancroft limited herself to swords of 20 inches. Instead of impressing audiences with the length of her swords, she dazzled them with volume by downing four blades at once in what she called her "sword sandwich."

From 1953 to 1954, the Bancrofts toured with the Ringling Bros. and Barnum & Bailey Sideshow. Betty performed as Fred's target girl and as the show's sword swallower. Called "Lady Beth," she included pink neon tubes in her repertoire. Like other sword swallowers, she experienced accidents with the neon though fortunately averted serious injuries. The first occurred in 1953 at Sedalia, Missouri, after the circus had been hit by a tornado and everyone was performing under emergency lights.

"It was the 'bug' season, and those 'bugs' just flocked to the lights, and, of course, they just swarmed into my mouth when I had my lighted neon tube inside me," she explained to a reporter. "I defy anybody to stand still under those circumstances. I just had to squirm and that's fatal in this game. Of course, the glass tube broke. I managed to spit the glass out. Could have cut my tongue or my jugular vein. I was lucky."

Another time, Bancroft was using a new tube that turned out to be flawed. It broke just as she raised it to her chin and prepared to swallow it.

Early in her career, while learning to swallow swords, Bancroft struck her voice box with a blade. Her voice never fully recovered, leaving it forever raspy. As she described it, it became "a sort of asset, part of my stock in trade. People hear me on the radio or on television, and they never forget my voice."

This can be heard today by streaming her April 4, 1954, television appearance on *What's My Line?* on YouTube. One of the show's panelists guessed her profession was in the circus, but no one deduced the correct answer. After her series of answers in her trademark hoarse voice, host John Daly announced, "Ms. Bancroft's having trouble with her voice; she's a sword swallower."

The Bancrofts continued performing for several more years, as long as they were able. Fred, who was seventeen years older than Betty, passed away on August 23, 1963, at age seventy-eight. By 1975, Betty retired to North Fort Myers, Florida, where she lived for the next ten years until her death on March 22, 1985. She was eighty-three.

Bancroft's obituary in the local paper touted her forty years of circus life and credited her as being the inventor

of the Wheel of Death. It's a claim that might have been disputed by the Gibsons—a husband-and-wife act from Germany who brought the wheel to New York in 1938 when they performed at Madison Square Garden with Ringling Bros. and Barnum & Bailey. Perhaps Bancroft witnessed the act and was just as impressed and inspired as she was watching Alex Linton just a few years earlier.

CHESTER DOLPHIN
1907–86

The only thing that Chester Dolphin could have done to make his sword-swallowing, juggling, and unicycling acts more entertaining would've been to do them simultaneously.

Born in Worcester, Massachusetts, in 1907, Dolphin worked in various circuses, sideshows, and fairs with the help of his brothers as prop builders. The versatile performer swallowed swords as early as 1929 in a sideshow with Lionette the Lion-Faced Girl, Koo Koo the Bird Girl, Armless Wonder Frances O'Connor, Jack Orr the Tattooed Marvel, and Capt. August Klint, an 8-foot, 4-inch giant.

By the thirties, Dolphin billed himself as "Champion swallower of swords, carpenter saws and stove pokers." The aforementioned large-toothed saw measured 23 inches, and in addition to his other championship claims, he also swallowed large shears and a 22-inch neon tube. He performed at the Ripley's Odditorium at the 1933 World's Fair in Chicago and, in September 1935, starred again with Ripley's at the Alabama State Fair. The *Birmingham News* marveled at his neon tube act: "After gulping it down, he turns on the electricity and the tube's reddish rays can be seen through him."

Dolphin's wife, Charmon, joined forces with him in the forties and fifties. She performed a comedy magic act and added sex appeal to the show. Chester added a balancing act to his repertoire, in which he did a headstand on a revolving globe ball and spun rings on each leg and each arm and one on a stick in his mouth. Together, they performed around the world, from Europe to Korea to Egypt. At Christmas the talented couple did shows for American servicemen stationed around the world. "It gives us a good feeling to be among our own people over the holidays," she told the press in 1958. The Dolphins occasionally shared the stage with much-bigger names, such as Bob Hope, Danny Kaye, and Jack Benny.

Years later, Chester returned home to settle in Worcester. Little is known about his final years, but he is believed to have died in 1986, at the age of seventy-nine.

CHARLES A. PRESTER

1913–2006

In 1966, while living in Fort Pierce, Florida, Charles A. Prester puzzled scientists with a unique ability. Not sword swallowing, but growing grapes. Prester's grapevines were yielding about 250 pounds of grapes a year, despite Florida's ground being inhospitable to most every kind of grape. "A field laboratory man wouldn't believe one vine could give such a yield—until he saw it," Prester told a reporter. He emphasized that he had no secrets or training as a viticulturist. After all, until retirement, he'd been too busy puzzling thousands of other people as a sword swallower.

Prester, born in Garfield, New Jersey, on April 24, 1913, learned to swallow steel when he was eighteen by studying with Alex Linton. By 1933, under the moniker "Prince Charles," Prester worked with Kent and Sussex Fair in Harrington, Delaware, before moving on to the World of Mirth show the following year. There, he met eighteen-year-old Anne A. Mukosey. She performed primarily as

a contortionist and worked illusion acts such as the blade box and the Headless Wonder. The two were married in 1935 in Chicago. Shortly after, the young newlyweds worked with Dodson's World Fairs, and, as evidenced by a photo of both swallowing swords side by side, they may have also performed as a sword-swallowing couple.

Over the next five years, the duo worked with the Hagenbeck-Wallace Forepaugh-Sells Combined Circus Sideshow, the Cole Brothers Circus, and the Dodson Shows. During that run, they also had a daughter, who assisted in their act once she was big enough to do so.

Prester was known to swallow up to five swords at once and displayed his props on two shields that held swords, knives, bayonets, long nails, fire pokers, and a keyhole saw.

He claimed to have settled in Fort Pierce in 1937, though he continued performing until at least 1940. He and Anne raised their daughter there and grew old together. In addition to being the first to grow grapes in Fort Pierce, Prester also worked as a carpenter and a nurseryman. When he passed away on September 25, 1990, at age seventy-seven, his obituary made no mention of sword swallowing. Anne, his partner in show business and life, lived to age ninety, passing away on December 15, 2006.

Prince Charles is seen in the bannerline among his fellow performers at a fair. *Collection of Warren A. Raymond*

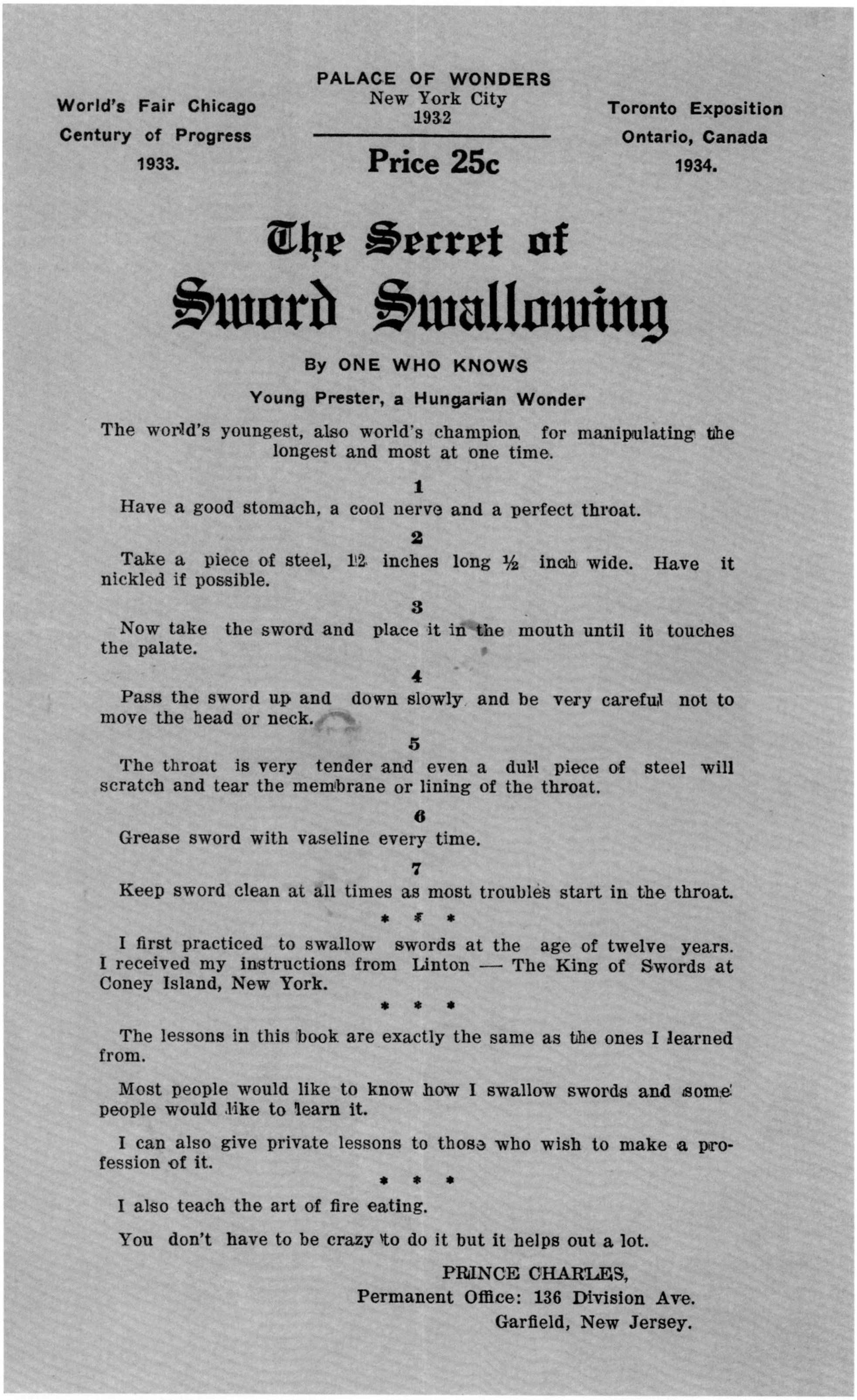

PALACE OF WONDERS
New York City
1932

World's Fair Chicago
Century of Progress
1933.

Toronto Exposition
Ontario, Canada
1934.

Price 25c

The Secret of
Sword Swallowing

By ONE WHO KNOWS

Young Prester, a Hungarian Wonder

The world's youngest, also world's champion, for manipulating the
longest and most at one time.

1

Have a good stomach, a cool nerve and a perfect throat.

2

Take a piece of steel, 12 inches long ½ inch wide. Have it
nickled if possible.

3

Now take the sword and place it in the mouth until it touches
the palate.

4

Pass the sword up and down slowly and be very careful not to
move the head or neck.

5

The throat is very tender and even a dull piece of steel will
scratch and tear the membrane or lining of the throat.

6

Grease sword with vaseline every time.

7

Keep sword clean at all times as most troubles start in the throat.

* * *

I first practiced to swallow swords at the age of twelve years.
I received my instructions from Linton — The King of Swords at
Coney Island, New York.

* * *

The lessons in this book are exactly the same as the ones I learned
from.

Most people would like to know how I swallow swords and some
people would like to learn it.

I can also give private lessons to those who wish to make a profession of it.

* * *

I also teach the art of fire eating.

You don't have to be crazy to do it but it helps out a lot.

PRINCE CHARLES,
Permanent Office: 136 Division Ave.
Garfield, New Jersey.

The Secret of Sword Swallowing for only a quarter. Please do not attempt to learn from these directions. *Collection of Warren A. Raymond*

ESTELLINE PIKE

1908–90

In 1928, sword swallower Lucky Ball was demonstrating his skills in Hoxie, Kansas, when an onlooker heckled him, proclaiming his act wasn't real. His wife, Estelline Pike, came to his defense. "Want to bet five dollars?" she challenged the cynic. The woman in the audience accepted the bet, and Pike stepped up to her husband, took one of his swords, and swallowed it. She collected her five bucks right after. At that moment, she decided that sword swallowing would be an easy way to make a living.

Pike was born June 5, 1908, as Estelline Mable Lovin, daughter of Ada I. Stevenson and Jackson Sperlin Lovin, a railroader in the town their daughter was named after: Estelline, Texas. The family moved to Kansas when Estelline was an adolescent. After graduating as valedictorian at Hoxie High School, she went to business school in Denver, Colorado, and then returned to Hoxie to work as an attorney's stenographer. Her life took an unexpected turn after meeting John Gregory Lucky Ball in 1927—a sword swallower who was spending the winter working with a local farmer and performing occasional shows. Smitten with each other, the two were married on August 16, 1928, and Ball wasted no time in teaching his bride to swallow steel. They soon hit the road and performed a successful sword-swallowing act together.

By 1935 the couple had a son, Jim. Two more children followed before Estelline and Lucky separated after twelve years of marriage. The single sword-swallowing mother was soon remarried to Dewey "Blackie" Pike. She left her act behind to help her husband run carnival shows and concessions, which included a snake show featuring a boa named "Oscar." Sadly, her marriage to Dewey was short lived. As a World War I veteran, he'd dealt with health issues suffered from mustard gas that had infiltrated his lungs. He passed away in 1947 at just forty-eight years old.

Following his death, Pike returned to sword swallowing. She even taught her son the art, who by then was twelve years old and asked to learn the family tradition. It took him several weeks, but sure enough, young Jim downed a blade and became known as the "World's Youngest Sword Swallower."

Back on the road, Pike worked for decades with Royal American Shows, the Ringling Bros. and Barnum & Bailey Circus Sideshow, various state fairs, and at Hubert's Museum in New York City. One of her most notable appearances came in late 1958, when she had the distinction of being the last American sword swallower to perform in Cuba before Fidel Castro took over on January 1, 1959. The revolution was taking place while she was there, and during one particular show she found herself competing with exploding grenades in a nearby parking lot.

Jim often traveled with his mother and worked various jobs on the shows. While Pike was with Dick Best's sideshow in Calgary, Canada, she was stricken with strep throat and had to take a few days off. Jim was selling tickets at the time and told Best he could fill in. "You can?" the showman asked. "Well yeah, I've been doing it since I was twelve," Jim explained.

Though the mother-and-son duo didn't perform side by side, they did appear on television that way. In May 1958, Estelline and Jim, who was then twenty-two years old, were featured on the popular TV show *What's My Line?* As the panel tried to guess their jobs with a series of

Estelline Pike added plastic swords to her souvenir pitch cards, as seen here. *Collection of Warren A. Raymond*

ESTELLINE
SWORD SWALLOWER

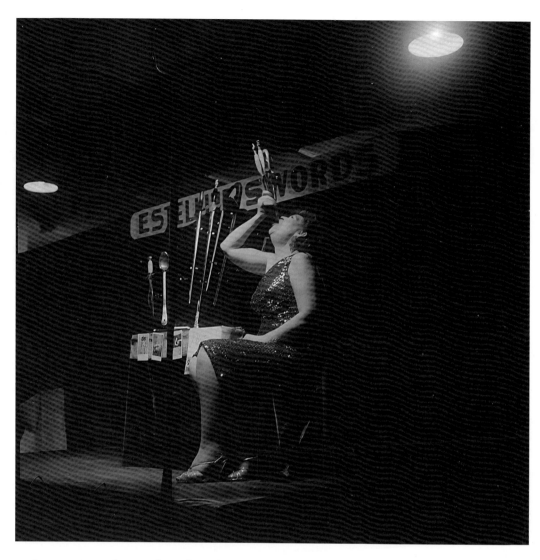

Estelline Pike swallows multiple swords onstage. *Collection of Warren A. Raymond*

yes/no questions, the sword-swallowing team acknowledged that anyone could enjoy their work, that it was enjoyable for groups of people to watch, and, eventually, that they did their work in either a circus, sideshow, or carnival. But when asked if it was "some kind of exhibition that requires physical dexterity," Pike responded, "No." That created a pause in the show while the host conferred with her and Jim and offered a new answer: "We will admit, if it were done properly there is a measure of dexterity required." This was, of course, an important distinction, since swallowing a sword without dexterity would likely be a one-time-only and potentially fatal performance.

By 1961, after thirty-three years of swallowing swords, Pike shared a few details of her routine with a reporter. "The trick to sword swallowing is to be completely relaxed," she explained. "You have to relax to control your throat and your emotions." At the time, she was swallowing a 22-inch sword, a "sword sandwich" of four blades, and, at the climax of her act, gulping six at once.

Pike also noted the importance of staying hygienic by using a medical antiseptic on her blades. "The skeptics want to handle them after a show. They think there's trickery involved and that I'm not swallowing real swords. The kids get cotton candy on the swords and the adults sometimes try to bite them." If anyone still doubted that her steel was real, Pike offered $1,000 to anyone who could make one of her swords fold up into its handle.

When asked how long she would keep swallowing swords, she replied with a smile the same way anyone with a job might: "Just as long as I keep getting hungry and the rent has to be paid." However, she had wished that income could have come from singing. "I really want to be a singer," she once told a reporter. "I've written more than fifty songs, and I'm a jazz pianist. An opera star once told me I should take up singing because I have a tremendous throat."

Though she eventually began selling tickets at Hubert's instead of performing, she continued swallowing swords at shows at Madison Square Garden and a resort in the Catskills. According to her son, Jim, her last few years were spent in retirement in New York City, until her passing on June 8, 1990. Her body was found in her apartment, having apparently suffered a massive heart attack.

LADY LOUISE CHAVANNE
1904–82

In Arthur H. Lewis's 1970 book, *Carnival*, Lady Louise Chavanne explained that "nerve is all you need to be a good sword swallower." Elaborating, she added, "Any doctor'll tell you when your head's thrown back your esophagus and throat are in a straight line and when you stick a sword in your mouth and down your gullet it won't touch nothin' till it hits the stomach."

By then, Chavanne had been swallowing swords, daggers, and other lengthy, pointy objects for thirty-eight years. Born in Atlanta, Georgia, Louise grew up planning on becoming a nurse. It was a profession her father, a cop, steered her toward, though she'd always been more interested in the performing arts. Chavanne was six months away from earning her registered-nurse degree when the C. P. Wertham Carnival came to Atlanta. She stepped into Johnny J. Bejano's ten-in-one sideshow, and suddenly her childhood dream took over.

"I met the talker, we fell in love and off I went," she told Lewis. "Never even collected my books and other things from the hospital." That talker was Jimmy Chavanne. The two worked for Bejano's sideshow from the mid-1930s through 1945. In the years that followed, Louise swallowed swords on the Kelly-Sutton Sideshow with James E. Strates Shows until as late as October 1968—before Sandra Reed became the show's featured sword swallower in 1969. Chavanne's last season as sword swallower was in 1971 with Pete Kortes.

Performing as Lady Chavanne, she would begin her act by swallowing a chrome fireplace poker. She'd follow it with a single sword, then gulp two blades at once. After withdrawing the swords, she'd wiped them off and tell the crowd, "Sword swallowing is a lot of fun! You should try it sometime!"

Though she surely had fun, she also suffered a few not-so-fun injuries and near disasters. One of them occurred in 1950 while performing in Illinois, when she pushed the sword down too far and nicked her stomach. She was hospitalized briefly. But as Chavanne explained in *Carnival*, the biggest danger wasn't pushing the blade too deep, it was performing while suffering from a cold.

"Everybody knows about opera singers worried about catching a cold and ruining their performance. Well, with opera singers all they can ruin is their profession. But with us, a cold can ruin our profession and us."

Difficulty with breathing while steel is shoved down your throat was the least of her worries. "The big problem is a cough," Chavanne said. "And a sneeze is even worse. That really can kill you, and I do mean it."

She claimed to have almost died during a show in Alabama when she had a cold but performed anyway. Someone in the audience sneezed violently just as she swallowed the sword. "It shook me, and that very second I felt one comin' on at the worst possible moment."

Luckily, Melvin Burkhart, best known as the Original Human Blockhead, saw what was happening and anticipated the worst. He quickly pinched her nose to prevent a sneeze and gave her time to safely extract the sword. "But it was an awful close call," she said.

As her career neared its end, she reflected on it with Lewis. "Been a great life," she told the author. "Wouldn't trade it for anything else. Met some of the most wonderful performers in the whole world." Among them were fellow sword swallower Delno Fritz, Betty Broadbent the tattooed lady, Sealo the Seal Boy, and William Durks, the man with three eyes and two noses.

Following her husband's death in 1965, Louise Chavanne lived in Gibsonton, Florida, where many other sideshow personalities wintered and retired. It's where she spent her final days, passing away in 1982.

JOHNNY NUGENT
1914–80

During the Great Depression, when jobs weren't easy to come by, sword swallowing could at least keep Johnny Nugent fed and traveling from town to town.

Nugent was born on November 24, 1914, in Petersburg, Virginia. A circus made its winter quarters in the local fairgrounds, and as a teenager Johnny began spending time with the performers. Among them was a sword swallower. Johnny was so intrigued that he became determined to learn the art. He started with a fly swatter and within a short time taught himself sufficiently enough—perhaps with help from the circus's wintering sword swallower—to eventually join the circus once the Depression hit.

Nugent worked as a sword swallower with an all-wagon show called the Brinson Bros. Circus and Shows through the late 1930s, at which point he formed his own traveling reptile show, "Johnny's 'Claw and Fang' Jungleland Zoo." He toured with various circus and carnival shows until World War II, when he was drafted into the US Army. Nugent answered the call of duty, sold his show, and went to war.

In World War II, Nugent served as a sergeant until an explosion severely injured him. He lost his right eye and had legs so badly damaged that doctors said he would never take another step. Yet, he overcame the odds and learned to walk again without a limp.

After the war, he started a new reptile show, but after a few years of traveling he opted to instead set up a permanent location in Colonial Heights, Virginia, called "Johnny's Jungleland Zoo." By the mid-1950s, he closed the show and took a part-time civil service job in Ft. Lee, Virginia, and started working part-time with circuses and sideshows during the show season. In addition to sword swallowing, Nugent also ate fire, threw knives, and performed magic, trick roping, and trick riding.

Nugent never married or had any children while he was on the road. When asked why he never married, he would always respond, "I was in one damn war, that was enough!" However, it appears he may have been married at one time to Helena C. Nugent (1890–1970).

According to a *White Tops* circus report, "Johnnie Nugent" filled in as a sword swallower with Hoxie Bros. Circus in 1961. By the mid-1970s he semiretired from the sideshow business but still performed at small local events and for the Kay Brothers Tent.

Nugent died on May 27, 1980, at the age of sixty-five, and is buried in the family cemetery plot at Saint Joseph's Roman Catholic Cemetery in Petersburg, Virginia.

THE TRACEY BROTHERS
GILBERT: 1907–68
LEONARD HARRY: 1909–97
ARTHUR: 1913–93

This book includes numerous claims of performers being the World's Youngest Sword Swallower and the World's Oldest Sword Swallower, but in the 1930s and '40s, the Tracey Brothers boasted a much-rarer title: World's Smallest Sword Swallower. Each standing at about 4 feet tall, Gilbert, Leonard, and Arthur were little people. Both Gilbert and Leonard swallowed a large pair of scissors and various Masonic Knights of Columbus swords.

Born in Baltimore in the early 1900s, the brothers were just three of fourteen siblings, though two died in infancy. According to a promotion leaflet, two others had dwarfism. A local showman, John T. McCaslin, signed the three Traceys to a contract (and had expected to sign the other two in the future) and exhibited them for several years through the mid-1930s.

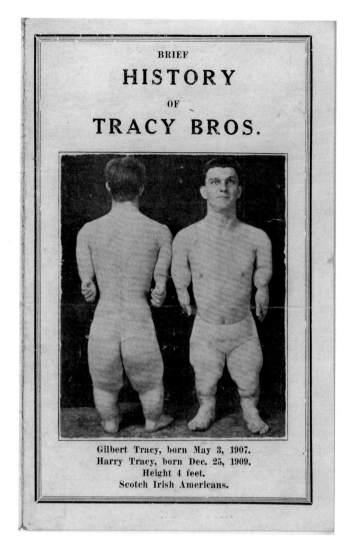

A Tracey Brothers promotional pamphlet. *Collection of Warren A. Raymond*

The diminutive trio later ventured out on their own and operated the Tracey Bros. Side Show, which, in 1939, featured Gilbert as sword swallower and inside lecturer, and Leonard and Arthur as "Mo and Ko," the midget boxers and wrestlers. The show also included a human pincushion, a mentalist act, and the blade box and electric-chair stunts.

The Tracey Brothers appeared with various outfits over the years, including Gold Medal Shows, Coleman Bros. Shows, J. George Loos' Greater United Shows, Bentley's All-American Shows, and the Crescent Amusement Company. At times, they performed individually as well. Leonard Tracey, for example, in an April 14, 1934, *Billboard* ad is showcased as the "Midget Sword Swallower" who swallows "the largest swords" for Marsh Brydon's International Congress of Oddities. In that show, Leonard performed alongside Jeanie Weeks, the "sensational acrobatic half girl" (who would later marry a giant, Al Tomaini), Big Bertha and Slim Jim, and the headline attraction, "'Snookie,' the $10,000 movie chimpanzee."

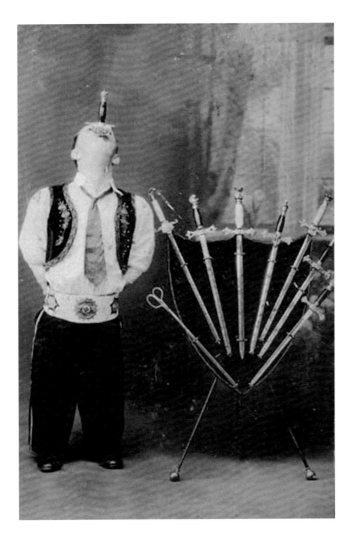

Gilbert Tracey and his many swords. *Collection of Dan Meyer*

NEREIDA CASWELL
1906–?

Nereida Caswell was a woman with many names and many talents. The sword swallower was also known as Helen Caswell, Miss Nerida, and, at times, just Merida, and performed various acts from the early 1930s to the 1940s.

One of her shows was a tank act—meaning she'd don a bathing suit and dive into a giant tank of water. At that time, seeing a woman in a bathing suit meant seeing a lot more flesh than was typically accessible. That made her an extra draw, starting at least as early as 1931 for the E. K. Fernandez carnival in Hawaii. Described by a reporter as a "shapely young lady," she would eat, talk, sew, and do "practically everything that a normal person can do with an unlimited supply of oxygen." Any suitors may have been out of luck, since newspapers reported in the fall of 1931 that she was engaged to Harry A. Rowher. Her husband-to-be stood 6 feet, 6 inches and weighed nearly 800 pounds. It's unclear if they were officially wed, or if the press was a sideshow-related publicity stunt.

In 1938, Caswell appeared at the Gray Wolf Tavern in Youngstown, Ohio, as the "Miracle Girl," who, according to an advertisement, "eats glass, phonograph records, razor blades." She was joined by "frisky, frivolous, flirtatious 'French models.'"

Two years later, Caswell performed at the Hubbard-McCaslin Museum in Washington, DC. She performed as "Merida" for her tank act and as Caswell for her sword-swallowing show. Johnny Eck the half boy and several other sideshow attractions entertained alongside her.

Caswell also appeared as the "Queen of Sword Swallowers" at Hubert's Museum in New York City in 1940. Sharing the stage with her (at least in a photo op that appeared in newspapers across the country) was retired baseball player Grover Cleveland Alexander, who was running a flea circus at the time.

The swimming sword swallower stayed on the move, dropping steel and performing her tank act with the World of Mirth carnival in 1941. By March 1943, she took part in a public discussion in Jacksonville, Florida, about the potential for carnival and small-time circuses to tour in the spring while about 800,000 show people awaited a green light from Washington.

"The war and tire and gasoline shortage didn't bother us much last year," noted showman Milton Cohen. It's unknown if she continued performing afterward, and if the war had anything to do with it.

It's unknown when exactly the Traceys left show business, but a "For Sale" ad in the July 31, 1948, *Billboard* indicates they may have sheathed their swords in that year. "Show complete, ready to do, $325.00," the ad read. It seemed that someone had been after their show for a while, considering a final note: "Warren, here's your chance."

All three brothers married. Gilbert retired in Gibsonton, Florida, and was a member of the Greater Tampa Showmen's Association and the International Independent Showman's Association. He also served in the town's volunteer fire department. Gilbert passed away at sixty-one in 1968. His brothers outlived him by decades. Arthur made his way back to Baltimore, where he passed away in 1993 at age seventy-nine. Leonard settled in Delaware, where heart failure took his life in 1997 at age eighty-seven.

Nereida Caswell at Hubert's Museum in New York City with Grover Cleveland Alexander, a former Major League Baseball pitcher turned flea circus operator, 1940. *Collection of Warren A. Raymond*

THE AMAZING BLONDINI
1922–96

Michael Costello was best known as the Amazing Blondini. But for someone who could swallow swords, pull cars with his teeth and have one drive over his head, eat fire and razor blades, have men stand on him while he lay on a bed of nails, stay buried in a coffin for months, and, on other occasions, lie in a coffin lined with explosives and emerge unscathed after the box is blown to bits, the word "Amazing" hardly does him justice.

Costello was born at a fairground in Dublin, Ireland, in August 1922. His mother was a fortune-teller, his father performed as a strongman under the name "The Mighty Atom," and his sister was a trapeze artist. Costello had no formal education and spent his youth on the fairgrounds of Ireland and England. In 1935, at the age of thirteen, his father told him it was time to learn an act.

Young Michael had seen a fellow performer at the fair, Zorro the Great, swallow swords, and decided it was something he could learn simply enough, especially since he thought the blades folded into the handles. His father approved, albeit begrudgingly, and informed him that there hadn't been a sword swallower in the family since his grandfather.

"What happened to him?" Michael asked.

"He accidentally cut his throat with a sword," his father answered. Still, the sword-swallower-to-be wasn't dissuaded.

Zorro quickly—and angrily—put an end to any thoughts of fakery within sword swallowing. After two weeks of apprenticeship, Michael finally succeeded and, at thirteen years and two months old, became the world's youngest sword swallower. His parents agreed to let him part ways with them and embark on a separate fair with Zorro, who continued to mentor the young performer. Billed as "The Marvellous Michael," Zorro would tell the gathering crowd that "his mother swallowed a spoon before he was born, so it runs in the family."

At fifteen, Zorro suggested he expand his act by combining it with fire eating. Zorro's friend, the Human Salamander, was just the person to teach him. Soon, the young teen was amazing audiences with both skills.

However, after Michael's sister fell to her death during her trapeze act, he felt disillusioned and left the fairgrounds and spent many years as a drifter, mostly around Dublin. By 1939 he'd joined up with a quack salesman and moved to London to peddle pills. But once Britain entered itself into World War II, Costello joined the army and fought alongside the other infantrymen. "I had become part of the Greatest Show on Earth," he said. "One that nobody laughed at for over six years."

Upon his safe return from the war, he returned to his roots and rapidly added to his repertoire. He mastered escapology, practiced self-hypnosis to put himself in trances, ate lightbulbs and razor blades, and learned the dangerous art of explosives. These skills allowed him to perform the numerous aforementioned stunts.

Armed with his new stunts, Costello began performing as the Amazing Blondini and continued inventing new acts. By the early 1950s he set his sights on becoming a human cannonball. Soon, he was shooting himself 80 feet through the air and into a 50-gallon tank of fire-coated water.

He'd experienced a few mishaps with the act, but one of the more unusual ones occurred in 1983, when someone stole his cannon. It had been mounted to the back of a 38-foot-long truck. He offered a reward for its return, telling newspapers, "It's the sort of thing you would notice if it passed you in the street."

Perhaps his most famous stunt occurred in 1975, when he was buried alive for seventy-eight days at Manchester's Belle Vue Fairground. Blondini was lowered into a brick-lined grave measuring 10 by 8 feet, where he lay in a coffin covered with a glass lid. The feat was instigated by a £500 wager. "I was really daft to do it, but it's a world record, you know," he told reporters after emerging from his self-imposed tomb.

Blondini performed his amazing acts in fairgrounds and theaters across Europe, America, Asia, and South Africa. He also worked as a stuntman for films and appeared on many British television shows.

Michael Costello died in Wicklow, Ireland, on November 20, 1996 at the age of seventy-four. "His death came as quite a shock," Blondini's agent, Frank Murphy, said in an obituary. "He had not been ill."

His life story is captured in a 1955 book called *Bed of Nails: The Story of the Amazing Blondini*, by Gordon Thomas. Though clearly, a second edition is warranted to cover the latter half of his extraordinary career.

JIM "LUCKY" BALL
1935~

Jim Ball holds several distinctions as a sword swallower, starting with earning the title of the World's Youngest Sword Swallower for learning at just twelve years old. Now, seventy-six years later as of this writing, he's the World's Oldest Sword Swallower and the World's Longest-Performing Sword Swallower. Each is a unique achievement, but then again, as the world's only sword swallower to have two parents as sword swallowers, his entire life has been unique.

Jim was born on June 28, 1935, in San Diego, California, to Estelline Pike and John Gregory "Lucky" Ball. With two parents so masterful in the art of sword swallowing, perhaps the most amazing thing about Jim's childhood was that he waited until he was twelve to learn. By then, his father had separated from Estelline and left him and his siblings behind at their home in Hoxie, Kansas. When the young boy finally asked his mother to teach him the family business, she gave him "a little beginner's sword" and some very particular instructions.

"It took me only about a month before I was able to ease that rascal down," Ball told us on a phone call in August 2023. "It was easy because Estelline told me what to do and what to expect and what not to do, and there was no fear. She told me to swallow a blade, and I just swallowed a blade."

Shortly after, just down the midway from where his mother was working, he found his way onstage with a Black revue show run by Madame Burleson. "That was the first time I swallowed professionally," Ball said. It was 1948 and he was still just twelve years old. Practicing for the show with friends kept him busy and, as he explained, kept "the carnival kids from running wild."

It wasn't until a few years later when Ball began swallowing swords more seriously. The opportunity came unexpectedly while working for showman Dick Best in Calgary, Canada. Estelline was the show's featured sword swallower, and Jim was selling tickets and working the canvases. Then Estelline got strep throat—and an opportunity presented itself.

"It got to the point where she had to take a few days off," Ball explained. "Dick said, 'We got a sword-swallowing banner down there but no sword swallower.'" Ball told Best he'd been swallowing swords since he was twelve and could happily fill in for his ailing mother. After that, Best made him a sideshow talker and had him working on the bally.

After that season, Ball and his mother worked separate shows. "You didn't want too many sword swallowers on the same sideshow," he noted. In the years that followed, he worked with Best again as well as with Walter Wanous's

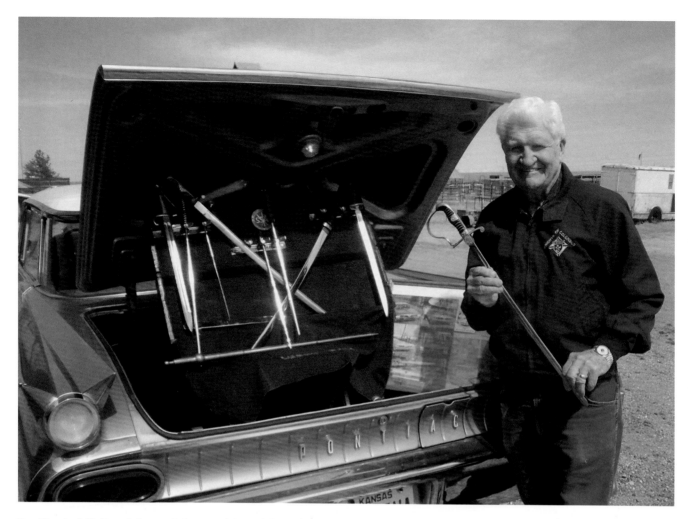

Jim "Lucky" Ball with his mobile sword board for a 2021 car show performance. *Courtesy of Jim Ball*

sideshow on Cetlin & Wilson Shows. During that time, he met Alex Linton at a performance in Columbus, Ohio. The legendary sword swallower helped Ball with his technique in downing multiple blades, though the young apprentice rarely performed the stunt.[10]

"My mother would swallow four or five at the same time, but she told me, 'If you don't have to do it, why do it?'" Ball said. Still, he greatly appreciated and respected Linton's skill. "In my estimation, Alex was the best sword swallower in the world."

Throughout this period, Ball was still just a teenager. By fall 1954 the young sword swallower decided to return to Hoxie, Kansas, to finish high school. He earned his diploma a year later and then promptly returned to the stage to work for his old boss, Dick Best, once more. Just like his first stint with the showman, he found himself filling in for his mother. This time she was suffering from food poisoning—leaving her in no condition to put steel into her system.

That winter, Ball returned home to Hoxie and took on a job that was arguably even more dangerous than swallowing swords. He worked as a lineman for Southwestern Bell Telephone, which meant laying wire and climbing poles in terrible blizzards. So, when Estelline called from New York and said that Hubert's Museum needed a sword swallower, he gladly accepted the gig. "I told Southwestern Bell I'm gonna take early retirement," Ball said. "I was about twenty years old."

While in New York, in addition to his job at Hubert's, Ball also worked with his mother for Ringling Bros. and Barnum & Bailey at Madison Square Garden. Their unusual claim to fame as a mother/son sword-swallowing duo caught the attention of television producers and landed them on the popular show *What's My Line?* in 1958. After a series of yes/no questions, a panel of celebrities eventually guessed their strange profession.

Between appearing in front of a national audience and performing for crowds in New York City, Ball's career seemed to be progressing. Until the US Army called. "I'd been bouncing around, but they finally found me," he said.

---

10   Ball learned everything from his mother, along with the lesson from Alex Linton. Unfortunately, he said he never learned anything from his father. After his parents divorced, the two never spent much time together.

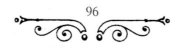

The Associated Press found him, too, and printed a story announcing that "Pvt. James Ball of Hoxie Kan., started his Army career by plunging a 26-inch rifle-cleaning rod down his throat, but people who know him won't be concerned by the news. He's a professional sword swallower."

Ball spent two years in the Army, including fourteen months on the front line in Korea. One of his generals witnessed his act and urged him to enter a military talent show in Seoul. He came in second. "I got beat out by a guy who'd take ten or fifteen tennis balls and juggle them off the floor," he said, admitting that it was "a terrific act."

Whether it was in the Army, at Hubert's, at fairs across the country, or even performances at classic car shows, Ball infuses an element of comedy into his performance to counteract the danger. Earning a laugh in addition to applause has been just as rewarding. "That was my plan, not to scare anybody."

He drew one example from an experience in Korea:

"We were heading to a Christmas party right on the DMZ, and I didn't have very many swords or anything. I needed something else. I saw this abandoned jeep in a ditch, so I went over and I got the oil dipstick out of it. I'd tell people, 'This is the most dangerous sword I swallow because it's so thin. You see the tip of the dipstick is rather sharp, so I have to be careful.' So, I'd put it down, pull it back out, then lay it over on its side and say, 'Oops, looks like I'm about a quart low.' And of course, laughter and applause."

Aside from dipsticks and swords, Ball also swallows a Japanese bayonet and, in more-recent years, has used a corkscrew blade given to him by Dan Meyer that once belonged to Alex Linton and his father.

"I doubt if there's anyone else who swallows a corkscrew blade like Dan gave me," Ball said. "Going down with that corkscrew blade is comparatively simple, but coming back out, you have to gently maneuver it, twist it, in order for it to come back out. It impresses the people. By the time I get it out, they know they've seen something special. Especially when I smile and bow and say, 'Thank you very much; I'm still okay.'"

Ball's life on the road came to a stop in 1975 after marrying a woman with three young children. "I was not going to subject them to the hardships of the carnival," he explained. Instead, he became an independent life and health insurance agent in Kansas but continued swallowing swords when possible. In 2005, for example, Ball was invited to perform on a reboot of *What's My Line?*, on which Ted Lange from *The Love Boat* removed the sword from his throat.

On World Sword Swallower's Day, February 28, 2008, at the age of eighty-two, Ball was inducted into the Sword Swallower's Hall of Fame and awarded the SSAI Lifetime Achievement Award by the Sword Swallower's Association International.

Ball's last professional show was at a Kansas car show in 2021. But he continues to perform for certain requests. In June 2023, he swallowed swords at a local family reunion. "I did the corkscrew there," he said. "No problem."

LADY PATRICIA ZERM
1910–86

Picking a fight with a sword swallower is never a good idea. In 1942, while working with the Ringling Bros. and Barnum & Bailey sideshow, Lady Patricia found herself in a crowded courtroom after a fellow performer, Baby Betty (billed as weighing 650 pounds), accused her of assault. As one headline about the case read, "Sword Swallower Hit Circus Fat Woman."

Those six words conjure quite a mental image, but fortunately Patricia had not attacked Baby Betty with her sword. After being provoked, she struck the fat lady with a Coke bottle in a skirmish quickly ended by the show's strongman. Sympathy within the court sided with the sword swallower. "The matter was dropped when the fat girl, who had a reputation for orneriness, took off for parts unknown before the case could be tried."

"I beat her up," Patricia recalled years later. "And she was a big one too . . . she was always causing trouble around the circus, and circus people have to know how to get along."

Aside from that unusual incident, the sword swallower got along with everyone for decades, including Franceso Lentini the Three-Legged Man, Grace McDaniels the Mule-Faced Lady, the Doll Family, and renowned clown Emmett Kelly. In fact, she and Kelly got along so well they briefly dated in 1944. Eventually she fell for and married Charlie Zerm, a talker and assistant general manager with Ringling.

Long before making headlines for attacking a fat lady and swallowing swords across the country, Lady Patricia was Patricia "Patsy" Nellie Kennedy. Born on September 1, 1910, in Kentucky, she found herself drawn to the carnivals and fairs whenever they visited town, despite her father's disapproval. As a teenager she tried to run away with the carnival but was caught before escaping the county.

Not long after, she dropped out of high school and found her way to Lexington. Young and eager for adventure, she found her way into show business by performing illusions for carnivals and sideshows. In 1935, she set her sights on becoming a sword swallower.

"I saw a boy doing it and decided I was going to learn, so I locked myself in a room where I was staying and I wouldn't let anybody in. It didn't take long. There is no trick. All it takes is practice, and I practiced with a small round rod that was about 18 inches long."

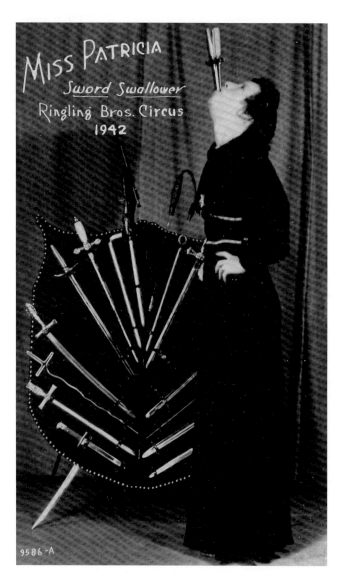

Lady Patricia swallowing swords for the Ringling Bros. Circus in 1942. *Collection of Karla L. Raymond*

Patricia Zerm with her neon sword board. *Collection of Warren A. Raymond*

By 1938, she was skilled enough to sign with Ringling, where she performed until 1951. In addition to swallowing swords, Lady Patricia downed Civil War bayonets, knives, and a 20-inch neon tube that illuminated her throat. Of the latter, she said, "That always makes believers of 'em." Occasionally Ringling would bill her as the "Neon Tube Artist," to promote the stunt and to separate her in the event of another sword swallower being featured alongside her.

Before leaving the show, she had caught the eye of Cecil B. DeMille, who gave her a cameo in the classic 1952 circus movie *The Greatest Show on Earth*. Credited as Miss Patricia, she's seen bent over, swallowing a curved sword.

After Patricia Zerm left the Greatest Show in 1951, she performed with her own sideshow and other small shows for years. She eventually joined Ward Hall and Chris Christ's World of Wonders following the death of her husband in 1968.

According to Ward Hall, "Miss Patricia was known for always wearing beautiful formal gowns. Patsy had a twangy voice with a Kentucky accent, and because of this, she never spoke in her act but instead would perform silently to the song 'Fascination' while the lights went low for her neon tube act. It was incredible! Patsy was a great cook, and she always cooked for Chris and me and Emmett Blackwelder, the Turtle Man."

In February 1975, at age sixty-four and still thriving onstage despite a few gray hairs and wrinkles, she told a reporter, "I keep thinking about giving it up, but there's such a demand for good sword swallowers these days. Besides, I like the bread. I like to dress good and eat good. When I first got in it, I did it for the thrills. Then I found you could make money too, and I do like money."

For her, the secrets to success were simple: "personality, costumes, and the ability to do the act." Throughout the years, she had been injured just once. It happened in Lexington while attempting to swallow the blade of a keyhole saw. She nicked her throat, and her doctor suggested she not try it again. She did it in her next show.

Despite her love of the act and the income, she had told Ward Hall she was going to retire upon turning sixty-five. On September 1, 1975, she stuck to her promise and reminded Ward that it was her birthday, then politely retired on the spot.

Zerm owned a home in Gibsonton, Florida, as did her sister, whose late husband had been a carnival electrician. After she retired, both Patricia and her sister sold their homes and moved from Gibsonton to Tampa. They moved into an apartment at the Baptist retirement home, where they lived out the rest of their lives. They had become religiously devout and no longer associated with their old friends. On January 8, 1986, Lady Patricia Zerm died at the age of seventy-five. After a lifetime of accomplishments, an obituary listed her simply as a "homemaker" and a member of the First Baptist Church of Tampa.

LEATHA SMITH
DATES UNKNOWN

Leatha Wade worked in sideshows but never intended or expected to become a sword swallower. Then she met her husband, Marvin Smith, and she found herself on the fast track to stardom. Leatha had been working with Hennis Brothers carnival in Shreveport, Louisiana, in 1938, when fate stepped in.

"I was just a nobody then, doing odd jobs like ballying out in front or standing for the armless man to throw knives at me," she told a reporter in 1947. "And then Marvin joined the show. We fell in love. I got married late that same year in St. Louis."

A day after their honeymoon, Marvin, who worked as the Anatomical Wonder, said, "Honey, how'd you like to be a sword swallower?" Leatha didn't think twice. The idea of being a headline entertainer thrilled her. Marvin wasted no time giving her a variety of shiny new blades, including a cutlass, a rapier, a scimitar, a saber, a couple of bayonets, and a short steel practice bar.

After her first attempt with the steel bar, Leatha wasn't sure if she'd ever succeed in her new career path. "But I kept trying and finally got so I could get the point 3 or 4 inches past my throat without gagging," she said. "By the middle of the winter I could get the bar down 18 inches, using plenty of olive oil, and then I began trying swords."

She began adding to her act by learning to arch her torso while swallowing a curved blade and mastered the art of smiling for the audience to disguise any discomfort while downing three swords at once.

By 1939, the young, blond sword swallower made her debut in Houston at the Fat Stock Show. Marvin set her up with a 21-inch neon-red tube to swallow for her grand

Leatha Smith on the bally stage with the Clyde Beatty Cole Bros. Circus Sideshow. *Collection of Warren A. Raymond*

finale. With her throat glowing red, the crowds went wild. Then one night, she withdrew the tube and saw it was no longer lit. "I kept on taking that thing out," she recalled, "and then I saw what was the matter. The end had broken off. What did I do? I went back into the two-faced man's ten, and was sick. And, brother, until you swallowed neon gas, you don't know what a real hangover is!" She remained calm and, knowing that she had another show in an hour, chose not to see a doctor.

"I got rid of the gas, and I figured I could digest that glass all right because neon tubing is not ordinary glass but is made of lead glass. And I guess I did, because it never bothered me."

In the years that followed, Smith continued using the neon tube finale, but she encased the tube in a slotted piece of steel tubing. It dimmed the light, but a faint red glow could still be seen through her throat and earned applause. It also helped ensure she'd live to swallow it again in the next show.

Leatha and Marvin performed together through the 1940s with the Clyde Beatty Cole Bros. Circus Sideshow, Biller Bros. Circus, and Al Wagner's Cavalcade of Amusements. Though she enjoyed the stardom, she once told a journalist—while crocheting between acts—that she'd be happy just selling baby clothes or doing something domestic.

"I don't mind telling you," she said, "these dang swords make me sick to my esophagus sometimes."

Leatha and Marvin settled in San Antonio in the sixties. Her swords, sword shield, and two dresses were added to the Harry Hertzberg Circus Collection, now housed at the Witte Museum in San Antonio.

LOUISE LONG
DATES UNKNOWN

Louise Long, also known as Lady Louise, swallowed swords with the Ringling Bros. and Barnum & Bailey Circus as early as 1944. She performed alongside many well-known sideshow attractions: the Doll Family, "The World's Smallest People"; Mr. and Mrs. Fischer, the Giant and Giantess; Percy Pape, the Living Skeleton; Rasmus Nielsen, the tattooed strongman; Singlee the Fire-Proof Man; and fellow sword swallower Patricia Zerm, who complemented Long's act with a neon tube.

Long spent several years with Ringling and by the 1950s continued her sword-swallowing career with Royal American Shows. Little else is known about Lady Louise's life or sideshow adventures.

Louise Long swallows a pair of oversized shears.
Collection of Dan Meyer

TONI DEL RIO
1924–87

Toni Del Rio was a snake charmer, dancer, fire eater, hypnotist, clairvoyant, and sword swallower. She was also a he.

Del Rio was born into a gypsy family of wire walkers who came from Andorra, a principality between France and Spain in the Pyrenees Mountains. They came to Tampa, Florida, for a circus booking by way of Cuba in the early 1920s. Del Rio was born there on April 2, 1924, as Nilo Garrido. Nilo grew up as a boy but was a pseudo-hermaphrodite. An accident on the high wire led to nerve damage in one leg, but being a kid surrounded by sideshow performers, he soon picked up a variety of skills, including sword swallowing from his uncle. Before World War II, he took advantage of his natural anomaly and worked with circuses and sideshows as a "Half and Half."

During the war, while serving in the US Navy as a registered nurse in Hawaii, Garrido's breasts began to grow, and he was given a medical discharge. Nilo underwent transgender surgery and became the second person in the United States to become transgendered. He changed his name to Toni Del Rio and went back to working with circuses and sideshows.

Del Rio enhanced her sword-swallowing skills under the guidance of Mimi Garneau while in her winter quarters in Gibsonton, Florida. Armed with some of Mimi's personal swords, Del Rio worked as a female sword swallower throughout the fifties and sixties. Standing just 5 feet, 2 inches tall, she would often pull a teenage boy from the audience to hold her waist as she placed a 17½-inch bayonet in her mouth. With the snap of a finger, the blade would drop down her throat. A flick of her pinky finger would thrust it into the air. After catching it in her hand, she'd ask the teen if he'd like a turn.

Del Rio performed with Johnny Meah on the Lou Walters Show during this period and trained both Eddie Miller and Red Stuart in the art of swallowing swords. In addition to gulping blades and performing her other acts, she also created her own attractions, such as the "Man Eating Fish." "When people bought their tickets and got inside, what they saw was a man sitting there eating a can of sardines," she told a reporter in 1976. "It was true—it's all in the punctuation."

A similar act was billed as "The boy who plays with a pink rattler." Behind the ticket booth, curiosity seekers found a little boy playing not with a snake, but with pink baby rattle.

"You gotta be able to do everything in the carnival," Del Rio said.

She continued doing everything she could into at least the mid-1980s. By April 28, 1987, however, Del Rio suffered a heart attack and passed away at Tampa General Hospital. As for Toni's swords, they were bequeathed to her star pupil, Red Stuart.

EDDIE MILLER
DATES UNKNOWN

Dressed in a black western costume resembling Johnny Cash, Eddie Miller made a living in the 1950s by hurling blades around a human target. But the knife thrower wanted to flirt with danger a little more intimately. It's why he learned to swallow swords in the early '60s from Toni Del Rio.

Within a few years, he was performing both feats for Ward Hall's World of Wonders Show and the John Bradshaw Sideshow, though knife throwing remained his primary act. However, Miller had a tendency to add an unnecessary element of difficulty into his performance: alcohol. In 1973, Miller's female assistant was pregnant and starting to show. Between his drinking and her putting a second life at risk, she was too nervous to stand at the knife thrower's board. In fact, his affinity for alcohol made it impossible to find any woman who'd allow a potentially drunken knife thrower to toss sharp objects in her direction.

Eventually, front talker Diego Domingo volunteered to be his assistant for an extra $10 a week for his bravery. If Domingo dared to watch the knives being thrown toward him, he would flinch in the wrong direction. Instead, he closed his eyes and moved only when he felt Miller's hand on his shoulder, indicating the safe end of the act, so he could go back to working the front.

As the years went on, Miller generally swallowed swords only when he needed to fill in for another performer. But when he did, he made it memorable with an arsenal of daggers, swords, and bayonets. While swallowing the bayonet, he'd get down on one knee, drop the blade down his throat, then flick it with his thumb about 8 feet in the air. As he stood up, the steel would stick in the floor between his feet.

His career appeared to end with less flourish. It has been rumored that he was last known to be working at a telemarketing job sometime in the early 1980s.

RICKY RICHIARDI
1931–70

In the early 1950s, Ricky Richiardi lived in Gibsonton, Florida, a small town south of Tampa where many show people wintered or retired. Being surrounded by such uniquely talented people, he decided to take advantage of their presence and learn a skill you couldn't learn in most other communities. So, Richiardi approached sword swallower Betty Bancroft.

"I went to her and told her I wanted to learn how to swallow swords," he explained to a reporter in 1968. "She told me to get a stove poker and sand it smooth and then come back." Bancroft instructed him to practice swallowing the poker. "It hurt, and I threw up and bled, but three weeks later I was performing as a sword swallower."

Richiardi, who was born Herman Kennedy Poss Jr. in Buford, Georgia, on August 8, 1931, eventually amazed audiences with his newly acquired talent while performing at New York's Madison Square Garden with the Ringling Bros. and Barnum & Bailey Circus in 1955. That season's sideshow also featured the Doll Family midgets, Frieda Pushnik the armless and legless girl, and Johann Petursson, the Viking Giant.

The young sword swallower went on to perform many acts for many shows. While working for the Hoxie Bros. Circus in the sixties, he swallowed blades up to 29 inches in length and was known to gulp seven at once. He also put the large blades in the blade box stunt as an attractive girl

A Ricky Richiardi pitch card. *Collection of Warren A. Raymond*

lay inside, performed a swinging ladder act with a girl doing aerial acrobatics, swung on a rope hanging from the big top, walked a high wire on his knees, and exhibited 15-foot pythons and 12-foot boa constrictors. Richiardi even shared the stage with a camel, leading it through various tricks, such as standing on a pedestal and drinking a Coke.

In the fall of 1969, while back in Gibsonton, Richiardi paid forward Bancroft's training and taught sword swallowing to an albino lecturer named Sandra Reed. He built her a sword shield, gave her three of his old swords, and taught her how to put together an act.

"He was a marvelous, marvelous man, and I mean super," Reed said in an early 1990s interview for *James Taylor's Shocked and Amazed! On & Off the Midway.*

Not long after mentoring Reed, Richiardi tragically was struck by a hit-and-run driver in a pickup truck while repairing a tire on the side of a road. It was January 30, 1970. He died a day later, at the age of thirty-eight. Some suspect that foul play was involved. As a member of the Greater Tampa Showman's Association and the International Independent Showman's Association, Richiardi was interred at the Showmen's Rest Cemetery in Tampa.

HENRY A. BURNS
1930–89

In October 1959, a bout of hiccups nearly proved fatal for Henry Amedeo Burns. The sword swallower, also known as "Jonda the Great," had two 21-inch neon tubes glowing in his throat at the same time while performing in Long Beach, California. When he hiccupped, he caused a short circuit, and one of the tubes burst. Burns removed the undamaged one and spit out as much glass as possible from the other. He was rushed to the hospital and treated for lacerations in the esophagus. According to the Associated Press, he was in good condition and, speaking from his hospital bed, "vowed to stick to swallowing steel swords."

Born on March 6, 1930, in San Francisco, Burns was a daredevil at heart. In his midtwenties, he found thrills in stealing cars for joy rides. Unfortunately, those rides led straight to a stint in San Quentin. While in prison he met a fire eater who promised to introduce him to circus life when they got out. By 1957, they regained their freedom, and Burns's friend kept his word. Not only did he begin a new chapter in the circus, but he also married his longtime sweetheart.

Burns learned sword swallowing and began performing in 1959 with fellow sword swallower Tony Mareno at an amusement park called the Pike in Long Beach. The daredevil had a new dangerous, but legal, outlet. Aside from his neon tubes, he also dropped curved swords and saws down his gullet.

In February 1960, while performing with the E. K. Fernandez carnival in Honolulu, he broke his hospital-bed vow and thrust an 18-inch neon tube down his throat, then bent over and broke it. Once again, he was rushed to medical help. It was his first show since being hospitalized months earlier. The United Press International suggested that it "might be a good idea" for Burns to "seek a different profession." This time, he did.

Jonda the Great quit sword swallowing professionally around 1961 but occasionally performed impromptu acts at the beach and at home for his family.

"I remember watching him and thinking, 'Oh my gosh, he's gonna get hurt,'" his daughter, Carolyn Burns Bass, told us in a phone interview in January 2024. "We liked watching him when he went to do the curvy one because he had to bend over and he had to curl his body. It was the craziest thing."

On one occasion he swallowed swords at a grand-opening event at a local strip mall parking lot. His wife had volunteered him for the gig. "He did it just to entertain people," Bass said. "Just because he could."

Even though he wasn't performing professionally, he was only in his early thirties and still had a spirited wild side, which led him into motorcycle racing. After about seven years of competition, he left the track and hit the open road with the Hessians motorcycle gang for three years. According to his daughter, a friend introduced him to sailing in the early 1970s and he shifted his passions into yacht racing.

The water soon became his home. He spent the last ten years of his life on a sailboat in Long Beach Harbor, California, where he passed away in his sleep of a heart attack at the age of fifty-eight in February 1989. Henry A. Burns was buried at sea. Sadly, his swords had been kept in a storage unit, where they were stolen and never recovered.

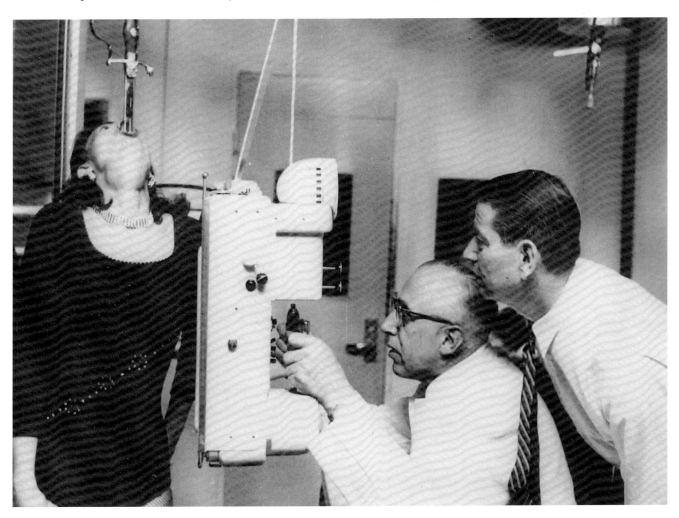

Doctors perform an x-ray on Turkish sword swallower Bella Haich in Copenhagen, 1960. *Collection of Dan Meyer*

DANIEL LYNCH— THE GREAT STROMBOLI

1926–2019

Daniel Lynch swallowed swords and ate fire, but it was the latter that earned him his stage name, the Great Stromboli. Lynch was born on July 7, 1926, in Dunfermline, Scotland, and by age fifteen served with the Royal Navy in World War II. During this time, he learned his unique skills and used them to entertain troops on long voyages. "They were sailing past an island off the coast of Sicily called Stromboli, which has an active volcano," his niece told the *Manchester Evening News* in 2019. "Apparently Danny was on deck and his friends said he could easily blow his fire higher than the volcano. It stuck." So did his love of performing.

Following the war, Lynch traveled the world as a showman for decades. After meeting a nurse named Silvia on a train in 1958, he made her his wife and his glamorous assistant. Together, they were Stromboli and Silvia, "The Strangest Show on Earth." Along with swallowing swords and eating fire, Stromboli strapped himself into a 16,000-volt electric chair and had Silvia pull a switch to apparently send thousands of volts through his body. Sparks flew and lightbulbs situated around the chair were illuminated.

In the 1970s, Lynch raised his fire-eating game to another level by setting a Guinness World Record for continuously blowing 136 flames from his mouth. He later claimed to break it with 214 flames, but the feat was not documented.

Offstage, Stromboli and Silvia performed for members of the British royal family multiple times. Lynch appeared in *Chitty Chitty Bang Bang* (1968) and in David Lynch's (no relation) *The Elephant Man* (1980) as a fire eater. He also earned film credits for appearances in *The Bride* (1985) and *Princess Caraboo* (1994) and was a frequent guest on British television programs. On one occasion, he swallowed a sword to demonstrate a new x-ray technique on *Tomorrow's World*.

Even further offstage, Lynch was a collector of oddities, which he amassed during his global travels. Among them were a two-headed calf, the skin of the world's longest snake, a mammoth's jaw, and a giant four-hundred-year-old shell he claimed was found on Madagascar and belonged to the extinct elephant bird. His acquisition of the egg in 2010 caught the attention of the press.

"These animals died out 400 years ago and are still a mystery to paleontologists," he told the *Manchester Evening News*. "They were highly prized for their eggs, which could feed an entire village, so to find a restored shell like this is very rare." Lynch often sold curiosities to the Ripley's Museum in Blackpool, England.

The Great Stromboli and Silvia's long, strange journey together came to an end in 2019. Silvia passed away at the age of eighty-seven on March 3, and Stromboli followed just five weeks later on April 9, at age ninety-two.

Stromboli and Siliva, a husband-and-wife team, performed various acts together for decades. *Collection of Dan Meyer*

FRANCIS DORAN
1908–79

Francis Doran began his sideshow career in the early 1940s as a female impersonator under the stage name "The Original Maxine," and a half-and-half as "Max/Maxine." His mother, Ivy, always traveled with him and juggled roles as a palm reader, cookhouse assistant, and ticket seller. By 1951, when Ward Hall acquired his first sideshow, Francis and Ivy were the first to join. All was good until Ivy fell ill and could no longer travel. Within a few years she passed away, which left Doran in such despair that he attempted suicide. Fortunately, a priest talked him into joining Hall's show on the road again, and his life began anew.

"He came with us as a front talker but was unhappy not being a performer," Hall recalled in his book *My Very Unusual Friends*. "Explaining that he no longer wanted to work in drag, he asked me to teach him to swallow swords." Hall had not personally swallowed swords, but he knew how it was done, and agreed to teach him on one condition: never swallow neon. A year before, an incident with a neon tube had severely injured another performer.[11]

Doran accepted the showman's proposal and got his wish. The newly trained sword swallower performed in Ward Hall's World of Wonders in 1960 and continued on and off throughout the decade. When he wasn't touring with Hall, Doran was a featured sword swallower with Wallace Bros. Circus and the Clyde Beatty Cole Bros. Circus.

Doran's sword-swallowing career was going along perfectly well, until June 16, 1969. On that day, it became clear he had broken his word to Ward Hall when a 36-inch neon tube broke inside his stomach and released gas and glass into his system. Doran, who was sixty-one at the time, had been performing with the Ringling Bros. and Barnum & Bailey sideshow in Houston when the accident occurred. More than two hundred people witnessed the tragedy. According to one of them, Doran was in an "inebriated condition" and "had somehow bent his body and broke the tube inside." An ambulance was called, and Doran was whisked to the hospital. The incident was actually the second time a tube had broken inside him, but the first to make nationwide headlines.[12] The *Miami Herald*, for example, wrote, "Neon Tube Explodes inside Sword Swallower." He reportedly spent eight weeks in the hospital and underwent two operations.

---

11   In 1970, Doran told a reporter that he'd been swallowing neon tubes for twenty years and steel for much longer. "Swords have been tickling his intestines since he was seven," the reporter wrote. He added that Doran claimed that both his parents swallowed swords, and, as Doran claimed, "It was easy for me to follow them." Sideshow is full of exaggeration, and swallowing swords at age seven seems to be a perfect example. We'll stick with Ward Hall's story, which may have its own degree of embellishment.

12   The first incident, fortunately, didn't cause serious injury.

"I wouldn't swallow another fluorescent tube for $100,000," Doran told a reporter a year later, after returning to sword swallowing (blades only) with Royal American Shows. He claimed that the tube had been poorly made and that the heat of his body caused the glass to explode internally.

Doran spent the rest of the seventies working with Ward Hall's World of Wonders once again, as well as Hoxie Bros. Circus and, toward the end of the decade, with John Bradshaw's ten-in-one sideshow. But by 1978 his health began to fail. Knowing his time on the stage was coming to an end, he decided to pass the sword-swallowing torch on to a new generation and began training Bradshaw's nineteen-year-old bally girl, Diane Falk.

"In the evenings, it became difficult for him to swallow sword because his throat really wasn't up to snuff and he was older," Falk told us in a March 2024 phone interview. "So he taught me to swallow swords because he genuinely was my friend, and I was so, in a way, enamored by him."

She filled in for him as needed and soon took over the show's role of sword swallower. Doran had worked as long as he could, but a case of pneumonia attributed to his neon accident ten years earlier was too much to overcome. After a long, colorful career, his curtain closed on October 18, 1979, at the age of seventy-one.

Doran was the last of his era to swallow swords in a Ringling Bros. show or other circuses of that caliber, but in training Falk—and bequeathing his swords to her—he helped ensure that a new era would keep the art alive.

"THE BARON"
BILL UNKS
1923–97

"Anyone could do it if he really wanted to," Bill Unks said of sword swallowing to a reporter in 1971. Of course, he was among the few who ever wanted to.

Unks was born on November 17, 1923, and started swallowing swords by age twenty-four (though he's also claimed to have started at eighteen). "I never touch the edge," he told the journalist, explaining how he removes only a fraction of the point to maintain the appearance of sharpness. "If you're going to swallow something, do it. Make it look dangerous." Just to prevent as much danger as possible, Unks always ran a silk stocking over the blade to ensure there were no nicks.

Of course, he was already used to danger. Unks had been in the US Army, and by 1945, shortly after returning home to Oakland, California, he found a job opening for a fire eater at a carnival and took the job—despite having no experience. He quickly learned the stunt and fell in love with carnival life—particularly the thrill-seeking crowds.

"In a carnival, you see more characters in front of the stage than you do on it," he told the *Oakland Tribune* in 1960. "Most people watch you because they expect you to cut yourself, set yourself on fire, or blow yourself up." Unks knew that all three were possible, having witnessed for himself a fire eater get severely burned after the wind changed directions and blew the flames back in his face.

In the early 1960s, Unks worked with showman George Surtees, who also served as guardian to famed sideshow pinhead Schlitzie (one of the stars of 1932's *Freaks*). Schlitzie was beloved by audiences and the sideshow community. He was a microcephalic whose real name was Simon Metz. If you've ever read a Zippy the Pinhead comic, that's who inspired it.

Several years later, Unks took a job as an orderly in a Los Angeles County hospital during the off-season. To his surprise, he ran into Schlitzie. Surtees had since died, and his daughter admitted Schlitzie to the hospital. When Unks saw him and heard the story from the hospital officials, he called a fellow showman, Sam Alexander. He came immediately. A state psychologist came as well, gave Schlitzie an evaluation, and allowed Alexander to take him into his custody.

"The state psychiatrist, having learned the background of Schlitzie, said that if they would institutionalize Schlitzie, which would have been the route they would have taken, that Schlitzie wouldn't have lived six months away from the love of the show people and the attention of the public," Ward Hall told me in a 2003 interview. "And the State of California made Sam the ward to Schlitzie. Schlitzie was legally taken care of by Sam. For the next several years, Sam had Schlitzie in his show." Going by that story, the off-season sword swallower saved Schlitzie's life.

Unks's life carried on too. In 1967 he landed a role in the movie *She Freak*, and in 1968 he was featured on a Jack Benny TV special. By 1972, he began performing as "The Baron" with Clyde Beatty Cole Bros. Circus. As the decade progressed, he moved on to work with Hoxie Bros. Circus and then with showman Bobby Reynold's sideshow in the early 1980s.

In 1985, Unks attempted to teach magician Penn Jillette to swallow a sword on television's *Penn & Teller Go Public*. After brief instructions, Jillette got the blade about halfway down before gagging and pulling it out. The Baron demonstrated the act, effortlessly dropping the steel down his throat. He then told Jillette that a typical day of work involved twelve shows, with five blades swallowed per show. Unks also explained that he could just as easily swallow swords sitting down—an unusual feat he adopted in his later years of performing that only added to his reputation. "I've never seen anybody do sword swallowing smoother," Jillette told him.

Unks had retired by the early 1990s but was flown out to Coney Island by showman Bobby Reynolds to train a young fire eater named Frank Hartman. Reynolds and Hartman's father were business partners, so to Frank, the impresario had always been "Uncle Bobby."

"The first thing [Unks] had me push down was a flyswatter," Hartman recalled in a phone interview with us. "So I actually learned with a flyswatter. But it took me all of a day or two to realize how uncomfortable that was, and I went out and bought a bayonet immediately. I swallowed it almost right away."

Hartman remembered Unks as a "sweet, old, retired sideshow guy" who was "extremely patient, soft spoken, and had a good sense of humor." He recalled meeting the Baron as a kid and watching him swallow a vibrator backstage one night, then turning it on "just for shits and grins." Reynolds called him the "Gay Blade."

Just a few years after teaching Hartman, Unks passed away on March 12, 1997, at the age of seventy-three.

JACK LOONEY
1925–2006

Jack Looney spent more than fifty years as a circus entertainer by working both as a clown and a sword swallower. Born in 1925 in the small town of Jenkins, Kentucky, he got his first gig as a teenager and never looked back. By age twenty, he'd joined the Ringling Bros. and Barnum & Bailey Circus.

"I just wanted to be in the circus," Looney told a reporter in 1986 while working as a clown with the Toby Tyler Circus. "It was so glorious to me. I thought I'd arrived. I was making $35 a week. I like the thrill of it. Making the children happy. Making them laugh."

After learning to swallow swords from Lady Patricia Zerm during his early years with Ringling, he brought the same joyful philosophy to every performance. Looney would pick a child from the audience and bring him or her onstage, swallow a sword, then kneel down at the young volunteer's level and give them the responsibility of safely pulling the blade from his throat. It may not have gotten the laughs that his clown act received, but he surely left them with a smile and a new sense of wonder.

Following his stint with Ringling, Looney frequently worked with the Clyde Beatty Cole Bros. Circus over the decades—occasionally alongside fellow sword swallower Rick Dennis. He also performed with Lewis Brothers Circus, King Brother's Circus, and Circus USA with Chris Christ and Ward Hall's World of Wonders Sideshow. On the national stage, he once swallowed a neon tube on the *Tonight Show Starring Johnny Carson*.

"I tried to quit the circus, but I couldn't," he said in 1986. "I once worked in a factory in Detroit. When the grass got green, I left. Whenever I hear a calliope in winter, I want to go back."

Though swallowing swords is always dangerous, it was those rare moments when Looney stepped away from the circus tent that he found himself in trouble. In 1956, while unemployed, he was sentenced to four years in prison after robbing a hotel clerk in Macon, Georgia. He served thirty-two months of his sentence, then found himself in trouble once again in December 1959 when he held up a store in Bristol, Virginia, with a toy cap gun and made off with $63. When the shopkeeper realized that the weapon was a toy, he pulled out a real gun and started firing. Looney ran off, surviving the hail of bullets. He then spent two months on the run, hitchhiking across the southeastern states, until he couldn't handle the sleepless nights and fear of being caught anymore. He surrendered to a sheriff in South Carolina in February 1960.

"I just couldn't run any longer," he told reporters. Yet, his motives were much the same as his reasons for clowning and swallowing swords: to make children happy. In this case, Looney had promised his sister's kids that he'd get them a bicycle for Christmas. "But I didn't have any money," he explained.

It's rumored that Looney suffered a stroke in the late 1980s. He had taken out an advertisement in *Amusement Business* magazine, saying that he was confined to a state nursing home back home in Kentucky and was asking for donations. He recovered enough to dress as a clown once again and entertain children in local hospitals until about 2000, when he was unable to get around any longer. Looney spent his final years in the retirement home in Jenkins, where he passed away on February 6, 2006.

JOHN "RED" TROWER
1939–

Like many sword swallowers, John "Red" Trower often had to convince a skeptical audience that his blade did not retract into the handle. Swallowing a pair of giant shears with looped handles did the trick. So did swallowing a neon tube with a glass hilt.

Trower grew up in Cheboygan, Michigan, in the 1940s but eventually sought more than Cheboygan had to offer. As Ward Hall recalled in his 1990 book, *My Very Unusual Friends*, Trower worked as a photographer during his teen years for a local newspaper and was given an assignment to cover Mills Brothers Circus, which had pitched the big top in town.

"John was so enamored by the circus, he left town with them, doing the only job available, cleaning up behind the elephants," Hall wrote.

Soon he started helping erect the big tent and quickly took on additional jobs as a lot manager, truck mechanic, elephant and chimpanzee trainer, aerialist, illusionist, and other positions. Trower eventually married and settled in San Antonio, where he ran a business maintaining TV and radio antenna towers. This involved climbing a lot of 1,000-foot-tall structures to service warning lights at the top. After a while, he realized that if he was going to live dangerously, it was better to do it on a stage. By 1973 he joined Ward Hall and Chris Christ's World of Wonders show. Trower had gone from elephant-dung duty to sword swallower and knife thrower, and when something needed to be fixed, mechanic.

"Without doubt, he is the greatest sword swallower of our time," Hall wrote. "He includes in his repertoire a stunt in which he removes the wooden stock of a rifle, swallows the metal part, and shoots the flame from a candle while the bar of the rifle is in his throat, thus combining sword swallowing and sharpshooting."

Trower's prowess entertained crowds at Hall's shows, at the Dailey Bros. Circus, and as a one-man show at amusement parks and fairs for years, until a neon tube broke inside him in the late 1990s. He was rushed to the hospital. Details from a medical paper in the *Texas Heart Institute Journal* described that "an esophagogram established the diagnosis, and surgical repair was attempted. However, nineteen days later, a persistent leak and deterioration of the patient's condition necessitated a transhiatal esophagectomy with a left cervical esophagogastrostomy. The patient recovered and resumed his daily activities at the circus, with the exception of sword swallowing."

Shortly after, Trower suffered another accident—though not from a sword. He fell out of a tree and was x-rayed for injuries. The images revealed that he still had 4-inch pieces of glass and pieces of the electrical connectors from the neon tube left in his stomach. Knowing his performance days were over, Red Trower retired to Houston with his wife, Alexandria.

CAPTAIN DON LESLIE
1937–2007

As a sixteen-year-old runaway, Don Leslie learned to swallow swords from an Argentinian fire eater named Carlos Leal while they were working with the Cristiani Bros. Circus. Now, ideally, one would learn sword swallowing from a sword swallower. Not a fire eater. Both stunts are dangerous, but otherwise they're quite different. In fact, Leslie later called Leal a "very inferior" sword swallower, though at the time he'd never seen another, so he couldn't make much of a comparison.

"I'll make a deal with you," Leal told Leslie. "If you let me send a telegram to your folks telling them that you're safe and well . . . I won't tell 'em where you are . . . then I'll teach you how to swallow swords."

Recalling the story decades later, Leslie said, "He did that, thinking, 'This punk kid will never make me take him up on it,' but I did!"

Donald Paul Leslie was born on December 26, 1937, in Boston, Massachusetts. Growing up with alcoholic parents, he didn't stick around for long. By age fourteen he ran away from home to join the Ringling Bros. and Barnum & Bailey Circus and sell hot dogs. Once found by his parents, however, he was yanked away from the show and sent to reform school. He didn't stick around there for long, either, and soon ran off to join another circus.

In 1952, having escaped homelife once again, he worked the pony ride with the King Bros. Cristiani Circus, which happened to be right across from the sideshow bally stage. During his ten-minute breaks from selling tickets and helping kids on and off ponies, he'd watch in awe as Leal ate fire and swallowed swords. Inspired, he decided that this was what he wanted to do. "This is where my destiny took hold, and I went with it!" Leslie said.

He connected with Leal and learned the art of fire eating before accepting the offer to study sword swallowing. Once Leal instructed him, it took seven months to down his first sword. During that time, he crouched over a toilet and gagged himself with his fingers, trying to suppress the reflex. He worked with screwdrivers, spoon handles, knives, and oil sticks. Finally, he graduated to the sword. And with every swallow, he'd gag and retch. Deliberately. Just as Leal had taught him.

While the teenager was polishing his act, he was also busily becoming a tattooed man. Leslie's earliest ink came from legendary tattooists Carol "Smokey" Nightingale and Lee Roy Minugh. After famed tattooed lady Betty Broadbent joined the Cristiani Bros. Circus, Leslie was inspired to become a fully illustrated man. In one instance, Californian tattooist Lyle Tuttle even worked on him in exchange for sword-swallowing lessons.

At age eighteen, Leslie hung up his swords to join the US Marines, but after only eighty-seven days, he was discharged due to a heart murmur. He couldn't serve his country, but he could certainly entertain it. Leslie grabbed his swords, returned to circus life, and picked up right where he left off.

In 1957, he performed alongside Harry Earles of the famous Doll Family midgets and star of Tod Browning's *Freaks*. Earles told Leslie he needed a stage name. Something

more memorable than "Don." So, he bestowed the title of "Captain" upon the nineteen-year-old with a very brief military career. From that day forward, the young sword swallower had a moniker that stuck through his entire career. Earles also introduced him to Alex Linton. The legendary sword swallower saw Captain Don and promptly told him to quit making the gagging noises. Linton took Leslie under his wing and helped him refine his skills and add flair to his performance and, by rectifying his bad habits, in all likelihood extended his career by decades.

Over the next few years, Captain Don became a complete ten-in-one act. In addition to being "America's most colorful sword swallower" and a fire eater, he became a talker, a grind man, an escape artist, a human blockhead, and a human pincushion and lay comfortably on a bed of nails and on a bed of glass. During the off-season, Leslie added to his income by adding "tattoo artist" to his repertoire.

In the early 1960s, Leslie married and had his first of four sons in 1962. He continued performing and working odd jobs while also operating his tattoo studio in Key West, Florida. As his sideshow career continued, Leslie eventually became known for swallowing five 30-inch swords with the blades perpendicular to the tongue instead of flat. It was a feat he began performing in the late 1970s, which would carry him through the next decade when he busked on the streets of Boston and at Fisherman's Wharf in San Francisco.

His shows also included other daring displays with swords. "I would take a piece of band steel, which was fairly soft metal, and swallow it and then would kind of bend my neck to pull it out bent," he told Madame Chinchilla in her 2010 biography. "It didn't hurt and was very impressive looking."

Leslie described rigging a microphone that worked off vibrations to a piece of steel to give crowds a particularly intimate experience: "I would swallow it and turn the volume up on the amplifier. It's right there next to the heart. It goes boom, boom, boom; my heart pounding against the metal blade would come out through the speakers. It would freak the audience out. If I swallowed a sword and you looked carefully and I held it for a minute, you'll see it throb. It is actually moving. That's my heart pounding against it."

Aside from various forms of steel, Leslie swallowed neon tubes. He was nonchalant about the danger until the death of Francis Doran, whose passing in 1979 was due to complications from a broken neon tube. Leslie retired that part of the act on the spot. Neon wasn't worth it. Yet, he didn't totally evade injuries. His worst occurred in 1989 while swallowing his five-sword sandwich in front of a packed house at the Center for Contemporary Arts in Seattle, Washington. It was the opening of a photo exhibit for the RE/Search book *Modern Primitives*. The blades scissored and lacerated his esophagus, causing serious internal bleeding that nearly killed him. After the accident, Captain Don gave up sword swallowing and passed most of his blades to fellow sword swallower Lady Diane Falk.

Leaving his trade behind wasn't so easy, however. By 1997 Leslie started swallowing swords periodically again at tattoo conventions, where he'd become a celebrity. Semiretired in Chico, California, he'd spent nearly fifty years with most of the major circuses, sideshows, and carnivals that trekked the United States and Canada from the 1950s through the early 1990s. In addition to the aforementioned, these included Ringling Bros. and Barnum & Bailey Circus, Great American Circus, Circus Bruno, Hanneford Circus, and Clyde Beatty and Cole Bros. Circus. He also performed in nightclubs, dance halls, and theaters in most major cities of the United States, Canada, Holland, Japan, and the Micronesian islands. That included a 1988 demonstration at a Guam legislative session hall to promote his upcoming act with Circus Bruno.

As he explained in the short 1997 documentary, *The Human Volcano*, his many dangerous stunts were a way to make a living:

> A journalist asked me one time, he said, "Why do you impale your flesh with shish kabob skewers and hatpins and why do you burn the mucus membranes on the insides of your mouth and your taste buds from your tongue with fire and why do you put steel blades down among your vital organs and why do you run 25,000 volts of electricity through your body and why do you this and why do you that and pound nails and ice picks up your nostrils to the base of your brain with a hammer?"
> And I said, "Well, did you pay to get in here?"
> And she said, "Yes."
> And I said, "That's why."

Offstage, Leslie appeared on a variety of TV shows, ranging from *The Dinah Shore Show* to *Captain Kangaroo* to *The Jerry Springer Show*. He was featured in several documentaries and made an uncredited appearance as the tattooed man in 1998's *Beloved* with Oprah Winfrey and Danny Glover. Outside of the sideshow arts, Leslie was also a musician and a songwriter (his first record was called "Tattoo Songs by a Tattooed Man").

Up to the last few weeks of his life, Captain Don still made occasional appearances at tattoo conventions and other events, occasionally performing with his favorite 1863 saber. His last appearance was in California in February 2007. By then, he had been diagnosed with cancer of the throat and jaw, brought on by decades of ingesting fire-eating fuel. Doctors had given him only four months to live.

Always one to push the limits, he hung on for six. Captain Don Leslie died at the age of sixty-nine at his home in Chico on June 4, 2007. His lifelong friend, tattoo artist, and former sword-swallowing pupil Lyle Tuttle was by his side when he passed away.

Leslie's journey was filled with adventure, but not always of the glamorous type. He often lived in trailers, bathed in a bucket, and for decades battled his own bout with alcoholism until giving up drinking entirely in 1980.

"He was a man of the world and an independent spirit," his son David told the *San Francisco Chronicle* for its obituary, "and he had one hell of a rollercoaster ride of a life."

As fellow sword swallower Lady Diane Falk added, "The Captain was old school. When you watched Captain Don, you knew you were watching history."

SANDRA REED
1945–2019

Lady Sandra Reed was known as the Queen of Swords, but she originally joined the sideshow to lecture on her albinism.

Reed was born in 1945 in the small rural town of Hermon, New York, near the Adirondack Mountains. Due to her poor eyesight resulting from albinism, she headed to Rochester at age eleven to attend the New York State School for the Blind. She finished high school at a local public school and then spent several years working as an aide in a nursing home. Then, in 1969, a fair came to Rochester and Reed found herself presented with an opportunity for a career change. In her interview with *James Taylor's Shocked & Amazed!*, she described how she saw a sideshow and started talking to showman Whitey Sutton. After their conversation, Sutton offered her a job as a lecturer and elevated her name to Lady Sandra. Reed's family supported the move. Her mother had a history of working in vaudeville and girl shows, her equally albino sister Doreen joined the show, and her father sold tickets.

"I gave lectures on myself, informing people what it's like being an albino," she explained in 1973. "I tried to convey that because you're different doesn't mean you're not intelligent, that you have sensitivity, likes, dislikes, and diversions like other people. People would come up to me saying, 'You poor thing . . . what a way to make a living.' But it's not distasteful . . . it's a living."

When Reed first began, sword swallower Lady Louise Chavanne was working the same traveling carnival. Reed was fascinated by her act. At the end of the season, the young lecturer decided she could hold a crowd better as a performer. That winter in Gibsonton she took it upon herself to master the art under the tutelage of a local swallower named Ricky Richiardi.

Lady Sandra Reed performs. *Photo by Diane Falk*

"It was no easy task . . . at first the swords just wouldn't go down," Reed recalled. "I wasn't holding my head back enough to line my throat with the esophagus, and I was too tense. That's a hazard because throat muscles tend to tighten, and accidents can result. Because I was so eager to start my act, I started with three swords, not an easy accomplishment for a beginner . . . it took much practice." Four months of practice, to be specific, just to get over the gagging.

By the next season, she was set to continue her albino routine until Lady Chavanne suffered a fall and was hospitalized. Reed stepped into the role and suddenly became a double attraction. In her act, the platinum-haired performer would swallow a French bayonet with a pointed tip and then down a World War II bayonet. Next, she'd swallow three swords at a time. Eventually she worked herself up to swallowing five Japanese ceremonial dress swords, with the weight of the handles combined with the weight of the blades amounting to about 5 pounds. In the mid-1970s, the Guinness book recognized this feat as a world record. While many sword swallowers used the term "sword sandwich" when gulping multiple blades, Reed liked to refer to her five-at-once sandwich as "the Dagwood." She later beefed it up even more by swallowing seven at once. The center blade was a Knights of Columbus–sized sword, while the outer swords were progressively shorter and made of thin, flexible steel.

If people ever started losing interest during her act, Reed would quickly recapture their attention with a dramatic drop to one knee while the sword protruded from her throat. "If the audience was asleep, it would wake them up," she explained.

Reed took great pride in her craft, which she often performed up to twenty times a day. "I want to make my act a work of art," she told a reporter in 1974. "I want to entertain people, not make people sick."

Throughout the seventies, Lady Sandra's sword-swallowing skills allowed her to travel the country with the Ringling Bros. and Barnum & Bailey Show, the Clyde Beatty-Cole Bros. Circus, the James E. Strates Shows, Ward Hall and Chris Christ's World of Wonders, John Bradshaw's Sideshow, and more.

While working with the Hall and Christ sideshow, Reed fell in love with its fat man, Harold "Big Jim" Spohn. Spohn, born in 1936 in Lancaster, Ohio, ran away from home at an early age to pursue a life in show business. The big man began as a clown before turning to professional wrestling. His increasing weight eventually prompted his sideshow career change.

The albino sword swallower and the fat man married and enjoyed show life together for several years. Sadly, by April 1980 their bliss came to an unexpected end after a sudden heart attack took Spohn's life. Following his death, Reed left the sideshow and retired in Tampa, Florida. She was unable to drive and claimed it was economically unfeasible to continue performing. In the years that followed, Reed received many offers to return to the stage again but turned them all down.

Despite once lecturing about her albinism, she loathed being called an albino. "That was one of the things she really did not like," fellow sword swallower Diane Falk recalled from her experiences working with her on John Bradshaw's sideshow.

Yet, Lady Sandra has been immortalized with that term in a 1970 photo titled "Albino Sword Swallower at Carnival, MD," taken by renowned photographer Diane Arbus.

At the time, Reed had never heard of Arbus. The photographer and a male companion had approached her just before a performance. "When I first saw them, I thought they were hippies," Reed told a journalist in 2004, noting that Arbus wore an entirely denim outfit. "She told me she was putting together a book, traveling around and seeking out people to photograph people doing things that people do." Arbus managed to convince Reed to pose for her lens in full costume, with swords swallowed in front of a canvas tent.

Prints of Arbus's photo have sold at auction for more than $25,000. In 2018, two silver prints from Arbus signed by Sandra Reed to Johnny Fox were sold by Potter & Potter Auctions as part of its sale of the Johnny Fox Collection. The prints received forty-eight bids, with the winning bid reaching $28,800.

JOE JAGGER
1947–2007

Every sword swallower has a certain level of oddness. After all, they swallow blades for a living. Joe Jagger, however, may have been the strangest of them all.

He was born Josef Zehetbauer on August 26, 1947, in Mauerberg, a hamlet in Garching an der Alz, situated in Bavaria, Germany. It's unknown how or when Jagger learned to swallow swords. But once he did, he added fire eating to his repertoire and eventually gained fame locally and throughout the region while performing at various beer gardens. Onstage he dressed in fitted black pants and a leopard-print vest over his bare chest. Any doubting audiences were shown x-rays of steel driven down his throat. With his unique style and daring feats, Jagger soon earned the title "The Most Famous Man of Mauerberg."

Looking to broaden his fame, he packed a sword and headed for the bright lights of Las Vegas. He allegedly swallowed his sword at a bar in town, then returned home and embellished his story by announcing he had performed in Las Vegas.

For a sword swallower, this all sounds perfectly normal. But after Jagger visited a local tavern, things began to change. Armed with a boosted ego, he refused a beer and shouted to the bartender, "I just came straight from Las Vegas! Bring on a carton of whiskey and an armful of bubbly!" He was enjoying a streak of success, until a need for alcohol began to dominate him. Jagger started missing performances and began adding the risk of drunkenness to sword swallowing. As his need grew, he would make a fool of himself for a liter of beer.

Then things started getting weird. Aside from his affinity for alcohol and swords, Jagger became a pet owner—his pets being an ape and a python. When Jagger was on tour and unable to care for his pets, the monkey would allegedly feed the snake—until one day when the snake bit the hand that fed him, and ate the monkey.

As the years went on, Jagger lost interest in sword swallowing and shifted his focus to wearing makeup, women's clothing, and high heels and riding a bicycle with a trailer carrying a coffin (presumably unoccupied). For the last few years of his life, he bicycled to rural German folk festivals, dragging his wheeled casket. At some point, after his python ate his monkey, and while he was parading a coffin around town while impersonating a woman, his home—an old caravan—burned down.

On May 31, 2007, Joe Jagger's bizarre story came to an end at the age of sixty under peculiar circumstances, when he drowned in a shallow pond in Bavaria. How this happened remains a mystery, as does the question of whether or not his traveling coffin became his final resting place.

Joe Jagger in Germany at a 1995 Volksfest performance. *Collection of Dan Meyer*

COUNT DESMOND
1941–2022

Count Desmond was not a count, nor was his name Desmond. But hanging upside down while spinning from a helicopter 200 feet over Niagara Falls while pushing a sword up his throat in 1980—that was completely real. And just to defy superstition, he did it on Friday the thirteenth.

Called the "Evel Knievel of the Sword" by Knievel himself, Count Desmond was born as Edward Benjamin on July 30, 1941, in Binghamton, New York. When he was about ten years old, a circus came to town with a sword swallower. Young Edward was so impressed that he ran backstage after the show and asked the performer to teach him. He obliged.

Until that point, Edward had been a self-proclaimed "Pentecostal preacher boy" who was teased at school by other boys and "picked on unmercifully."

"I thought if I could do something no one else could, I would be popular," he told a reporter in 1977. He started

On the back of this Count Desmond pitch card, it offers these directions for sword swallowing: "Tip Head, Insert Blade, Swallow, Practice Ten Years, Be Very Careful." *Collection of Dan Meyer*

practicing with a coat hanger and "had a lot of sore throats" while he trained. "It took me six months to get to the point where I could swallow the whole thing."

After mastering coat hangers, he moved on to drumsticks, pool cues, and, of course, swords. By the late 1950s, armed with his newfound talent, Edward adopted the name "Count Desmond" and performed with the Shrine Circus as its ringmaster, sideshow talker, and fire manipulator.

In August 1967, Count Desmond worked on the Circus Bartok sideshow bally doing fire eating and sword swallowing, as well as announcing in the big top and managing the show for Milton (Doc) Bartok. His wife, Loretta, performed her own daring act as a hair-hanging artist. Over the next few decades, Count Desmond worked at various nightclubs, burlesque shows, and even the Guinness Book of World's Records Museum in Myrtle Beach, South Carolina.

His unique skills were complemented by an equally unique look. Count Desmond stood more than 6 feet tall and wore bushy hair and a goatee. A saucer-sized pendant with a dead wood spider and a sword stained red by his own blood hung from his neck, while he flaunted a satin tuxedo with copious rhinestones and rings on every finger.

In 1978, he set his first of several Guinness World Records with eight swords swallowed at once. Eventually he pushed the Guinness record of thirteen 23-inch swords, as listed in the 1984 book. During the record-setting attempt, blood appeared on the swords upon their withdrawal, which spooked Guinness and led to the following note after his listing: "This category has now been retired and no further claims will be entertained."[13]

13   Guinness has since recognized sword-swallowing records once again.

The injury, however, was nothing new to Count Desmond. In the late seventies he told a reporter that he'd performed in nearly eight hundred shows and "been carried out seventeen times and injured sixty or seventy other times." One of those mishaps resulted from a table knife accidentally slipping from his fingers into his stomach. It had to be surgically removed.

He also exposed himself to greater risk than most sword swallowers. Oftentimes performers will allow a member of the audience to slowly withdraw a swallowed sword from their throat. Count Desmond opted to involve his audience earlier. During his act, he'd invite someone onstage to push the sword straight down his gullet. As if that wasn't dangerous enough, he'd offer perhaps too much trust and let them do it while he was blindfolded. "One woman ripped my esophagus right near my heart," he said. He called it the "Suicide Show" and noted that it wasn't in the book of records "because no one will allow someone else to thrust the sword."

Always one to keep things interesting, Desmond was also known to swallow a vibration microphone with the sound system cranked up so the audience could hear the sound of his heart pulsating throughout the room. Rapidly.

His creativity led to several bold proclamations to the press, such as the time he planned to truly live up to his Evel Knievel nickname and ride a motorcycle through a 30-foot tunnel of fire with a sword sheathed in his throat. "Coming out of the tunnel, I will flip the blade free and ride 50 feet more into a wall of fire," he announced. "I won't be steering the motorcycle—someone is taking me through." No further reports indicate whether he pulled the stunt off (or didn't).

Yet, it was this kind of audacious thinking and successful daredevil antics that kept audiences watching. As he once stated, "People come to watch me because they think they might watch me die. They want to watch the danger, not the performance."

Having repeatedly eluded death for decades, Count Desmond retired in 1994. Eleven years later he was honored with a Lifetime Achievement Award by the Sword Swallowers Association International for his many sword-swallowing feats, including being the first to mix daredevil stunts with swallowing swords. He was also honored with a gold medal from Japan for placing in the Top 15 Daredevil Acts of the world, by hanging 35 feet in the air, spinning upside down from a rope while his wife inserted a sword up his throat.

Mortality finally caught up with him on December 18, 2022, when Count Desmond passed away not over Niagara Falls or in a tunnel of fire, but with his family—the most-important fans of all—at his side.

STAN MARYE
1937~

When Daniel Mannix wrote *Step Right Up!* in 1951, he became the first sword swallower to capture his adventures as a sword swallower and a fire eater between two covers with a major publisher. But for fourteen-year-old Stanley Andrew Marye, the autobiography was more than a book. It was a career path.

Marye, born on October 18, 1937, was so enthralled with becoming a sideshow performer that while reading Mannix's words he singed his eyebrows and burned a hole in the carpet before getting to chapter 2. "My mother tanned me good," he recalled years later.

By age sixteen, feeling confident in his newfound skills, the lanky teen packed a few belongings and ran away from his Wellsville, New York, home to pursue a career in outdoor entertainment. Eventually, he found work at a sideshow with Glades Amusements in Florida. He met Tiny Cowen—a 741-pound fat man—who offered more training than Mannix's book. With Cowen's training, Marye quickly improved his fire-eating skills and learned to dance on glass, walk on swords, and lie on a bed of nails. He also developed a contortionist act, which he credited to a bout of rheumatoid arthritis and rheumatic fever as a child that left his joints unusually loose.

In 1957, during a week of working at the Arizona State Fair, Marye met another influential entertainer: a sword swallower named Don Ward. The young performer studied his act and sought tips afterward. Between Ward's tutelage, Mannix's memoir, and a close connection to key pages in *Gray's Anatomy*, Marye began practicing diligently with a coat hanger. Though it wasn't easy, by 1958 he'd succeeded in his longtime goal. "I learned the art by trial and error—mainly error!" he once told a reporter.

As Marye developed his own act with an assortment of long, sharp pieces of hardware, he became known as "the only sword swallower who didn't swallow a sword." First, he'd swallow a bent coat hanger, then a 20-inch stove poker, a 15-inch-long Army serving spoon, a bayonet with a 16-inch blade, a 22-inch barbecue skewer, and eventually, just to truly live up to the title of "sword swallower," a 25-inch saber.

All the unusual objects helped prove to audiences that the stunt is real. Marye, like many sword swallowers, found disbelief to be common among crowds.

"The kids, even some grown-ups, they think we press a button and it curls up into the handle," Marye told a reporter in 1968. "Actually, it's practice, learning to relax, control muscles. Once you've done that there's nothing to it. Besides, I have a double esophagus."

With audiences feeling more convinced, he hoped, after he'd swallowed various objects without handles for

blades to fold into, he progressed further into the sword portion of his act. His "Hot Sandwich" routine featured two swords with a lit cigarette wedged between them. After removing the blades, he'd continue smoking the cigarette. Marye also swallowed a sword sandwich of up to five swords, though an injury eventually led him to thin out his meal to just three swords. One reporter referred to him as "an omnivorous gent who downed broadswords like they were oysters."

After four years of touring, Marye took a brief break to join the US Navy. His duties, however, didn't stop him from performing. He was known to entertain recruits with his unique talents.

Once returning to civilian life, Marye found his way back to the sideshow stage, working stints with James E. Strates, Royal American Shows, King Brothers Circus, Clyde Beatty-Cole Bros. Circus, Ward Hall and Harry Leonard's sideshow, and more. In the early 1960s, while working for showman Jerry Lipko, he even teamed up with another sword swallower, Vickie Pope, who doubled as a Fat Lady act. Along the way, he met another woman who didn't swallow steel but became his wife. The two continued crisscrossing the country, bouncing from sideshow to sideshow as he swallowed swords, performed his many other acts, worked as an outside talker and concessionaire, and even helped rig high-wire acts and set up tents.

By 1965, Marye was ready for another break from the business. He took a "real job" in construction, but it lasted only three years before the urge struck to swallow swords again. He continued working sporadically over the next two decades with gigs spanning everywhere from Bridgeport, Connecticut, to Johannesburg, South Africa. In 1987 he very well may have claimed the odd distinction of being the only person to have swallowed a coat hanger for the crew of Kool and the Gang.

JOHNNY MEAH
1937~

The spectacle of a sideshow starts before performers ever set foot onstage. It begins with colorful sideshow banners hyping the most amazing and wondrous, the biggest and smallest, and the absolute strangest people the world has ever known. All to lure visitors inside the tent. Johnny Meah, known as the Czar of Bizarre, not only painted many of those banners: he was one of the featured acts.

Meah was born on December 12, 1937, in Bristol, Connecticut, and his artistic journey started at an early age under the influence of his father, Harold, an editorial cartoonist for the local newspaper. By the age of eight, Meah began honing his skills by sketching caricatures, following closely in Harold's creative footsteps. His father influenced his artistic sense further with childhood visits to fairs and amusement parks and cultivated an affection for the circus at the same time. Meah's uncles helped too, since they had a background in circus arts, having performed an aerial act in vaudeville.

At fourteen, Meah immersed himself in the world of the King Bros. and Cristiani Circus during a transformative summer. His uncles had introduced him to the legendary Hugo Zachinni, the original Human Cannonball, who mentored him in the world of clowning. The multitalented Zachinni also painted banners for the circus and taught Meah how to embrace vibrant colors, bold lines, and exaggerations. In the mornings, Johnny contributed by painting small signs, while his evenings were dedicated to performing as a clown. As his apprenticeship continued, Zachinni taught him a variety of circus acts, giving him a broader, more diverse repertoire. Meah knew that more acts would lead to more money.

In 1954 he joined the Hunt Bros. Circus as a clown and continued his training in other skills. Soon Meah had mastered seventeen of them, including juggling, aerial stunts, fire eating, and sword swallowing.

"It's a very unpleasant thing to learn," Meah told a reporter in 2003. "You wind up spending a lot of time decorating your shoes."

During his teen years, he eventually returned home to attend the Rhode Island School of Design for one semester. But the call of the circus was too strong. Merging his two passions, he began painting sideshow banners in 1957 after a female impersonator named Leo/Leola (whose real name was Homer Tracy) was impressed with his work. He/she had sent a few of his paintings to renowned circus artist Snap Wyatt for his opinion. Wyatt, too, was impressed, and Tracy hired Meah to create banners for his sideshow, which at the time toured with Ross Manning Shows. Meah's banner-painting career was launched. That year, he also began performing professionally as a sword swallower with Tracy's show.

Over the next two decades, Meah traveled the world working as an artist with numerous circuses and sideshows, including Ringling Bros. and Barnum & Bailey, Royal American Circus, and Circus USA. By his estimation, he's painted more than two thousand of them, portraying such acts as the "Fire Worshipper," "Popeye: The Man with the Elastic Eyeballs," and "Pricilla the Ape Girl."

"I measured my banners at 110 feet so the average person has to take thirty-three steps to walk by them," he told the Los Angeles Times in 1997. "You are trying to make a banner that is going to stop them, intrigue them, and motivate them to want to buy a ticket and see the things portrayed on the banner."

By the 1980s, there were fewer circuses left to paint for, leading Meah to return to the stage as a full-time sword swallower with the Ward Hall & Chris Christ World of Wonders Show. Armed with his 2-foot blades and a neon tube, he performed with World of Wonders and other shows through the '90s. But he also found another revenue stream: selling banners to art collectors.

After a 1980 exhibition at the Smithsonian that was centered on the outdoor amusement business featured some of Meah's work, things took off in ways he never imagined. The exhibit led to a 1983 *Life* magazine article, which led to a call from a Chicago art gallery. Suddenly, his work was sought after and selling for thousands of dollars.

"At that time there was no real value to the things," Meah told the *Chicago Reader* in 2001. "We had just made a monster bonfire with probably 50 banners that were shot. Now, hindsight being the wonderful thing it is, that bonfire would be worth $20,000. Then it was just crap we were getting rid of."

His work has since been exhibited in other museums, including the Barnum Museum in Bridgeport, Connecticut, and at Intuit: The Center for Intuitive and Outsider Art.

Several books have featured Meah's art as well, including 1995's *Freaks, Geeks, and Strange Girls: Sideshow Banners of the Great American Midway* and 2018's *Painters of the Peculiar: A Guide to Sideshow Banner Artists and Their Respective Work*. In 2003 he traded his paintbrush for a pen and published *Polidore*, a novel about the dark recesses of show business. Meah's vast and varied experiences also earned him a role as an advisor on the HBO series *Carnivale* (2003–05).

As part of the World Sword Swallower's Day celebration on February 28, 2008, the Sword Swallower's Association International awarded Meah an SSAI Lifetime Achievement Award for his years of service to the art of sword swallowing.

WALTER HALL
1953–90

At 6 feet, 11 inches tall, Walter Hall had little competition in billing himself as the World's Tallest Sword Swallower.[14] Having a longer torso than others, he claimed to be able to swallow longer blades. In 1978 his maximum length was 27 inches while performing at the Skowhegan State Fair in Maine.

Hailing from Wilmington, Delaware, Hall first worked as the "Cowboy Giant" on the Lawrence Carr Show. But after sword swallower Toni Del Rio left in 1974, Hall learned

---

14   At 7 feet, 3 inches, George "The Giant" McArthur has since surpassed Hall as the world's tallest sword swallower.

"SIR WALTER"
WORLD'S TALLEST
CIRCUS
SWORD SWALLOWER

Pitch card of Sir Walter, sword swallower. *Collection of Warren A. Raymond*

the art from showman Dean Potter and half-man/half-woman Jadi Easton. No longer just a giant, he swallowed swords under various stage names, including Sir Walter, Tall Tex, Tall Paul Adams, and Sebastian.

With the King Brothers Circus, Hall performed an act called "The Spider Web," in which he swallowed multiple swords, then pulled them out and spread the blades. The saliva between them created the effect of a web.

In December 1978, while performing with the Clyde Beatty-Cole Bros. Circus in West Palm Beach, Florida, a bewildered reporter asked the twenty-five-year-old sword swallower if he felt uneasy about his act. "What I feel isn't paranoia or stage fright . . . It's just the jitters," Hall responded. "But once I begin my act, I loosen up and everything is smooth."

The giant sword swallower continued performing into the 1980s but passed away in 1991. The cause of death is unknown.

LEO GRIEP
1946~

Leo Griep once said he saw his reflection in the window as he was carrying a torch outside as a teenager and at that moment decided he was going to eat fire. Growing up in Los Angeles as the son of an El Salvadoran mother and a German father, he buried himself in books about anatomy, magic, and comedy and started swallowing small objects tied to strings and then bringing them back up. Soon, he'd learned enough to become a fire eater and sword swallower.

When his parents enrolled him in a Catholic seminary, he began earning money by getting away from it. Griep took to the streets as a performer and skillfully gathered large crowds that filled a hat with money. He worked as a busker for several years until he eventually met up with the Big John Strong Circus in the mid-1970s. Griep claimed that his mother clutched her rosary beads and wept about it until her death.

Wearing a turban, a black-and-gold vest, colorful pantaloons, and curly shoes, Griep would perform in character as "Swami Amazo Benbota" as he ate fire, swallowed swords, and served as an assistant ringmaster with Strong's show from 1976 to 1983. His wife, Marsha, performed alongside him for several years with three aerial acts.

Onstage, Griep used three blades of steel: the first was a thick bayonet about 8 to 10 inches long and 2 inches wide; the second was a longer bayonet with an 18-inch-long blade that was also thick and wide; and the third was a saber from the Spanish-American War with a 22-inch-long blade. Rollick finished his act by swallowing all three blades at once and ending with a bow from the waist.

"Leo did things that I'd never seen before," John Strong III told us in a March 2024 phone interview. "He'd swallow a sword and then throw it up into the air 20 feet, and all of the saliva would come flying out of his mouth. Every show that he did he would get a standing ovation. He was just that good."

When not working with the Big John Strong Circus, Leo and Marsha returned to their street performance roots with shows on the road from California to Colorado. By the mid-'80s, they settled in Colorado Springs and left the sideshow arts to focus on political activism. Their efforts were directed toward issues concerning Central America, notably protesting against the potential US invasion of Nicaragua in 1984.

Leo Griep as Swami Amazo
Benbota, 1977. *Collection of
Dan Meyer*

Rick Dennis performs his sword-swallowing act. *Collection of Dan Meyer*

RICK DENNIS
1952~

In 1966, Rick Dennis was working with the Clyde Beatty Cole Bros. Circus as a fire eater and magician. During his time with the sideshow, he studied sword swallower Francis Doran and secretly began teaching himself, using a straightened coat hanger. He graduated to swords soon after. By then, Dennis was all of fourteen years old—and was promptly billed as "The World's Youngest Sword Swallower."

Born on June 5, 1952, in Vestal, New York, Dennis started juggling and performing magic by age ten. As his young career quickly progressed in the circus, he ran into trouble when a fire-eating magic trick backfired and left him in serious condition at a Binghamton, New York, hospital for six weeks. The experience never caused him to shy away from danger though—especially when it came to sword swallowing.

"After I got the hang of it, it used to be a lot of fun," he told a reporter in 1973. "For example, I would swallow pool cues. I could say: 'If I lose the game, I'll swallow the cue.' No one would believe that."

In perhaps his most dangerous feat, he allowed his girlfriend to slide the sword down his throat. If she slid it down improperly—even just slightly—his act may have been over, permanently. He had hoped that the truly rare stunt would land him in the Circus Hall of Fame in Sarasota, Florida (a search online shows he didn't make it—nor has any other sword swallower).

Dennis's daring act added knife throwing, the bed of nails, and a straitjacket escape, which he performed for Sells and Gray Circus, Ward Hall's World of Wonders show, and Carson and Barnes Circus Sideshow. He also toured with a small group of performers (and a giant python) as the Dr. Demon Show, playing at colleges and other venues. By the end of the seventies he was running his own ten-in-one show under the ominous but alluring name of Dr. Blood. Dennis continued his act through the early nineties before retiring from performing.

JOHN STRONG III
1958~

When your parents own a circus, you start learning acts at an early age. For John Strong III, it was earlier than most. By age eleven, he'd swallowed his first sword.

Born on October 16, 1958, young John grew up in the business: the Big John Strong Circus. The budding performer was just ten years old when showman Jack Waller taught him to eat fire. John was not yet a tween when he began advertising his new talent, along with a magic act and a two-headed calf he owned on the show's banner line. That banner also promoted a sword swallower who worked for his father.

One day after the crowd had paid fifty cents for the show, they started shouting for the sword swallower, who was nowhere to be found. He'd just quit the show and left. "I had about three hundred people in there, and I didn't want to return $150," Strong recalled. "At eleven years old back then, it was a lot of money."

Strong's dad had bought the sword swallower's blades before he took off, and young John was determined to use them. "I went into the truck real quick, grabbed my sword—it was a bayonet, about 19 inches long, and I just swallowed it," he said. "I was trying at it for a while, but I said, 'It's now or never,' and I pushed it all the way down. I was really happy because now I'm a sword swallower and everybody clapped."

The young performer also added juggling, plate spinning, and a one-finger handstand to his act. By age seventeen he was managing the sideshow for the Ringling Bros. and Barnum & Bailey Circus at Circus World in Haines City, Florida, near Orlando. On one occasion in 1977, Olympic gold medalist Bruce Jenner showed up, and Strong invited him to smash a block of sidewalk cement on his stomach as he lay on a bed of nails. "I told him to hit the rock as hard as he could," Strong said. "I shouldn't have done that because I almost had to be peeled off that bed of nails."

Strong also continued working for his father's circus and eventually took it over in 1995. Though he's swallowed up to sixteen thin swords at once, as the owner of the show he's been able to hire other sword swallowers—such as Dan Meyer and Katya Kadavera—and attend to managing and promoting. In addition to human oddities, Strong's show has included a freak animal exhibit with live two-headed turtles, a two-headed bull snake, a two-headed tortoise, and more.

Outside the tent, the sword-swallowing showman has spent several years training celebrities for CBS's hit television show *Circus of the Stars*. Among them were Loni Anderson and Brooke Shields, whom he taught to walk across glass, and Hervé Villechaize from *Fantasy Island*, whom he instructed in fire eating.

Strong's greatest brush with fame, however, came with a role in Tim Burton's 1992 film, *Batman Returns*, where he landed a role as both a sword swallower and a fire eater (see page 140 for more).

After forty years of swallowing steel, Strong rarely does it anymore. He remains active in the sideshow world, however, and as of this writing is exploring an event in Orlando, Florida, with rides and live shows. Undoubtedly, a sword swallower would be among the performers.

RED STUART
1951~

It takes some sword swallowers months or years to get their first blade down. Red Stuart claims to have done it in about ten minutes. After four tries. Granted, he had a good mentor in Toni Del Rio, but ten minutes is still record timing. Perhaps a little royal blood helped.

He was born in New Jersey on March 21, 1951, and John "Red" Stuart XXVIII's numerous Roman numerals refer to his position in the lineage of Mary Stuart, Queen of Scots. His youth, however, didn't quite reflect that prestige. When he was just four years old, Stuart's mother put him up for adoption in Philadelphia. Young John grew up in an orphanage and a series of foster homes until graduating high school in 1967, at which point he sought change and adventure. He found it by hitchhiking across the country and landing a job at a carnival during Mardi Gras in Louisiana. There, he met Del Rio, who not only taught him sword swallowing but also trained him to perform other sideshow acts as well.

"It was like monkey see, monkey do," Stuart told us in a March 2024 phone interview, regarding all of Del Rio's training. Pounding a nail into his nose for the human blockhead routine was the first stunt he learned. "She took a nail, touched the tip of my nose, shoved it in, and told me to leave it there. I held it there for about two minutes." He pulled it out, blew his nose, then did it again till he figured out the proper placement to push it all the way

John Strong swallowing a sword in front of Alice from Dallas and a sideshow banner painted by Fred Johnson. *Courtesy of John Strong*

Red Stuart swallows his giant 54-inch sword at Tattooed Mom, a bar and restaurant in Philadelphia, 2004. *Photo by Liz Steger-Hartzman*

into his head. Stuart soon added fire eating, hot-coal dancing, the human pincushion, glass eating, and the sword ladder to his résumé. Swallowing steel was the final lesson in his crash-course sideshow education.

"With the sword swallowing, the first two tries I hacked and coughed and gagged," Stuart said. "Even then I still swore up and down that the sword folded up in the handle. With all the teachings I was taught about the seven deadly tortures, I figured that there was always some sort of gimmick or preparation to get it done, but there really wasn't." After that, Del Rio handed him a broken Knights of Columbus sword with no handle on it. On his third attempt he pushed it down just below the collarbone, then pulled it out and coughed.

"Red, you did it—but you didn't do it," Del Rio told him. "If you say you can do it, you can do it. If you have the slightest doubt, fear, or hesitation, you will never do it. You had it properly aligned, you went down, but you stopped. You shoulda went all the way."

Stuart took a moment to concentrate, then gave it another try and got the blade all the way down. "It was

one of the strangest sensations I ever had," he said. That milestone, on March 24, 1967, marked the beginning of a sword-swallowing career that continues today.

His quick mastery of the art soon took it to another level. In 1969, Stuart was labeled the only sword swallower to swallow broadswords and car axles. He's also put coat hangers, giant screwdrivers, bayonets, neon tubes, and a 54-inch long, 2½-inch-wide sword down his throat. The oversized blade drops about 24 inches into his body. Stuart showcased these feats at many shows throughout his career, including numerous seasons with Ward Hall and Chris Christ's World of Wonders sideshow.

Over the course of many decades, the sword swallower has kept busy with more than just steel. He's also helped set up rides, handled electrical and maintenance duties, and run girl shows and reptile shows. While working the latter, Stuart found that snakes could be even more interesting if they were swallowed. Using an indigo snake, he let it slither down his throat head first, with its jaw held shut by his esophagus. In *American Sideshow*, he described an even more intimate stunt that he called the "Kiss of Death." In the act, he offered his tongue for the snake to bite, then brought his tongue and the clamped-down head back into his mouth. "I didn't do it too often. It hurt like hell," he said. "I'm not sadistic."

Stuart has helped many young performers who share the same fearlessness learn to swallow swords. As of this writing he's teaching his sixtieth student while working at Pexcho's American Dime Museum in Augusta, Georgia. Stuart has been swallowing swords there since January 2019, with the 1-inch-thick car axle serving as the grand finale of his performance.

"I will swallow the car axle till I die," Stuart said. "I'm planning on staying here till I either fall off the stage or go to sleep and not wake up."

DIANE FALK
1959~

Diane Falk didn't know what a sideshow was when she started her career with showman John Bradshaw in 1979. But that was a minor detail for the nineteen-year-old student at Virginia Commonwealth University.

Falk first met Bradshaw at a local coffee house, where he was playing blues guitar. As a fan of the genre, she spoke with him afterward, and he explained that he'd be hitting the road in a week and invited her to join his sideshow. The semester had just ended, and she went home to her parents' house in northern Virginia. But the promise of adventure percolated in her head.

"I said, 'You know what? Let me do it. What the heck?'" Falk told us in a March 2024 phone interview. She hitchhiked to Richmond and survived the ride with the "very strange people" who picked her up. "I guess that was the carny in me before I knew I had it in me. I have a pretty good way of dealing with dum-dums."

She met Bradshaw at the coffee house and they headed out, en route to a career that college could never have prepared her for. Falk began as a bally girl, meaning she'd stand on the stage and help gather a crowd for the show inside.

"I held a snake, and back in the day, people would scream and that would be exciting," she said. "Nowadays people are like, 'Yeah, frickin' snake. Look, I got one round my neck too. So what?'"

One of her fellow performers was sword swallower Francis Doran. "He was a charming, grumpy old man," she said. "I took a liking to him; I really liked Francis." Doran had health issues and was facing the end of his career. Knowing he'd struggle to keep up with his sword-swallowing schedule, he took Falk under his wing and taught her the ancient art.

"When you really like somebody, and when you're nineteen years old, especially, you learn stuff quickly—so I was a rather good student," Falk said. After about a month of training, she would fill in for him when he wasn't feeling well. "That was my beginning."

After a few years with John Bradshaw's show, Falk continued her career with numerous other shows, including the Sutton Sideshow Circus, Ward Hall's World of Wonders Show, Coney Island Sideshows by the Seashore, and on a boat tour of the Micronesian islands and Guam in the South Pacific with Captain Don Leslie. It was Leslie who suggested her stage name in the late 1980s after finding out she didn't have one. As Falk tells the story, the process was a quick one:

"Captain Don said, 'Diane, so what's your name?'"

"I said, 'I don't know.'"

"He said, 'How about Lady Diane?'"

"I said, "Okay.'"

She's been Lady Diane ever since. Leslie also taught her to eat fire. "This shit is hot!" Falk chuckled, as she recalled her thoughts while learning.

While at Coney Island in the late 1980s, Lady Diane had the good fortune of being in the right place at the right time to meet Bruce Springsteen and his producers as they cast members of the sideshow for the "Tunnel of Love" video. "I still have a picture of Springsteen pulling the sword out of my throat," Falk said.

Though she traveled frequently with her various troupes, one of her nonsideshow performances unexpectedly landed her in the *New York Times*. In 1993, much like during that initial leap of faith in 1979, she was in search of adventure and brought her swords to Washington, DC, for President Bill Clinton's inauguration.

"I really liked Clinton—and I didn't care what happened underneath his table," she told us.

Despite being among 400,000 people, swallowing steel was a surefire way to stand out. The *Times* noticed Falk and wrote about her as "a streetside sword swallower" who "showed up in full costume, attracting crowds of astonished gawpers."

Lady Diane has always appreciated the sense of wonder that accompanies not just her performances, but her travels. "To summarize sword swallowing—what I really like about it was it gave me an opportunity to see things," she told us. Falk continues to swallow swords to this day and still owns many of Francis Doran's blades. "I'm honored to have them."

JOHNNY FOX
1953–2017

When Johnny Fox was ten years old, he read that Houdini practiced swallowing and regurgitating items by swallowing a piece of potato attached to a string. "I thought, wow, that was brilliant; if it got dislodged, he could digest it," Fox remembered. Inspired, Fox swallowed a piece of spaghetti and brought it back up. The event would prove to be a precursor to his career as "The King of Swords."

Born on Friday the thirteenth in November 1953, Johnny Fox never considered himself unlucky. Instead, he had the good fortune to simply do the things he loved. Growing up in Connecticut, Fox developed an interest in magic and theater. He also developed unusual abilities that he'd use to amuse his friends.

"I used to bend myself around in knots and tie myself—I was Rubber Boy, Pretzel Boy," he said. "I hung around pool halls learning trick shots in pool; I learned coin tricks and card tricks, learning hustles, obscure knowledge, martial arts, and street fighting."

By the age of twenty, Fox began performing sleight-of-hand magic and comedy in Florida restaurants. In the years that followed, he added other stunts, such as fire eating, which helped him gather crowds for street performances. In 1978, he began training to swallow swords. Fox spent six to eight months slowly perfecting the art. "I didn't want to look like I was struggling. I wanted it to look really natural in front of a crowd," he said. Having achieved a level of effortlessness, Fox swallowed swords for thirty-seven years at the Maryland Renaissance Festival, as well as fairs in Colorado, Sarasota, and Chicago.

His mastery of the blades has led to numerous television appearances, including the *Late Show with David Letterman*

Johnny Fox at his New York City museum, the Freakatorium, 2000. *Photo by Liz Steger-Hartzman*

and a 1992 performance on *The Jonathan Winters Show* in which he swallowed sixteen swords. At the time, he asked the Guinness Book of World Records to document the feat, but they informed him that the category remained closed.

In the early 1990s, even doctors took notice when the Johns Hopkins medical department documented Fox's skills in an x-ray film produced to help people with swallowing disorders. Fox's repertoire of stunts also includes contortion, glass eating, coin tricks, and the human blockhead. The latter was first inspired by old photos of Leo Kongees, a blockhead from the 1930s. "I was using a spike, which was really like a nail. I noticed people in the audience were grossed out and disgusted. So I stopped doing it," Fox said. That lasted until he discovered photos of Melvin Burkhart using a giant twenty-penny spike. "That's the way to sell that trick. That way people from the back row can see it." Fox combined his inventory of talents with storytelling and jokes in a one-man show. And in one instance, for a Maalox commercial. In the ad, he looks at the viewer and asks, "Are you like me?" He then lifts a hammer and smashes a lightbulb. "Do you occasionally eat things that don't agree with you?" Then he eats the shards of glass.

Skilled as he was, he continually sought new original material to expand the act. For example, he developed a stunt in which he'd swallow the handle of a giant spoon, bend over, and crack an egg into the bowl of the spoon protruding from his mouth, then cook the egg while the handle was still down his throat.

Aside from performing, Fox was the founder of a museum dedicated to sideshow memorabilia, called the Freakatorium, El Museo Loco, which was located on New York City's Lower East Side from 1998 to January 2005. The collection featured carvings by armless man Charles Tripp, a two-headed cow, a mummified cat from an Egyptian tomb, conjoined piglets in a jar, and an incredible display of old photos, posters, artifacts, and more. "New York needs a place where people can come see the history of freakdom," Fox said of his collection. "I want it to bring happiness, or wonder, or awe, or disgust to people. Whatever it stirs up. Something like that should always be in Manhattan."

Following the museum's closing, Fox relocated to Connecticut and continued performing in Maryland and elsewhere. However, life took a dramatic turn in early 2017, when Fox was diagnosed with stage 2 liver cancer. Due to the large size of the tumor (10.3 cm) and five to six smaller tumors, his doctors said there was nothing more they could do for him, since there was no conventional treatment available for his situation. They gave him a prognosis of only six months to a year to live.

On March 20, 2017, Fox slipped and fell on black ice at his home in Seymour, Connecticut, which greatly exacerbated his liver condition and left him in critical condition, fighting for his life. Doctors didn't expect him to make it through the night, but he survived.

Money raised by friends and supporters helped Fox receive treatment at a naturopathic center in Mesa, Arizona. He began improving and even made an inspirational return to the Maryland Renaissance Festival by the end of August. He refrained from swallowing swords but performed his brilliant version of the cup-and-balls tricks, his "holy water from India" routine, and other acts.

Sadly, his miraculous recovery was fleeting. On Sunday, December 17, 2017, at 2:24 a.m., Johnny Fox died of liver cancer at the age of sixty-four at the home of a friend in Damascus, Maryland.

"It was a peaceful transition," his friend said. "We were grateful that it was peaceful. He passed with a smile on his face. After he took his last breath, the five of us gave him a standing ovation."

Weeks later, fans, friends, and coworkers gathered at the Maryland Hall for the Creative Arts in Annapolis to celebrate his life. Fourteen sword swallowers from around the country gave a twenty-one-sword-swallowing salute in his memory. He was further honored when the Maryland Renaissance Festival renamed the stage he performed on as the "Johnny Fox Stage."

There is no end to the history of sword swallowing. But the twenty-one-sword salute to Johnny Fox honored the death of a legend who began at a transition point in the world of circus and sideshow. Sword swallowing along the midway had already been declining since the latter half of the twentieth century. Performers such as Fox, Red Stuart, Diane Falk, and John Strong bridged an era, keeping the art alive at fairs and various shows and events. Soon, sword swallowing would enjoy a renaissance bolstered by the rebirth of the sideshow at Coney Island in the mideighties, led by John Bradshaw and Dick Zigun, as well as the success of the Jim Rose Circus as it toured with Lollapalooza in the early nineties. Todd Robbins, who began performing sideshow arts in the early eighties, later served as dean of the Coney Island Sideshow School in the first few years of the 2000s. They've all helped inspire and train a new generation of sword swallowers who are continuing to shock and amaze audiences everywhere, from traveling sideshows and fairgrounds to nightclubs and private parties.

CUTTING UP JACKPOTS

Charles Prester, as seen in the 1930s scrapbook of Agnes Schwarzenbacher, the Rubber Skin Lady.
Courtesy of Dori Ann Bischmann

Behind the sideshow tent was an area the local rubes would not get to see—the "backyard" where performers would sit around cutting up jackpots. (If you're not with it, that's lingo for swapping stories.)

So grab some popcorn, pull up a chair, and listen to these modern-day sword swallowers as they keep history alive and cut up jackpots about the strangest, funniest, scariest, and most unbelievable experiences on and off the stage. All the stories are in their own words, just as they shared them with us.

And remember, these are all trained professionals. Don't try to imitate them on your own—or your story may end up being your last.

GROWING PAINS

HOW TODAY'S SWORD SWALLOWERS
LEARNED TO PUT STEEL DOWN THEIR
THROAT FOR FUN AND PROFIT

SWORD SHOPPING

I did a lot of juggling, and I thought, "Man, it would be cool if I could do something a little more original." I wanted to do TV shows, and I remembered my grandfather telling me that when my dad was a boy, he took him to a show in my area and they had a sword swallower. I remember asking my grandfather if it was real. This was long before I ever swallowed swords. He said, "Well, it sure looked real." I thought if I could swallow a sword and add it to my juggling routines, it would make it more unique.

I lived in a university town, so I had a friend with an anatomy book from anatomy class, and it said about how long the average esophagus is. So, I took a measuring tape to my local army/navy store, and I started measuring swords. I found one that the blade seemed to be about the right length and width. There was nobody in the store, and I thought, "I hate to buy this sword and then I can't swallow it. I wonder if I could try it." I meant to be saying it to myself, but I guess I said it under my breath, and then unbeknownst to me, the clerk had walked up to me, behind me, because I heard this voice saying, "Well, I guess so." He didn't know what I was talking about.

I held it flat like a tongue depressor and pressed the back of my tongue down, and lifted it up, and slid it down. I was so thrilled. It was such an odd feeling –that cool blade going down for the first time. I took it out, laid it on the counter, and said, "I'll take a couple more."

—**Brad Byers**, sword swallower since 1981

CONEY ISLAND INSPIRATION

I'd worked my first season in Coney Island—half the summer for John Bradshaw. I would do outside talking, magic, the electric chair, the blade box. Then the following year was when Bradshaw split and Dick Zigun started the show. So, the cast was me, Todd Robbins, Michael Wilson, the illustrated man, and others. A crew came in to scout for the Bruce Springsteen "Tunnel of Love" video. And I was told I wasn't visually interesting enough, and that's when I was like, "Screw that; I'm learning sword swallowing." The show actually didn't have a sword swallower at that time. So, I was like, all right, I'm gonna do this. I had a coat hanger I was trying to swallow, but it wasn't gonna go down. Everyone at the sideshow was like, "Oh, sword swallowing, that's yoga." I had no clue what yoga was. I was like, "What? Yogurt?"

So, I went to a yoga center in the East Village, and that whole winter I was going to classes. That was really my on-ramp to learning sword swallowing. I was going a couple of times a week, and then and during that time, I tried, like, five times to get the coat hanger down and it wasn't going. Then on Palm Sunday that following year, it just went down.

I chalk a lot of it up to just really being in the actual space of the sideshow. Like the moment I was in that space, and my body knew the level of final relaxation of yoga to do it. Then it was easy peasy. I started performing that day.

I performed that weekend with a hanger— my shtick was always to bend it while it was inside me. That week I went out and I bought my first sword off the wall from the Medieval Times storefront in Times Square. I took it to the glass workshop and they belt-sanded the sword smooth.

I did the neon tube for a while too. I also bought a curved sword at a flea market in Maine, and I'd bend my body over to the right side and swallow it. I was the first person I ever saw that did that, although I'm sure that goes way back.

—**Fred Kahl**, a.k.a. **The Great Fredini**, sword swallower since 1992. Influenced by Melvin Burkhart while he was performing at Coney Island and Daniel Mannix's book *Step Right Up!*

SEPARATING FACT FROM FICTION

When I began learning (read: researching and self-teaching) sideshow stunts in the late '80s and early '90s, sword swallowing was incredibly rare and nearly impossible to get good information on. I was driven to figure out how to do it from a personal desire to achieve such a feat of mind over body, and by the belief that it would be a huge benefit to my goal of becoming a professional performer.

It was very difficult to learn—and the fact that I was trying to separate fact from fiction without the benefit of any instruction didn't help. I gave up a few times, but eventually I managed to swallow a *sai*, then a car antenna, and then worked up to actual swords. I spent weeks sitting on my couch with a bucket between my feet for vomit, shoving fingers down my throat till I couldn't take it anymore.

Since succeeding, I've swallowed an octagonal *sai*, a small cane designed for BDSM play, several variations of swords, a bayonet, pool cue, large soup ladle handles, various plastic-handled instruments, and probably some other stuff I'm forgetting. The *sai* was particularly hard and a horrible choice early on, and the pool cue was very rough going down.

—**Erik Sprague**, a.k.a. **The Lizardman**, sword swallower since 1996

ON LEARNING FROM A LEGEND

When I was twelve years old, I saw a sword swallower and fire eater perform on a bally stage in Bakersfield, California. I was amazed at what the human body could do—in my mind that was real magic. Later on in life, when I was approximately twenty-one, an incident occurred in my life that made me have a fear of fire. So, I decided to learn fire eating, just like when I was scared of heights I decided to bungee jump. I started learning sideshow stunts one after another. And I always wanted to learn sword swallowing. I finally ended up meeting Bobby Reynolds, which I then found out later was the owner of the sideshow that I saw when I was twelve years old. Bobby was getting ready to go on the road to Amarillo, Texas, to do a fair. He asked me to go on the road with him. I had just lost my job in radio as a board operator and on-air personality, so I said I would go under one condition: that he would teach me sword swallowing. He had said that he himself

had been a sword swallower but had decided to quit because he didn't want to affect his voice, which is what he really makes his money from.

Before we left for Texas, he had told me to get a button with a string on it to swallow it, pull it up, and concentrate while doing it to relax the muscles and the sphincter so I can swallow a sword eventually. Then he got a coat hanger and bent it into the shape of a sword and gave it to me. He said that after a week of doing the buttons, we would then swallow the coat hanger. After we got to Amarillo and set up, I tried to put the coat hanger down. I could not do it. I kept trying for around an hour. Finally, he came by and screamed at me, telling me I was a big wuss and I can't believe I couldn't swallow it, and to just push it down my damn throat. And then I pushed it down. My body reacted, and as my body was collapsing on itself and trying to get the coat hanger out, I yanked the coat hanger out and threw it across the lot.

Bobby then told me to do it again. I hesitated, but I was able to do it a little bit easier. And he kept having me do it until I was able to swallow the coat hanger without a problem.

—**George "The Giant" McArthur**, 7-foot, 3-inch sword swallower

FROM BELLY DANCER TO SWORD SWALLOWER

I started belly dancing in 1993 and I performed with swords, which is actually a little taboo. Huge, bloody, very, very heavy swords. I loved them. They would be on me head and my hips whenever I performed. That's how it started—and it gravitated. And not rapidly. It took me being in the belly dance world about three and a half years. I was becoming more and more popular, and it was strange because I was small, blonde. Not your typical belly dancer at all.

One day I had a huge performance here in New York City. At the end of it, I bowed and kissed the tip of the sword. My own mentor was there and went crazy mad on me and embarrassed me in front of hundreds of people—with a microphone, no less.

"There is Natasha," she said. "I hope she understands that never do you kiss the sword."

I turned beet red. I was so upset, didn't say a word. I was crying, then turned to my husband, Terrance, and said not only would I always kiss the sword because I had a great show, I'm now going to swallow the darn sucker.

Natasha Veruschka swallows at sword on World Sword Swallower's Day at Ripley's Believe It or Not! in New York City, 2010. *Photos by Marc Hartzman*

I guess you could kind of say it was pure hatred. Terrance, who is dead now, he died in my arms, looked at me and says, "If anybody can do it, you can."

So, I placed an ad on the back of a little newspaper called *Circus Spectrum* that said—no joke—"Care to know the art of sword swallowing and looking for swords to swallow." I put me phone number in, and I got some of the rudest comments, like, "I'm going to show you what to swallow," you know, and shite like that. But the only good answer I got was from Mr. John Bradshaw. He wanted to get rid of some swords that he had no use for any longer. Okay, set a price. He said 275 bloody dollars. All right. He didn't think I'd do a bloody thing with it. Boy, was he wrong.

It was like second nature to me. It takes the average person quite a long time to swallow a sword. And everybody who was in the sword-swallowing biz told me to stop; you'll kill yourself. Stop it. But John Bradshaw helped, so did Red Stuart over the phone. So I start, and within five and a half weeks I was up to a 27-inch sword.

—**Natasha Veruschka**, belly dancer and sword swallower since 1997

ILLEGAL IN ICELAND

When I was a little kid, about six or seven years old, there was a circus show on Icelandic national television once a year, and I was always waiting all year to see that one show at the end of the year. There was a guy there doing a great fire routine, doing dragon's-breath blowing fire, and at the end, swallowing a long sword. And I thought to myself, *I want to do that!*

As the years went by, I became a magician. I was doing magic tricks with some sideshow tricks, escape, straitjacket, a fire routine, things like that. But there was always in my mind swallowing swords, so I looked in the magic world to find out how to do it. I went to the international magic institute in UK, but they always said to me, "No, no, no . . . this is a bad thing, don't do it!" I bought a book from Abbott's Magic called *Strange Secrets*, and in that book, they told how it was done. I practiced like it said, training for three months, three times a day, each time three times. So, I was self-trained, and it took me over three months to learn.

I found out that I was doing both sideshow and magic blended together. Sword swallowing was one trick in my magic show, but it's not a trick, it's a real thing, of course, but it's the trick behind swallowing swords. Though the hardest trick is getting swords in Iceland, because in Iceland, we can't have swords, except the Freemasons and things like that. Iceland is a Viking country where everyone used to have swords. Today it's illegal unless you have a license. Now, today, I can have a sword because I do have a license. But the cops got my swords right now because I did the world record. And they destroyed my sword in 2002 because I was swallowing it.

—**Pétur Gisli Finnbjörnsson**, a.k.a. **Pétur Pókus**, Reykjavík, Iceland. Self-taught in 1997 at age twenty-four after three months of practicing nine times a day. Guinness World Record holder, Iceland's only local sword swallower.

RED TO THE RESCUE

My first season at the sideshow I was super green. I was able to swallow the sword, but I had very little experience working a show or knowing how to maintain my props. I had a big Knights of Columbus sword I had been using. It was about 30 inches long, and the edges were dull as a spoon, but the tip was unworked and still pointed. I had been using it in my shows before working at World of Wonders and was even stupidly doing hands-free drops with it. I didn't know any better! In a moment of sheer luck, the legendary Red Stuart was working my first spot with the show. He beckons me over and, with his deadpan expression, utters: "Lemme have a look at those things." I sheepishly hand over my swords, and he zeroes in on the Knights of Columbus immediately.

A mix of disbelief and amusement crosses his face as he exclaims, "You big dummy, what are you trying to kill yourself?!" Classic Red! Without missing a beat, he takes it upon himself to give my sword a makeover. The pointy tip gets a trim, the length gets a sensible adjustment, and suddenly, I've got a weapon that won't inadvertently turn my act into a human sacrifice.

Honestly, he not only saved me from potential disaster that day but became a close mentor and friend. Without Red's no-nonsense wisdom, I wouldn't the person I am today. Thanks, Red!

—**Tommy Breen**, a.k.a. **The Great Gozleone**, owner of the World of Wonders sideshow (purchased from Ward Hall and Chris Christ in 2017). Began learning sword swallowing at fifteen after reading Jim Rose's book *Freak Like Me*.

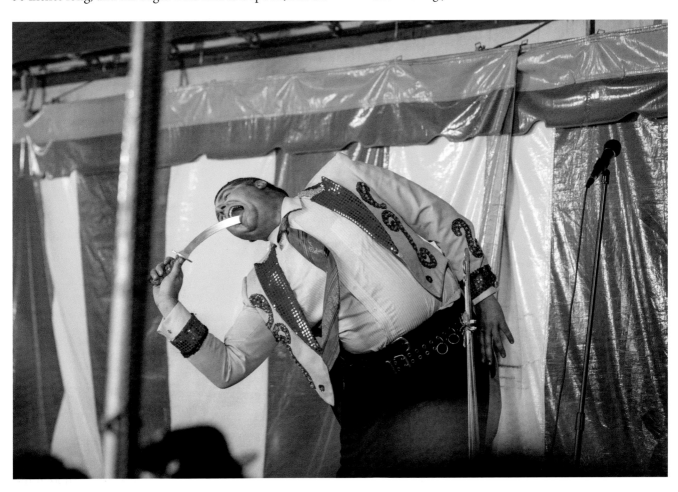

Tommy Breen at World of Wonders at the National Cattle Congress in Waterloo, Iowa, 2018. *Photo by Maggie Gulling*

A SIDESHOW LOVE STORY

A lot of modern-day sword swallowers decide to find somebody who will teach them or teach myself or whatever. For me, it wasn't like that. I met Tyler [Fyre] and we fell in love. We got married and he was gonna leave for a tour. Obviously, I'm gonna go, but how do I do that? So, we went through a bunch of different scenarios, and the best thing to do would be for me to learn acts, and obviously, the big payoff is sword swallowing.

I was doing the Palace of Wonders in DC when I when I met Tyler, so I was already involved—I'd been doing burlesque and stuff. So, it wasn't too far of a stretch, but it wasn't like I wanted to be a sword swallower. I was kind of sort of talked into it: "If you could swallow swords, then we could do like a couple swords-swallowing act." And that would be a good thing to bill. So, I said, "You're absolutely correct. How does one swallow swords?" I remember Tyler teaching me in our little 196-square-foot apartment in Washington, DC, and he told me, "Look, it took me three years. There was a lot of vomiting in the sink. Frank Hartman taught me reluctantly, and it took me three years to really be able to do it in a show."

Then it took me three months. And he was so mad.

He was like, "That is bullshit. It took you so little time to learn to swallow a sword." I just didn't feel like it was that hard to learn.

But then being the sword swallower, I definitely realized the power that the act holds. When you go out and you do the bed of nails or something else, you can see the audience thinking, "Well, I mean, I could dance around with snakes. I could lie on a bed of nails." You can see them thinking it, and you have to do the extra showmanship to make the act grand and make it entertaining. But with sword swallowing, I felt like I could just go up and swallow a sword and everybody's blown away.

—**Jill Fleet**, a.k.a. **Thrill Kill Jill**, sword swallower since 2007. Taught by her husband, Tyler Fleet, a.k.a. Tyler Fyre.

FROM VENICE BEACH TO NATIONAL TV

For me, growing up at the Venice Beach Freakshow, sword swallowing was the top thing you could do. The hardest skill, the one that a lot of people don't do. It's scary; it takes a lot of training, a lot of work. So, I had to do it. It was the ultimate crazy thing—I *had* to do it.

I picked up tips in my environment, but I'm mostly self-taught. I was doing it at home, trying to get the hanger down, but I was severely terrified of throwing up. Everyone said I couldn't do it if I was afraid of throwing up. Well, watch me. Luckily, I threw up only a couple of times while I was learning. It was just a weird fear that would make me panic. The thought of this crazy act, where throwing up was part of learning, meant I really had to tap into another mental level to do it.

I also have anxiety, where the body tenses up when I feel it. So, while filming the *Freakshow* episode where I could show this new skill I had learned, I had to really tap into that mind/body connection to calm my body down and allow it to relax. I was also a teenager still figuring myself out and being filmed on national TV while doing this life-threatening thing. It was thrilling for sure—a lot of emotions at once!

—**Asia Ray**, sword swallower since age nineteen, performed at the Venice Beach Freakshow, owned by her father, Todd Ray. AMC turned the venue into a TV series, *Freakshow*, from 2013 to 2014.

VOLUNTEERS GONE BAD

TALES FROM THE DARK SIDE OF AUDIENCE PARTICIPATION

CHEERLEADER CONFUSION

Working at the sideshow, during the blade box pitch we would hold out the incoming crowd so they didn't walk in just as we were asking for more money. So, it was a busy day, I was holding out the crowd, and they were restless and annoyed they couldn't come into the show they just paid for. I thought, instead of being the carny they were all mad at, I'd be the hero and throw a little impromptu excitement into the mix! I grabbed one of my swords and picked one of the people in the front of the line to be my assistant. She was a smiling teenager in a cheerleading outfit—a friendly picture of wholesomeness. What could go wrong? I told her I'd swallow the sword and she could pull it out. I swallow the sword, bend in half, and give her the signal . . . and then instead of gently pulling it out, she reached out and pushed the sword deeper into my body! It was terrifying! Still bent in half as it's going farther down my throat, I reached up and grabbed the sword to stop it from going through my stomach.

After I stood up and pulled out the sword, she just looked confused. I don't think she knew what she was doing was wrong, or that she could have killed me, and although I was really angry and pretty scared, it was time to let them in! Showtime! I opened the doors and then walked around the tent to assess if I was going to die. There was no blood and no weird pain inside . . . I was miraculously unscathed.

From that day forward, I vowed to be more discerning in choosing my assistants and, most importantly, to provide crystal-clear instructions on what should (and should NOT) happen during my acts.

—**Tommy Breen**, a.k.a. **The Great Gozleone**, owner of the World of Wonders sideshow

BLOODY NOSE

I was doing blockhead once, and I had a lady punch me in the nose with the nail in there. I pulled the nail out, plugged the other nostril, and just blew blood all over her. I don't know if she was just scared or an asshole or wanted to hurt somebody. But that was my reaction. I don't know what was going on in the lady's mind, but her shirt full of blood changed her mind about everything. After getting punched in the face with a nail, I was apprehensive about having someone pull a sword out of my throat. That kinda went by the wayside.

—**Frank Hartman**, sword swallower since 1994. Taught by Bill Unks at Coney Island.

ALMOST A HOLE IN THE PANTS

I was doing a shopping-mall grand opening, and I pulled a guy out of the audience to push a sword down my throat. I got down on one knee and gave him all the instructions about how I'd like him to press the sword down—I'd be giving him hand signals. I had a joke about holding my hand up to stop, and said if he isn't following my hand signals, I'd have to mend a hole in the seat of my pants. So, I gave the signal, and he starts pushing.

I had always used a sword that was kind of long—but I'd just give a signal and people would stop. I noticed this guy was kind of nervous, but it didn't seem alarming at the time. He started pressing the sword down, and I gave the signal to stop. Of course, I couldn't talk. He put his other hand on top of the hand already on the sword and started pushing harder! That sword went down farther than it's ever gone down before.

I pulled it out and looked to see if there was any blood. There wasn't. I thanked him, and nobody in the show knew any different. Then I finished the act as usual. I swallowed a bunch of swords, and when I pulled those out, every blade had blood on it. I wiped them off really quick. The guy in the front row said, "Hey, is that blood?" I said, "No, no, that's just saliva on it."

—**Brad Byers**, on a nervous-turned-dangerous volunteer

DOROTHY

As a performing sword swallower, one of the things I have always thought important is to make sure at least one person in the audience leaves the theater knowing beyond a shadow of a doubt that it's real. So, one of the standard operating procedures anytime I did a show was to go down into the audience and let a random person handle the sword and see it with their own eyes.

On one such occasion in 2012, while performing on a cruise ship, I explained this to the audience and said I needed a volunteer. Immediately several people began to point and shout, "Dorothy! Dorothy!" Then additional members of the audience took up the chant, and next thing I knew, twenty or thirty people were all shouting excitedly, "Dorothy! Dorothy!" Raising my hands placatingly, I said, "All right, all right, where is Dorothy?"

Following the direction everyone was pointing, I made my way down the staircase into the audience, and toward a little old woman, who now was raising both of her hands in the air in a "V" shape. Making my way over to her, we made eye contact and I asked, "Dorothy?"

"That's me," she said excitedly.

Her once-gray hair had gone all white, and the skin on her face was freckled by many decades of life. Despite this, her eyes sparkled with a youthful vigor.

"Well, Dorothy, would you like to help me out?"

Unbidden, she stood up and pumped her fists in the air like she'd just been called down on *The Price Is Right*. The crowd cheered her on wildly. It was an unusual reaction. I figured she must have come on this cruise as part of a family vacation; it was the only explanation I could think of as to why so many in the audience seemed to know her.

Extending the sword out to her handle-first, I said, "Take this, examine it, make sure there's no way for the blade to bend, fold, collapse, or retract into the handle."

She wore thick glasses, with a little lanyard attached at the hinges. The lanyard itself was a string of clear gemstones, which wrapped around the back of her neck to keep them from being lost if they fell off. If you searched the word "Grandma" on the internet and then clicked on images, she's exactly what you'd expect to see.

She made a show of examining the sword, even bending the blade so far that I worried she might put a permanent curve in the steel. Then she looked at me with those bright, mischievous eyes and stabbed the sword straight at my stomach.

Reflexively, I backed up an inch or two, causing her thrust to fall short, and laughed it off, saying, "Oh, careful there." But then she took one step forward and thrust forward a second time with intent. This time I had to legitimately jump back to prevent her from skewering me on the blade. I still tried to laugh it off and keep the energy light, but then she shifted her grip on the handle, placing it into her right hand in an overhand stabbing slasher-film position. She sidestepped into the walkway that led from the back of the room down to the stage, then proceeded to come after me. Chopping the sword to and fro aggressively with each step.

"Whoa, whoa, Dorothy, can't we talk about this?" I shouted as I retreated toward the stage. The crowd roared with laughter, feeding into her madness. I ran up the five steps that led to the stage, and she followed me right up. Her little white sneakers, with knee-high, skin-tone hose pumping vigorously with each step. I ran across the stage, and she followed, sword still waving wildly. Reaching the other side of the stage, I considered running down the other staircase but worried that if she tried to follow, she might lose her footing and fall. Normally I made a point of helping every volunteer offstage, always extending a hand to ensure their safe passage, but these were unprecedented circumstances. Glancing to my left at the audience, I saw an empty couch in the second row. Having no other option, and being endowed with the superhuman abilities given to performers whenever they are onstage, I leaped from the edge of the stage, over the heads of the audience members seated in the front row, and landed gracefully onto the open sofa.

Turning to face Dorothy, I saw that she had stopped at the edge of the stage right where I'd departed.

"What are we gonna do now, Dorothy?" I asked.

She stood there thinking, looking genuinely disappointed that I'd ended the game. Then she turned and made a beeline straight toward my performance partner—a juggler—who'd been standing next to his prop case throughout this debacle. She approached him threateningly, sword held high. But he stood his ground and, speaking softly, lifted his left arm the little he could. "I'm sorry, Dorothy; my arm is broken."

This stopped her in her tracks, and she looked down at the large sling cradling his shattered limb as if realizing his predicament for the first time. The day before we'd been scheduled to fly out for this contract, he'd had an accident and broke it. After he had rushed to the hospital and gotten x-rays, the doctor had told him that the earliest they could do surgery would be the following week. I was carrying the load of the show until he could heal.

As if his week weren't already hard enough, he now stood in front of a sword-wielding silver alert named Dorothy. Tearing her eyes off the sling, she looked into his blue eyes, trying to discern whether his arm was really broken or if this was all part of the show. But he just stared back, and giving a little shoulder shrug, he shook his head side to side and, looking genuinely sympathetic, said, "I'm sorry."

Somehow she accepted this explanation, and turning her attention to his prop case, she set a new course for her havoc wreaking. She picked up his bowler hat and put it on her head. Then she grabbed a roll of toilet paper and threaded it onto the sword, followed by two more rolls to make a sword-and-TP shish kebab. She picked up his juggling clubs and tucked them under her arms and held them in her armpits.

As she did this, my teammate looked up toward the sound booth and said, "Security?" The audience cracked up at this, not knowing if he was kidding or serious. From where I stood on the couch in the second row, I also wasn't sure if he was serious. Which made me wonder, at what point do you call security and have an eighty-year-old sword-wielding and prop-stealing woman removed? I dunno, but I'm pretty sure it's not in the performer handbook.

Once her hands were just about as full as they could be, she reached out one last time and grabbed a soccer ball. Awkwardly hiking up her knee-length flapper dress, she tucked the ball between her knees and, squeezing it tight, began to penguin-walk back toward the stairs that would lead to her seat. She took six or seven awkward steps before props began to yard-sale all over the stage. The clubs under her arm slipped out one or two at a time, the soccer ball fell out and rolled away, and now that her hands were freed up, she grabbed the toilet paper rolls off [the sword] one by one and threw them wildly in different directions. Then she dropped the remainder of the things she was carrying, letting them flop noisily to the stage. She turned to the crowd, raised her arms triumphantly, and curtsied dramatically. The crowd went crazy, applauding and whistling and shouting, "Whoop whoop whoop, Dorothy, we love you." She walked to the stairs, gave another curtsey, then continued down the stairs to return to her seat.

As she did that, I made my way up the other staircase while my teammate said something that made the audience laugh. He always knew just what to say when things got weird. Then we got on with the show. During a later routine, Dorothy stood up once again and threatened to return for a second cameo, but my teammate convinced her to relax and enjoy the show, which she did.

Afterward, we spoke to the sound tech and asked if he'd noticed anything strange about our show. "Oh, you mean Dorothy? Yeah, I heard you ask for security, but I wanted to see how you'd handle it. You did good though, way better than the other acts."

"Other acts?!" we asked.

"Yeah, she's been doing that all week. On the first night, she charged up there during the Welcome Aboard show and tore the microphone away from the cruise director. Then on the second night, she did the same thing to the comedian. He made the mistake of making fun of her, and she made his life hell. But you guys, you handled it really well; we were all laughing our asses off in the booth."

And that's how our very first contract on Carnival Cruise Lines went.

—**Bill Berry**, the taller half of the comedy juggling duo Rootberry

LICKED TO THE HILT

At the North California Renaissance Faire in October 2023, I pulled someone up onstage, and after they pulled the sword from my throat, I said as a joke, "Hey, one more thing, would you like to smell it?" This guy grabs my wrist, then while making very creepy eye contact licked the blade of my sword from hilt to tip with the creepy smile and creepy eye contact and then finally let go of my hand. I sent him back to his seat after that, then gave the sword a very firm cleaning with mouthwash.

—**Cyrus Pynn**, a.k.a. **Cydeshow Cy**, sword swallower since 2014. Inspired by watching Johnny Fox at the Maryland Renaissance Festival and Dan Meyer on *America's Got Talent*. Self-taught.

BLIND, NO BLUFF

I've had some memorable experiences with volunteers throwing up and/or crying when pulling a sword from my throat. One of the best was when there was a blind guy in the front row, and I just had to pick him. He stayed seated, and his partner guided his hand to the handle after I explained what was going to happen, and he worked by touch. He said it was an interesting sensation knowing that the resistance was the blade sliding along my throat.

—**Erik Sprague**, a.k.a. **The Lizardman**, sword swallower since 1996

INJURIES HAPPEN

SWORD SWALLOWING IS DANGEROUS, AS MANY PERFORMERS ARE UNFORTUNATELY REMINDED

NEON NIGHTMARE

In around 2003, Coney Island had a new neon guy who also did all of Old Navy's neon signs. He called me one day and said, "Hey, Tyler, I've got all this leftover red Italian glass and it's really cool. You don't get it much, and I think it'd be perfect for making a neon sword for you."

So I said, "Yeah, it's awesome." It's red glass filled with red neon and glows red—it's like the reddest red sword! So, he makes his neon sword and tells me he put a piece of monofilament fishing line inside the tube before he bends it.

"This way, if it breaks, you can get the glass back out," he said.

"It's not gonna break," I said.

I wouldn't do it if it was gonna break. A couple weeks later in Coney Island, it's the Sunday show, at noon, so we might be looking at a dozen people in the audience. But, you know, five people or five thousand people, you give them the best show that you've got, right? I get to the end of the sword act, and I'm just not feeling it and my hips are too far back, which puts an unnecessary strain on the sword. So, just the tip of it pokes into my stomach—and it has a tension point there.

Then the glass breaks.

And it's this crack sound like when the dentist taps your teeth with a metal instrument. It's like a sound that you feel, not like one that you hear, you know? It's loud and the light on the handle goes out. For a second, I thought, "Oh, is this the moment I always wonder about? What would happen if the sword breaks?" Of course it's not gonna, right? But it did. And I realized it's still plugged into a 5,000-volt transformer on the side of the stage.

I'm thinking, what am I gonna do? I'm staring at the ceiling, and I don't have much choice. So, I start to tug on it. And I can feel the sword start to move, and it feels like it's cutting me, but as long as it's moving, I'm not going to stop it and let it get stuck anywhere. So, I just tug the whole sword out. The bottom 3 inches of the Horseshoe Bend had broken free from the rest of the tube. The whole thing comes out, and I'm looking at the bottom piece of it swinging in the lights there, but it cut from the top of my stomach to the back of my mouth.

I look out toward the audience and see Scott Baker, who was the outside talker on the show that year. He had just come in to get a snack out of his locker and just happened to catch that moment in the sword act. I don't know what to do, and Scott's standing there. Scott can do every act in the show—he's a great guy to have on your team—so I said, "Ladies and gentlemen, up next, Scott Baker!" He wasn't up next, but I couldn't go on. Scott walks up from the front of the stage and just takes over the show.

I went back to the dressing room, and a handful of people had seen what happened or caught that the act wasn't normal, and popped their head around to see what was going on. So, what do I do? Go to the hospital? Except it's Coney Island Hospital, and they're really good at bullet wounds and broken arms, but if you go in there and tell them you have a sword-swallowing injury, they're gonna tell you to sleep it off because they think you're on drugs. Instead, I did what anyone without health insurance would do, and went to the bar. I drank a combination of whiskey and aloe vera juice—which ended up being what I did for the next thirty days.

And then after that, I went back to work again.

—**Tyler Fleet**, a.k.a. **Tyler Fyre**, sword swallower since 2001. Taught by Frank Hartman at Coney Island.

A CUT WITH A SILVER LINING

When you're learning to swallow swords, you can go only so far with someone and what they know. And when you're trying new stuff, there's not always someone to ask, especially as a female. A lot of men, for example, are not going to be cinched tight in a corset onstage—which is how I hurt myself. It all made sense after it happened, since you're squeezing all your organs together.

In 2016, I was touring a show in Australia called *Limbo* and had decided to perform with my new stack of six swords. Though I wear a costume onstage, I don't usually think I need to do a dress run when I'm practicing a new stunt at home. So, when putting the two together—swallowing the stack with a corset on for the very first time—I cut myself! I tore my esophagus. And it was one of those things that I could have guessed, but I didn't think of because no one else had performed this before, so it never happened yet.

I ended up staying in the hospital for two weeks. It took that long just to lay my bed down flat. It hurt so much to straighten my torso. Thankfully, they let me heal naturally rather than having a scar like a lot of sword swallowers when a procedure is needed. But it was pretty full on, especially dealing with nurses and doctors who don't take you seriously. That was probably the hardest part. They try to be nice but are just talking to you like you're a child. I thought it was really condescending, but I'm happy they let me heal naturally. I didn't swallow a sword for probably a month, and the next season for my show I performed fire only, no swords, just for some added healing time.

It was a great learning experience for me—and it spawned one of my best tricks of all time. This is the silver lining. I can't swallow a stack of six to eight swords with a corset on. I needed to come up with a transition where I can remove it. So now I do this two-sword drop, where I put the two swords in and they're stuck partially in my throat. It looks like I can't get them down, but then when I take off my corset, the swords drop the rest of the way. It's on a music beat and a lighting change, which helps it look pretty epic. It's everyone's favorite trick. The audience goes nuts. This would have never happened had I not hurt myself!

—**Heather Holliday**, sword swallower since 2004, mentored by Todd Robbins

PERFORMING THROUGH THE PAIN

Right after I learned, in about 1997, I got booked to do a party in Ísafjörður Vestfirðir, in the west of Iceland. This was a country party with a DJ, and I was on the stage at two o'clock at night.

Everybody was drunk, everybody was saying, "You're never gonna get the crowd." But I said, "It won't be a problem."

I had been performing all day in the parade, and warming up for the night show. So the DJ introduced me, and I went onstage, and I tried to swallow this sword. But the sword stopped in the middle of my chest. The audience was screaming and applauding and going crazy because I was the last act in that show. So, I took it out and I look at the crowd, and I put my sword back in, and it stops somewhere in my lung. I took it out and held it

Tintype of Heather Holliday swallowing eight swords.
Photographer: Myron Hensel, 2023

up for a second time. And the crowd was screaming, "Yeah, yeah, yeah!" So, I did it a third time, but this time I pushed it down. But something hurt this time—and you cannot go after the show and say, "I have to go to hospital," you know, in Vestfirðir, and with all the crew there. I just thought I would go to Reykjavík, because it hurt a lot. I couldn't complain.

It took about six hours to drive back to Reykjavík. When I came to Reykjavík, I went to the hospital, and I sat down with the woman at the desk.

"What happened to you?"

I said, "I was swallowing swords in Ísafjörður, and I think I hurt myself."

"What are you saying?"

"I was in Ísafjörður swallowing swords, and I think I have hurt myself."

She said, "I'm not working here to play with you, to have fun . . ."

And I said, "I'm not here to have fun either. I'm telling you, it's an old stunt, I was swallowing swords, and I think I have really hurt myself."

She took a long pause, and the pause went on. I went to three specialists, and they put me in an x-ray and let me drink some kind of shadow drink. When I was drinking the barium shadow drink, they tried to take photos, to see if something was leaking, but they did not see anything wrong. But after a few takes, they finally saw something. When I left that office, the three doctors came over to me. They were very nice, and I think they respected me that I was a sword swallower. One of the doctors shakes my hand, and he said to me, "And you will *never* do that again . . ."

I took hold of his hand, and I said to him, "This was just the first time . . ."

—**Pétur Gisli Finnbjörnsson**, a.k.a. **Pétur Pókus**, Reykjavík, Iceland. Self-taught in 1997 at age twenty-four after three months of practicing nine times a day.

FROM REN FAIRE TO ER

It was the fall of 2003 or 2004, and I was working at a renaissance faire, performing classic sideshow stunts, including sword swallowing. I had done hundreds of shows, swallowing swords multiple ways during each set. Up until that day, I had never had a mishap. That was about to change.

I displayed my swords on a sword stand, and during my show I'd remove them from the stand as needed. What I didn't know was that before the show, my assistant had accidentally knocked one of the swords free, and it hit the ground backstage. Before I returned, she had replaced the sword on the display, then failed to tell me about it. I can't fault her for the accident, as I should've checked the blade before swallowing it. That's something any good sword swallower should do, but I had gotten too relaxed due to having no injuries. Big mistake.

During the show, everything went as usual. Finally, it was time to swallow the swords. I took the first sword from the stand, discussed the history of sword swallowing, and took it down. Gulp, no problem. It was the second sword, the longest one with a 20-inch blade, that caused the issue. I lifted it from its cradle, threw my head back, and slid it down my throat. That's when I knew I was in trouble.

I felt a sharp scraping all the way down my esophagus. I immediately knew there was a problem. My heart sank, my eyes got wide, and I paused, trying to think about what to do next. Something was obviously very wrong, and I knew I'd been cut. I didn't know if it was bad, but I did know it had to come back out. As I pulled the sword up and out of my throat, I felt that same scraping, all the way up. I moved slowly, but it made no difference; there was a pink sheen to the polished steel when I slid it out of my mouth. I saw it, and the audience saw it, but it wasn't until I coughed and spat out a wad of blood that people began to get concerned.

I thanked the crowd and explained that I was going to the hospital. They knew it was no joke, and all I could do was hope it wasn't serious. I was able to drive myself to the ER and walk in on my own, although I was still coughing up blood. The nurse wasted no time in getting me into a room to be seen by a doctor. After the doctor inspected my throat, it turned out to be just a deep scratch, not a full cut. Come to find out, when the sword fell, it created a burr on the edge of the blade that caused the sword to snag on my esophagus and scrape all the way in and out. I was put on a liquid diet and prescribed a nasty chalky, gooey medicine I had to swallow every few hours. Funny thing was the specialist they called in to "talk to me" about why I had done that to myself. Boy, did we have an interesting conversation . . .

—**Jesse House**, a.k.a. **Ses Carny**, renaissance faire performer, learned in 2002 at age twenty-two with tips from Todd Robbins

BAR FIGHT

In around 2015, I was performing at a bar in Augusta, Maine, called Shenanigans and doing a meet and greet. I was taking photos with people for a fee—swallowing a sword of my choosing for $10 or a sword of their choosing for $20—to post during the show.

While I was swallowing a Nippulini sword, a bar fight broke out. Two people bumped into me from behind, and I got knocked to the ground with the sword in my throat. I tried putting my arms out to catch myself, like in a push-up position. But I failed to do that. The pommel of the sword hit the ground where the wall and the floor meet, right at that 90-degree angle. And because of the angle at which I was falling, and the momentum, the sword bent inside my throat—like a coat hanger would be bent to prove that it really is being swallowed. I panicked and freaked out, but I was able to bend my neck straight as I pulled the sword out. I didn't feel any pain in my stomach, which is where I thought the injury would occur if the pressure of the pommel hitting the floor pushed the blade into my stomach. That didn't happen.

I sat around for about half an hour and then went to the hospital to get checked out just in case. There was no injury. Everything was fine. It was just a very freaky, panicky moment where I thought that I had severely injured myself.

—**Nick Penney**, sword swallower since 2007. Self-taught.

BLOOD EVERYWHERE

I had a blockhead accident. I was performing at a haunted house and I'm doing the power drill. I've performed in wind, and my hair was blowing in the wind and gets attached to the power drill and goes into my nose. The hair wraps around the drill bit, goes inside my face, the drill goes all the way to the back of my nose, and I'm bleeding everywhere. But they booked me for blockhead and swords, so I have to do the sword act next. And I'm doing Red Stuart's poem:

> Like to become a sword swallower yourself?
> Between the lips and over the tongue,
> Behind the heart, between the lungs,
> Watch out stomach, here it comes,
> This is the way sword swallowing's done.

And I have the bloodiest nose I've ever had in my entire life. I'm dripping blood. I was on somebody's SnapChat that day. Blood everywhere.

—**Lydia Treats**, sword swallower since 2014. Taught by Eric Odditorium and Sally Marvel, with additional training on the World of Wonders show.

PUNCTURED, BUT NOT PENALIZED

I had my accident in early December 2017. I was trying for the world record for most swords swallowed while juggling with three objects. I tried to swallow fifteen—the previous record was thirteen. But I didn't get to juggle because the swords didn't go down right. It was a little bit chilly there—maybe that was the reason; I'm not sure—but the swords splayed and punctured my esophagus. My voice changed to something that sounded metallic. The ambulance came and took me to a hospital in Munich.

At first the doctors told me this cut is not so bad, and they only want to watch me for a few days or a week to see how it heals up, and then I should go home. But the problem was my throat was cut; I got an infection, and this put me in the hospital for about five weeks. They put me in a coma for about a day. A Munich newspaper even wrote a story of my accident.

I spent Christmas and New Year's in the hospital, and then I go back home. I think it was the fifth of January. They let me out in the morning at about ten o'clock. And my girlfriend, Andrea, was working. So, she can't pick me up. I have to wait for a lot of hours there for Andrea, or I could take the train. I didn't want to wait for five hours or more in Munich, so I took the train.

On the way, I had to change trains, and I forgot to take a ticket for the second train. I was sitting in the train—and I also have to say, in all those five weeks, I didn't shave myself, so I had a full beard. I was sitting in the train and heard in the back, "Tickets! Tickets!" Oh my god, I forgot to buy a ticket for this train. So, I tried very fast to buy a ticket with my phone, but that didn't work.

The conductor was standing by my side, and I said, "I'm so sorry. I just came from the hospital from five weeks. I'm so sorry. My brain wasn't there; I forgot to buy a ticket." Then she looked at me and said, "Are you the sword swallower who had that accident?"

I said, "Yes, yes, that's me!" She recognized me—even with the beard—from the newspaper story of the accident. Then I just had to pay the regular price. She didn't make me pay the penalty fee.

—**Franz Huber**, based in Germany, sword swallower since 2013, inspired by Joe Jagger and self-taught. Holder of nine world records, including the most bowling pins knocked down while sword swallowing, the most sit-ups while sword swallowing, and swallowing the most curved sword (133 degrees).

Phoenix Blaze at the 2017 Escondido Renaissance Faire. *Courtesy of Edward Robinson*

DOWN THE THROAT AND THROUGH THE EYE

I learned to breathe fire from Brian LaPalme—he's a big-time circus performer who taught Ricky "The Dragon" Steamboat to breathe fire. I watched his act and learned. He also did a sword-balancing act, and I watched that act so much I learned to do it too. I started doing it with a swallowed sword. So, I swallowed one sword and then did a sword-balancing routine on top of the swallowed sword, and then I had a spinning sword balanced on the handle of that one. So there were three swords in play. While I was doing it, I messed up and they came down. The spinning one hit my eyeball and scratched my cornea. I had to wear a mask for months. Not fun. I have never gotten all my sight back.

—**Edward Robinson**, a.k.a. **Phoenix Blaze**, Ren Faire sword swallower from 1984 to 2017, taught by Red Stuart

STONED STEEL

I had an injury, not because of my talent but because I was stoned. And irresponsible. I had a bunch of weed/edibles at 4 a.m., and then I went to bed. I had two shows the next day where I was sword swallowing, and it was irresponsible. I was practicing and somebody touched my throat because they didn't know. I perforated my esophagus.

I was in the hospital for almost six weeks in 2017. I also have to tell you, doctors love sword swallowing. Those people—that was the most exciting thing in their medical history lives. But thank you, modern medicine. I made it out. I did have nerve damage for a while, because I was rushed to the ER. It was bad. I am okay. I have been able to take swords down since then, but I haven't been able to perform.

I do miss that feeling when the sword drops into your throat when you don't have to touch it; it's one of the best feelings I've ever felt—like you feel like you're connected to the divine.

—**Sati**, sword swallower since 2016. Taught by Dan Meyer.

THE STALKER

Courtesy of Gigi Deluxe

Gigi Deluxe swallows the 20-inch blade of a giant pair of shears. *Photo by Echo Roo McNeill*

I started learning in 2011, when I was living in Chicago. I started practicing with a hanger, and once I felt comfortable with the hanger, I started doing it with a sword. It was going okay for a while, but then my ego started getting involved. I had my daughter film me to track my progress—and I pushed myself way too hard. I swallowed the sword, but then something went wrong because this wave of heat went over my body. I felt very nauseated. I pulled it out. My daughter said, "Are you okay?" I couldn't talk for a minute. It was like the wind just got knocked out of me, and I was on my knees on the floor. Then everything was okay, and I went into the bathroom to check for blood. There was a little, but nothing major. I felt swollen, but fine. I thought, "I probably just overdid it this time."

Afterward I went shopping at the grocery store with my daughter. Then this wave of heat and nausea hit me again. I gave her my card and said, "Pay for this. I gotta go to the bathroom." I splashed cold water on my face. Every step I took was so painful. I never felt pain like this in my life. Breathing was painful. And it just got worse.

I managed to drive us back to the house. My ex-husband's an ER doc. We were divorced at this time, but he was living downstairs on the second floor of a three-flat family house so he could still see the kids with his crazy schedule at the ER. I was in excruciating pain. I'm not a wuss; I can handle pain—I had twins. But this was like nothing I've ever encountered. I could barely talk. I told my daughter, "Tell your dad he needs to drive me to the hospital. If he's gonna give me a hard time about the sword swallowing, call me a cab."

So, he drove me to the nearest hospital. We're doing intake, and I explained what happened. "I was practicing sword swallowing, and I feel like something terrible went wrong. I don't know what." And they're like, "Excuse me?" And I said, "Yes, I was sword swallowing." So, I had to go in for x-rays. At this point the pain was unbearable, and they said they had to transfer me to a trauma hospital. That meant a twenty-five-minute ride in the back of an ambulance all the way out to the hood in Chicago. I could feel every single bump and every little rock in the road. When they did my intake, they took me up to ICU, and then immediately to surgery. I had torn my esophagus in three places, which they sewed up. I have a scar on my neck.

At the same time, there was a doctor doing his internship who was following me on all my social media, messaging me, asking me out. He was young, in his early twenties. And he was just a pain in the butt. So I told him, "I'm not interested."

After my surgery, I'm in the ICU, and I was coming out of anesthesia. I was in that twilight period where you're

kinda out of it. I wake up and this intern is in my freakin' hospital room! Out of all the hospitals in Chicago, he happened to be working in the same hospital. I knew his face. But I couldn't talk. At first, I thought it was a dream. But I was like, no, this is real. I had that little call button by my hand since I couldn't talk, and I started pressing it. When he saw that, he left the room and he was gone. The nurse finally came in. I could whisper, so I asked her about him. She said, "Yeah, that's one of the interns. But he doesn't belong in the ICU. I don't know why he was here."

After I got out of the hospital, he was still messaging me on my Facebook performer page. So, I wrote him and kindly asked, "Did you visit me when I was in the hospital?" He said, "Yeah, I was working in intake. Everyone was talking about a weird surgery that came in from a sword-swallowing accident. I thought it was you, so I thought I'd check up on you." I told him straight out, "If you ever contact me again, if I see you anywhere in my vicinity, I'm gonna report you to the board, and you will get your license taken away for stalking." It was the most bizarre story. I couldn't make this up. I almost died. I was in the ICU for two weeks. But then I wake up out of surgery, and this stalker is in my room. It was so crazy. Never heard from him again. Never saw him again. Nothing.

—**Gigi Arroyo**, a.k.a. **Gigi Deluxe**, studied archery for ten years before teaching herself sword swallowing in 2011 with tips from Red Stuart and Coney Island's Sideshow School

BRUSHES WITH FAME

SWALLOWING SWORDS WITH THE STARS AND OTHER BIG MOMENTS

BATTLING BATMAN

My greatest story with sword swallowing is when I was playing Malibu Beach with a 165-foot sideshow. There was a big festival with the largest carnival on the West Coast, and there's all kinds of movie stars walking by. Danny DeVito came up with Rhea Perlman, his wife, and his couple of kids, and they had Telly Savalas with them. They asked if they could come into my show.

So, of course, I invited them in, and we were doing the bed of nails, the electric chair, glass walking, and traditional sideshow acts. Then I blow the balls of fire, like Leo [Griep] taught me—I could blow pretty big balls of fire, like 30 feet.

Danny DeVito said, "I'm going to be the Penguin in the new *Batman* movie, John. We've been looking for someone that can do the fire eating and the sword swallowing in *Batman Returns*. Tim Burton is the director—here's his card. Go see him on Monday and audition for the fire-eating and sword-swallowing roles. Tell him I sent you, and I'll put it in a good word for you."

That Monday, I blew a ball of fire and almost caught his secretary on fire on the second story by the offices there at Warner Brothers. Tim Burton says, "You're hired. I don't have to see another person. This is the man I'm hiring." He tells me how much I'm gonna get paid, and I was just so happy because, I mean, it's a role of a lifetime.

Then he said they're trying to find the sword swallower. "I heard there's only about seventy sword swallowers in the world; do you know any sword swallowers?"

I said, "Well, I'm a sword swallower, Mr. Burton."

He says, "You are? All right, then I'll give you the part. You could be the sword swallower and we'll put a mustache on you, we'll put a long wig on you, and we'll change your costume." So, I had sword fights with Batman, we had firefights, and then fire from the Batmobile burns me up.

Batman changed my whole life. It was a whole new realm. So many other doors opened—I got a free trip on a cruise ship to do Batman stunts on seven different islands in seven days in the Bahamas. I got a Pepsi Cola commercial. I got a McDonald's commercial. Then I did *Joe versus the Volcano*—I was the witch doctor blowing fireballs. I've made over a million dollars in residuals and pay in all the years since just that one movie alone. I was probably the highest-paid sword swallower and fire eater in the history of fire eaters and sword swallowers just from that one gig.

—**John Strong III**, sword swallower since age eleven, cast member of 1992's *Batman Returns*

ROSEANNE BARR

Around 1998, Roseanne decided she wanted to be a sword swallower. I didn't bring a sword with me. Roseanne had a collapsible sword she wanted to swallow. I had never seen one before. We were waiting for the commercial break. I asked her if I could see it. She handed it to me. It was so fake and cheap looking that I decided to collapse it in front of the audience before the cameras came on to ruin it. She grabbed it and lightly hit me on the head with it and then threw it side stage and didn't do the stunt. So, I kept sword-swallowing integrity, and it didn't cost me anything. She let me back on her show several times after that.

—**Jim Rose**, founder of the Jim Rose Circus, defending sword swallowers on *The Roseanne Show*, 1998

A LATE SHOW WITH LETTERMAN

The most nervous I ever was while swallowing—which wasn't based around the swallowing—is when I swallowed a stick with a plate spinning on top for David Letterman. But my worry was nothing to do with the swallowing part and all to do with the plate, because the idea of the plate messing up and falling on the Ed Sullivan stage worried me until the gig was over. But just being able to spin a plate and swallow a stick on Ed Sullivan's stage, for me, meant quite a bit.

—**Keith Nelson**, a.k.a. **Mr. Pennygaff**, cofounder of the Bindlestiff Family Cirkus

DUMBRELLA

I had a few people come up to other performers that I worked with, and also calling my wife and father, telling them that they were sorry that I had passed away after they had watched an episode of *1000 Ways to Die* where I was portraying an individual that died swallowing an umbrella. The segment was called "Dumbrella."

—**George "The Giant" McArthur**, on an episode that aired in 2009

SWORD-SWALLOWING CELEBRITY

Brianna Belladonna, brief star on CBS's *How I Met Your Mother*. *Courtesy of Brianna Belladonna*

I was sword swallowing for only about two weeks when I got a call from Todd Robbins, who said that Neil Patrick Harris was looking for a sword swallower for *How I Met Your Mother*. He said, "You swallow swords now, right?"

I said, "Yes."

He said, "How long have you been doing it?"

I told him about two weeks or so.

He said, "Well, I'm going to tell him you've been doing it longer than that."

I had just started swallowing swords, and *now* I'm on *How I Met Your Mother*. I look back, and obviously I wasn't as polished as I am now. But it was a great experience. I was so lucky to get that amazing of a gig right off the bat. That same year, Neil asked me to come and perform at a Halloween party at his house, which was pretty crazy and awesome.

Another time I was at the Magic Castle, and Jason Alexander came up to me and I was like, "Oh my gosh, it's George Costanza!"

He said, "I know who you are! You had a show in Vegas—*Freak*, right? And you're the sideshow girl. I'm sorry, I can't remember your name, but I know your face and all your tattoos."

I could feel myself getting kind of bashful and turning tomato red. Wow, I was on cloud nine after that. Jason Alexander knows who I am!

—**Brianna Belladonna**, sword swallower since 2008. Taught by Andrew Stanton.

HAPPY WORLD SWORD SWALLOWER'S DAY

Believe It or Not, since 2008, World Sword Swallower's Day has often been celebrated at Ripley's museums across the globe on the last Saturday of February. Yes, the official day honoring the art is as real as sword swallowing itself.

The event and the day itself were conceived by this book's coauthor, Dan Meyer. "There's President's Day, Secretary's Day, Nurse's Day, Boss's Day, Magician's Day, Juggler's Day; why not have a Sword Swallower's Day?" he told me in 2010 when I wrote about the celebration for AOL Weird News. "After four thousand years of being neglected, let's let everyone know we're still alive."

Meyer approached Ripley's with the idea and found an enthusiastic partner. "I didn't have to think twice about it," recalled Tim O'Brien, vice president of communications at the time for the company. "There's an incredible history that Ripley has with sword swallowing. They go clear back to the first Odditorium at the Chicago World's Fair in 1933."

The event has featured many highlights across the various Ripley's museums. The 5-foot, 3-inch female sword swallower Natasha Veruschka set a new SSAI women's record by downing a 29½-inch blade. Red Stuart once put down fifty-two swords—at once. Bundled together, the very thin blades

measured nearly an inch in thickness. And in a display that surely made audiences wince more than usual, Travis Fessler swallowed steel with a mouth full of Madagascar hissing cockroaches. No insects were harmed during the stunt.

But the purpose of Sword Swallower's Day goes beyond entertainment and verification purposes. Since February is National Swallowing Awareness Month, World Sword Swallower's Day also recognizes the contributions that sword swallowers have made to medicine and science over the years.

MINOR MISHAPS, MISADVENTURES, AND OTHER MEMORIES

SOMETIMES SWALLOWING THE SWORD ISN'T THE HARD PART.

TSA GETS TOUGH

For several years I lived in Alabama and would fly in and out of the Huntsville airport. One time I was flying out, and I had to take a glowing lightsaber, kind of like a neon sword of the old days. But this one was an LED lightsaber I had made in Sweden. It was pretty expensive, so I didn't want to ship it in the suitcase—I wanted to carry it on the plane. I packed it in a brand-new padded rifle case. Well, of course, when I walk into the airport carrying a rifle case, you can just hear the radios going and all that stuff.

So, I get in line and put the rifle case on the conveyor belt, and it goes through the x-ray machine. Of course, it's got like twenty-four batteries and a bunch of wires on it. The guy there called a bunch of other guys over, and they're all pointing at it, looking at it, you know, scratching their heads like, "Oh, we got a bomb here," or something. As it comes out the other end, they said, "We're gonna have to come and take a look at this." There were five of them standing around the case, nervously contemplating opening it. First, they wiped it down with the swabs to see if there's any gunpowder on it. Then they opened it very gently, very gingerly. You could tell they were tight as a spring. Like they're gonna explode, you know? They opened it up and said, "What is this?" I didn't want to say it was a sword or anything that sounds like a weapon at all. Instead, I just downplayed it—and I never, ever call myself a magician—but on this occasion I did.

"Oh, it's a stage prop," I said. "Like if I were a magician. It's something I use onstage for my shows."

"What do you do with it?" they asked.

"Well, it's a lightsaber," I said. "It's just a bright light, that's all. And I swallow it." And they just didn't quite get it. I said, "Can I show you?"

"Okay," they said.

They were very skeptical, so I flipped a little switch on it. It explodes into a bright yellow light so bright that they all jump back at once as if a firecracker went off. I swallow the thing very slowly down my throat as it shines through my neck. I turn and look around, and everybody waiting in line has their eyes wide open as they're watching me swallow this glowing lightsaber. I pulled it out and looked back at the people waiting in line behind me and said, "Man, this TSA sure is getting tough. You're next."

—**Dan Meyer**, Huntsville, Alabama, 2008

BUSTED AT THE AIRPORT

We were flying into Phoenix, getting ready to do a convention and waiting for my sword case to come out of the conveyor belt at the end. Well, they had obviously inspected it and not closed the latches, so as soon as it went on the conveyor belt, it busted open all over the place where everybody's waiting on their luggage. They're seeing everything—and maybe I should've prefaced this by saying I already look suspect when I'm in an airport, period. You know, when you look like I do. And I'm on my knees because it's so low, and crawling around as fast as I can try to grab everything. Not only swords, but the hammer, the

nail, the mousetrap—everything that you could pack in a sword case, up to 50 pounds, of course, so you don't get charged more. I'm crawling around on the floor like a madman with a bunch of weapons in an airport. And I'm way too old to get tased, I'll tell you that for a fact.

—**Chris Steele**, a.k.a. **Captain Stab-Tuggo**, 2023. Sword swallower since 2000.

Chris Steele swallowing seven swords at the Sideshow Hootenanny at Coney Island, April 6, 2024. *Photo by Marc Hartzman*

HARDEST WORK EVER

We were on tour in the mid-'90s, and since the Bindlestiff's beginning we've always honored our past, our mentors, the folks who paved the road we're on. And we were passing through Gibtown and reached out to Ward and said, "Hey, could we stop by and hang out?"

He and Chris treated us extremely well for a couple of days. I think they even housed us for a night. And then it was during that stay that Ward asked a few of the Bindles, "Hey, I'm gonna be heading out this summer; would you guys be interested? What's the least amount of money you would work for?"

And we told Ward what that is, and he came in about $10 less than our least amount. And I said yes. So myself, David Hunt, and Daniel Browning Smith, a.k.a. the Rubber Boy, went and joined Ward's troupe at that point. As we're driving into the fairground, you see that it's three days until the fair starts, and we were there to help him put up a tent. Watching a rubber boy try to work with a jackhammer was pretty amazing, because Danny's body would basically wrap around the hammer as he was trying to use it. So, we took him off heavy lifts.

For me, it was my first time working with folks who were simply attractions. The bearded woman that I've worked with over the years here in New York, she's a wire walker, juggler, stilt walker. Everybody that I've worked with previously that were natural-born freaks also had circus skills, but working for Ward was the first time that I was working with folks who didn't. The bearded lady would stand up and wave, and that was it. Bruce the fat man would get up, do a little jiggle, then sit down and go back to reading a sci-fi. It was kind of an amazing experience. Never walk by the fat man's trailer, cuz urine gets slung out the window. You pick up a lot of little things on that tour.

But I really think it was one of the most instrumental periods of my sword-swallowing history. It was having the opportunity to do twenty to thirty shows a day with Ward. And, you know, when you're doing that sort of level as a beginning sword swallower, you learn how the body works, and feel a sore throat from all the friction and keep pushing forward. Being in that kind of setting with that many times a day to rehearse, if you will, was just an opportunity that I think very, very few people today get. It's the hardest work that I've ever done. So pretty much any gig after that, it's been a breeze.

—**Keith Nelson**, a.k.a. **Mr. Pennygaff**, cofounder of the Bindlestiff Family Cirkus. Sword swallower since the early 1990s, self-taught.

Keith Nelson performing with Ward Hall and Chris Christ's World of Wonders show. Pete Terhurne is seen eating fire next to him, with Chris Christ at the ticket booth. *Courtesy of Bindlestiff Family Cirkus*

THE WORLD'S YOUNGEST AUDIENCE

I was booked for a camp show. I've done hundreds of camp shows, and I'll always ask if they want me to swallow swords. I have so many other feats for kids shows, if the director or whoever books me doesn't want sword swallowing, I don't do it. So, I'm booked through an agent to do a camp show, and they specifically ask for sideshow feats. I review the set list with the agent: blockhead, swords, feats of strength . . . and I get approval. Well, I get to the camp, set up my gear, and in walk the campers . . . toddlers and kindergarten kids! Now I've done plenty of camp and school shows, but when the entire group is under five? They need something different.

Anyway, I got approval from the agent, so I begin with a kid-friendly blockhead routine and move to swords. After I swallow the first one, the director storms the stage, chastises me, and insists I stop. These were preschoolers. They were actually well behaved and just sort of sat there. Some took the opportunity to take a nap. I wasn't insulted. That age needs a clown dressed in primary colors doing silly gags, not a dude who looks like a biker playing with sharp objects.

—**Adam Rinn**, a.k.a. **Adam Realman**, artistic director at Coney Island USA, and sword swallower since 2001

GETTING PAST THE BOUNCER

I got hired to do a show in 2008 at a bar in Cincinnati, and the bouncer would not let me in with a sword. "You can't bring that in here," he said over and over again.

I said, "I'm doing a show; this is a prop sword."

The bouncer just wouldn't believe me. "No swords allowed," he kept saying.

Finally, I asked him to call the owner—he was the one who hired me. Eventually the owner came out and said, "Hey, let him in. He's working here tonight!" I thought, man, someone's more likely to bust someone over the head with a beer bottle than get hurt by my sword.

—**Travis Fessler**, sword swallower since 2003

PULLING OUT MORE THAN THE SWORD

I was working Pier 39 in San Francisco in 2016. The night before a show, I threw a big party and had a massive hangover the next day. I had a show at 12:15. I got there late and had fifteen minutes to get my stage set up. Because of my hangover, I grabbed a coffee from a nearby coffee shop called Aunt Fannie's and downed it. I slammed the entire thing. Then I'm doing my forty-five-minute show, and at the end I had a lady come up onstage and pull the sword out. I'm up on my platform, and I told her I was going to lean over, she's going to grab the sword, pull it out, she's going to raise her hand, and everyone's going to go nuts.

She said, "All right."

So, I do the drop, sword goes down, I lean over, she pulls it out. But she whipped it out so fast that a perfect sphere, like a brown ball, trailed right after it. It looked like it had a hang time that seemed like an eternity up in the air. Then it went straight down to the ground, hit the stage, and made a perfect circle of liquid. The lady looks at it, she looks at the sword, she looks at me, and just says, "Nice."

It was the one time I threw up onstage. I knew that everybody could see it coming out, because I could see it. There were a good, solid six hundred people there. Fortunately, the woman said she was a nurse and wasn't grossed out easily.

—**Lynx Kim**, studied under Johnny Fox in 1989, started sword swallowing in 2013.

UNEXPECTED DISCOVERY

I had extreme chest pain and thought I was injured from sword swallowing. Every time I would breathe, it was hurting in a certain way. I got an endoscopy, and the stomach doctor said that I was probably in pain because I probably have a gluten intolerance, and my system was just inflamed. Nothing was torn. I ended up getting a blood test and ended up being allergic to gluten.

—**Asia Ray**, sword swallower since age nineteen. Self-taught.

UNDENIABLE PROOF

In 1998, I got a call from a big national newspaper called *Séð og Heyrt* (a popular yellow-press newspaper sold at checkout lines that published large, flashy photos with catchy headlines and short texts).

They said to me, "Pétur, we're going prove to the world that you are not a sword swallower, that you are just faking it. We're going to expose you!"

I said, "Really? How are you gonna do that?"

"Put you in an x-ray!"

And I said, "Great!"

I went back to the same hospital that treated me after my injury, and they took x-rays with a 52-centimeter sword inside me so I could show them that the magician was not fooling them by any tricks.

After that article, my phone rang off the hook again, and I got very famous around Iceland—and around the world.

—**Gisli Finnbjörnsson**, a.k.a. **Pétur Pókus**, Reykjavík, Iceland. Guinness World Record holder, famous as the only local sword swallower in Iceland.

TOP THAT

I did an after-party show for the APP, which is the Association of Professional Piercers. And I made a joke, because everybody always battles about who's got the coolest, craziest piercing, and I was like, "Oh yeah? I pierced the bottom of my stomach, and this is how I change the jewelry." And then I swallow the giant forceps. It was ridiculous how many people came up to me afterward and thought I was being serious. Why would I pierce the bottom of my stomach? What end does that serve?

—**Brianna Belladonna**, sword swallower since 2008

SUPERSTITIONS

In Thailand, there are superstitious beliefs. Before you perform in a nightclub, you have to knock on the door. I didn't know that. My agent picked me up, we went to the club, and I got ready to swallow my swords. I'd be doing it for fifteen years already at that time. I tried to swallow the sword—it wouldn't go in. It was stuck! I couldn't swallow

it. The next night, I went back, and the same thing happened. My agent said, let's do the superstition. Let's knock on the door. Then everything was good. I'm not saying I believe it; maybe I was just excited. I don't know. But that was a strange one.

—**Mighty Torrent**, sword swallower since 1990. Learned in the Philippines from his father and grandfather, both of whom were circus sword swallowers.

BRIBERY WORKS

I've got a Tesla coil and a rifle that I swallow, and I travel around the world. So obviously, I'm in a lot of airports, and sometimes I get called off the line of the plane and have to talk to the police in the basement or some other place. I've been taken into weird military police basements in Germany, Dubai, and the United Arab Emirates where they thought my Tesla coil was a metal detector.

But the weirdest thing that happened with my Tesla coil and my rifle was when I was in Israel doing a tattoo convention, and I had to fly to New Orleans to do a grind show for Mardi Gras in 2016. There was a transfer in Kyiv, Ukraine. It was around the time that Crimea was taken by Russia, and Ukraine was getting more guarded. So anyway, I transferred there, I landed in New Orleans, I looked at my suitcases, and my Tesla coil was completely taken apart. And my rifle is not there. I usually take my rifle apart when I travel, so I had the handle, but the actual metal gun part was gone, and there was a note in the suitcase in Ukrainian from the police.

I was with a friend who was from Belarus in New Orleans, so he translated the letter and said, "Oh, the police have your rifle. And they're holding it because you can't bring a rifle through there."

I was really devastated because the rifle meant so much to me. My older brother shot himself with a gun, and that's how he died. And I was swallowing a rifle to remember him and to cheat death. I had to get this rifle back. I didn't want to modify another rifle to swallow. That's the one I wanted. So, I called a friend from Norway who I knew had a lot of friends all over the world. He's in a sideshow called Pain Solution and goes by the Headmaster. He's into body suspension and had a friend in Ukraine who also does body suspension—he jumps off buildings with bungee cords attached to hooks in his flesh. So, he connected me with him, and he looked into it and said it was a little too dangerous. He didn't feel comfortable talking to the police about a rifle. Instead, he recommended a lawyer and introduced me to her. I got on a call with her, and we started talking about it, and then she said, "Okay, here's what we're gonna do. We're gonna bribe the police." I'm like, "What? You're my lawyer. I didn't expect you to say that."

But I took her advice and sent her the money to bribe the police, and she bribed them $50. That's all it took. She got the rifle back and then tried to send it to me. But no post office would send a rifle. So, she said, "Look, you're gonna have to come to Kyiv to get the rifle." I found a fairly inexpensive ticket and flew out there. I just had to get papers saying that the rifle had been demilitarized for stage performance, which I got through a theater company that I worked for. Then I flew out there and met her in front of a McDonald's in the middle of town, and she had my rifle wrapped in cloth.

That night I was flying out, so she came with me to the airport, and we had to bribe some other police. But she got me on the plane with my rifle, and I came back.

—**Eric Broomfield**, a.k.a. **Jellyboy the Clown**, sword swallower since 2006. Taught by Red Stuart and Andrew Stanton.

A BRIEF SCARE

When I was first learning sword swallowing and pulled the sword out, the tip was covered in red, and I thought I was dying. It wasn't until I smelled it and remembered I had just eaten tomato soup.

—**Natalie Grist**, a.k.a. **Pippsy Pinwheel**, self-taught in 2016 after three years of study

EXCALIBUR SAVES THE DAY

There was a time where this beard-and-mustache competition forgot to follow up with a booking with me. So, I thought the booking was forgotten and they just moved on. Then I had a date, and I saw that there was a beard-and-mustache competition happening about forty-five minutes away. This is when I was in Vegas.

My date and I both have beards, so I said, "Hey, you want to go to this random beard-and-mustache competition? You want to check out our competition?"

He said, "Yeah!"

So, he picked me up, and we drove to the competition, and it turns out it was the one my friends were trying to book me for. They were glad I showed up, and asked what swords I brought. I told them I wasn't prepared. And I hadn't had a chance to really talk to my date about the fact that I'm one of the most dangerous sword swallowers alive.

The Amazing Zilla swallows Excalibur at a beard-and-mustache competition. *Courtesy of the Amazing Zilla*

There's no dainty way to bring that up. So anyway, we're trying to find a Home Depot, Lowe's, or a place like that, where I could find various things that I could modify on the fly to be used for the gig. There wasn't a hardware store anywhere nearby.

It turned out that the Best in Show prize for the beard-and-mustache competition was a giant sword from the original Excalibur hotel. I looked over at that sword, and I looked at my date, and I said, "I think I could do that." He was like, no way. Well, let's find out, let's do it.

We tried to find tools to be able to adapt the blade, and after much searching and resourcing from local supplies that we had there on-site, my date, it turns out, is a skateboarder, so he sacrificed his skateboard as I hand-polished and hand-shaped this sword on it. There was a tattoo artist there, so I was able to properly clean and sterilize everything. I managed to fix up that sword in about twenty minutes, and I had it ready to swallow onstage. It was the craziest thing; that sword was 3½ feet long, and about 3 inches wide at the top of the taper.

As for the competition, I took second place in the partial-beard category. Another bearded lady was there, and she took the silver in the full-beard category, so the bearded ladies cleaned up.

—**The Amazing Zilla**, bearded lady performer, and sword swallower since 2007

METAL STICK SWALLOWING

I was doing a show at the Renaissance Festival in Phoenix, and there was this little kid sitting towards the back. When I asked if anyone thought it was fake, his hand shot up. He was like ten or eleven, and he was being real snotty—imagine that for a ten- or eleven-year-old. So he shoots his hand up. And I said, "What do you think, they fold up?"

And he said, "No."

I said, "Fake throat?"

He said, "No."

"Well, then what do you think?"

He said, "I don't think they're sharp!"

"Well, they're not sharp. You can't swallow a sharp sword more than once, you know." And he thought about that for a second. Then he shot right back at me as snotty as he could and said, "Well, then you should call it metal stick swallowing!"

—**Geoffrey Cobb**, a.k.a. **Thom Sellectomy**, circus clown, busker, and Ren Faire sword swallower from 1987 to 2021.

RUSTY LUNCH

In March 2024, I was working at the American Dime Museum in Augusta Georgia. For lunch, I go next door to a German restaurant. As I'm waiting for my sandwich, I see this old case with antique knickknacks, and at the bottom is an old bayonet. I ask the waiter, "Is that for sale?" He says, "I don't know. It's been here longer than I have!" So he opens the case, and it's an antique French bayonet, super greasy and super rusty. So I buy it for $100 and take it over to the Dime Museum where Red Stuart is outside smoking. "Hey Red, look what I bought!" Red pulls it out of the sheath and says, "It needs to be cleaned up," puts it back in the sheath, swallows the rusty bayonet inside the rusty sheath, pulls it back out and says, "Yeah, that's a good find." I'm like, "Thanks, Red. I wanted it to be the first to swallow it! But I'm gonna clean it up and tell that story every time I swallow it!"

—**Jax Silvertree**, World of Wonders performer, sword swallower since 2024

PUSHING THE LIMITS OF DANGER AND CREATIVITY

TAKING THE ART OF SWORD SWALLOWING TO ANOTHER LEVEL

PREGNANT AND SWORD SWALLOWING

We were trying to get pregnant, and it was a bumpy road. Then, in 2011, one of the pregnancies finally stuck, but we had all these shows booked. I thought, well, I'm just gonna swallow swords until I can't anymore, I guess because it was . . . it's the act and you can't skip it. It's our opener, and we're both swallowing swords and we can't skip this act. So, I'm just going to do it for as long as we can. Because we have so many shows booked and I'm pregnant. And then it just turned out that I could just keep doing it. I got pretty pregnant, but I wasn't too pregnant to be able to swallow a sword. I mean, by the time I was nine months pregnant, I could still totally swallow a sword. I found that it was actually easier to swallow a sword while pregnant because I didn't have to wear a corset. Wearing a corset and swallowing swords is much more difficult.

I already knew how powerful sword swallowing is to the audience. It's intense. That's the act they never challenge me on. And I don't have to work so hard for it. But then being pregnant, and swallowing swords? It was just like shooting fish in a barrel. Everybody was just blown away by this crazy pregnant lady toddling out in high heels and swallowing swords. It was some of my best audience feedback. I will always remember those days as my absolute favorite in sword swallowing. I won't ever get that again—but I did have three pregnancies.

—**Jill Fleet**, a.k.a. **Thrill Kill Jill**, mother of three

THE TOILET PLUNGER SWALLOW

The plunger is the most normal thing that I swallow all the time. It's always in the repertoire. Because I can take a swig of water and choke on that, and hate water, and keep choking and then have to do the toilet plunger. I don't need any other props to do that subset of a routine. All I need is a toilet plunger. Plus, I can carry it on the plane.

—**Harley Newman**, a.k.a. **The Professional Lunatic**, performer and historian. Sword swallower since 2002.

SWORD SWALLOWING AT 55 MPH

I was the first guy to ride a motorcycle and swallow his sword. *Guinness Book of World Records* has refused my record. I believe that 52 miles an hour was my max speed—maybe 55. But I know I can go way faster. I went just a little over a quarter of a mile because I know I could go way longer, and I wanted to be able to blow my record out of the water eventually on a sport bike.

So, for Guinness, what I did was I went to the *World Records* book online, and I copied the entry for "the longest distance ridden on a unicycle whilst swallowing a sword." Word for word. I just took out the word "unicycle" and I put in "motorcycle." I submitted it, and they never responded. So, I just went and did it, thinking that then they can't refuse it.

Well, they came back and said, "No, you didn't do it right. You gotta have it verified and blah, blah, blah, blah, blah. And the motorcycle must be going 8 miles an hour the entire time. The motorcycle must be moving before the sword is swallowed."

Now, I'm sorry, but the guy that rode that unicycle didn't start riding a unicycle and then swallow a sword. I know this because I ride unicycles—I could swallow a sword and then ride a unicycle just like I can swallow a sword and ride a motorcycle. Why does the bike have to be moving when the unicycle guy didn't? Everyone asks me to this day if I got the Guinness World Record. They all knew about me because there was such a buildup to me riding this motorcycle and swallowing a sword. And they wouldn't give it to me.

—**Ted Campbell**, a.k.a. **Will Rotten**, sword swallower since 2008, taught by Mike Harrison

BELLY GLOW

I was swallowing a glass neon tube for years and years. You do it for your throat to glow—it's a really good way to prove to the skeptics that this is real; it's actually happening. There's a skeptic all the time. People think it's a projection, or lighting guys are projecting; they have an answer for everything. But anyway, my neon is really long. It looks like it's longer than my torso when I hold it in front of me.

When I perform, I always wear high-waisted costumes, because I like that vintage, old-school showgirl look, so my stomach was always covered. But in Switzerland a few years ago (in 2022), I did this "sexy circus" show, and I wore a much-smaller costume. This girl filmed my act one night, and when I looked at it, I saw that my belly button was glowing. And I said, "What the hell is that?" She said, "Oh, you didn't know that happened? Heather, it happens almost every night." My belly button is glowing?

So, I had no idea that this had been happening. I have a doctor friend in London, and I sent the photo to him and said, "What part of my body is this? It doesn't even make sense. Behind my belly button is intestines. What's happening?!" And he said, "No, you stretch your stomach, so you're just pushing your stomach lower." That was crazy. So that made me go get my Guinness World Record for the longest neon. I've never heard of this happening to anyone before.

—**Heather Holliday**, Guinness World Record holder for the longest neon tube swallowed (21.41 inches) and the largest curve in a sword swallowed while seated (90 degrees)

BREAKDANCING INTO FAME

In 2008, I was living at home in Moldova, Romania, and I was breakdancing, working on acrobatics, and fire eating. I saw Dan Meyer on *America's Got Talent*, and that really inspired me. It was so inspiring to see the reactions of people that had never seen sword swallowing before. I was so impressed that I just had to try it. But I had to hide it from my parents because they didn't approve of hobbies like that. So, I practiced at night. When you practice at night, you injure your throat pretty much every time you practice. By morning, you've already healed up overnight and can have some food in the morning. That meant night was the perfect time for me to learn and be functional during the day.

It took me three months to learn, practicing every day. Even after three months, it wasn't solid. The technique has to be so good that you could do it in any circumstance; you have to take your breathing pattern into account. In a normal situation, when you're calm, you can swallow a sword, but when you're under pressure with five thousand people watching, you might have a different breathing pattern that can be an obstacle to swallowing the sword. Once I could do it comfortably, my idea was to combine it with breakdancing. After winning the Green Card lottery in 2010, I moved to Los Angeles to become a star break-dancer on the streets on Hollywood Boulevard. I didn't even know English. I was dancing with the music and, at the end, swallowing the sword. During one of those shows, somebody recommended I should audition for *America's Got Talent*. I hadn't even dreamed of being on *AGT*, but later on it kind of pushed me toward that direction.

In 2013, I got into Chinese pole dancing and started to combine it with breakdancing and sword swallowing. Since I was just starting out as a pole dancer, I applied for *America's Got Talent* as a Chinese pole act. They said, "That's nice, but what else can you do?" I said, "I can swallow swords . . . I can also do some breakdancing." They said, "Hey, you're a sword swallower first, then you can do the rest. You're gonna do sword swallowing with breakdancing." They let me skip auditions with producers or anybody else and just put me right in front of the judges, right in front of the cameras. So, I did the act without the pole. I got four yes votes, all good.

Then for round 2, they say, "Okay, we need your second act with the sword," but I wanted to do the pole. And they're like, "No, no, no. . . . Everybody knows you as a sword swallower, so you have to do the sword swallowing." I started to brainstorm how I could combine all three together, and I came up with lots of tricks and combination acts. All these ideas come at night, when I cannot sleep, and that can be till 4 a.m. But by 4 a.m., I have the whole act ready in my brain. So, a couple of nights like these and I came up with the act—swallow the sword, do acrobatics, pole dancing, then a headfirst dive with the sword down my throat. I started to practice in a circus school in LA, one block from my place. By then I was coming up with crazy tricks, one-arm moves, combination acts nobody else was doing on the pole. After they saw me slide down the pole with the sword down my throat, the circus school decided it was too risky to have me, so they kicked me out.

After doing three episodes on *America's Got Talent*, I started doing two other "Got Talents" back-to-back—*Italy's Got Talent* and *Russia's Got Talent*. I wanted to do more daring, live stunts, invent more tricks that people have never seen before and cannot repeat. *Italy's Got Talent* was the second Got Talent where I came up with so many new pole tricks that by the time I landed on the floor, it was time to swallow the sword, but I was out of air. I was breathing heavy because of all the pole tricks, and I couldn't catch my breath, couldn't swallow the sword. That's the moment when three months might be enough to just swallow the sword, but to swallow it under any condition, that's different. So I pushed too hard, and it went down, and I finished, and the audience didn't even notice. Maybe it was a delay while sword swallowing, maybe a second. But that second was an eternity for me, an eternity when you've got to make a decision because five thousand people are watching, and all these cameras are capturing everything. So it was a quick one, and I did it, and I don't regret it, because it was still an amazing experience—both for them and for me. But on the sword dive, I always risk my life. That's why I'm not aiming to perform this two times a day in regular shows, because there's too much risk. It's just a matter of time when you're going to hit it. It messes with your head. So, I do this only on special occasions, just the coolest events.

After I won *Russia's Got Talent* in 2014, my prize was to open the Winter Olympics in Sochi, Russia. But there were logistical issues. It was hard to have my pole installed and disassembled. So, they took a motorcycle and installed my pole on a passenger carriage. A driver steered the motorcycle with the carriage next to it, and I was on the pole doing acrobatics. What an amazing experience! I have never heard this kind of noise from a stadium—it was like walls of people, all screaming like crazy. We're not talking five thousand people, ten thousand people . . . This was like forty thousand people screaming, and it was unreal! I was thinking I will never experience anything like this, ever again.

Altogether, I did fifteen "Got Talents." Each one was like a Disneyland when I would come onstage and say, "Okay, we need a bed of nails or drill bits. And the next one is going to be a running chain saw, and I'm gonna fall." In Ukraine, they did crazy drums with the fire rim around it. I was going bananas with all my energy, all my fantasies, and they were doing crazy cool construction with all the props. From that moment, I didn't stop, and I'm continuing to improve and create new swords and new acts.

—**Alex Magala**, Moldova, self-taught in 2008 after watching Dan Meyer on *America's Got Talent*. Winner of *Russia's Got Talent* (2014) and competitor in fourteen other global "Got Talents."

THE FLAMETHROWER SWORD

I think the best-known sword of mine is the flamethrower sword. It's got a flamethrower in the handle, a torch coming up, and a gas can with a trigger on it. If I line up the gas at the flame, I can shoot it.

I came up with that because I had a torch on my sword, and somebody was breathing fire off it. Lots of other sword swallowers have done that. I was doing this show—like a grind show—and my handle melted off over time. So, I decided to take the same sword and make a new handle, and the handle was a flamethrower. I could do a fire jet out of the sword, unassisted, without having another person breathe fire off it. It turned out to be a lot cleaner because the gas doesn't spray all over the place the way a fire breath does. And it's just cool, because it's original.

I can shoot it only horizontally, so I have to swallow the sword and then bow. As I'm bowing, I line up the flame on the torch with the jet of gas coming out of the can. I can shoot a 4-foot jet of flame out of the handle of the sword. When I do it, people freak out. They're really excited. And if they're really close to it, they feel the heat and they get a little scared.

—**Eric Broomfield**, a.k.a. **Jellyboy the Clown**, cofounder of the Squidling Brothers Circus

Jellyboy's flame-thrower sword at Coney Island, 2009. Banner art by Marie Roberts. *Photo by Liz Steger-Hartzman*

THE RIFLE SWORD

I got the idea to swallow a rifle from Red Stuart, who was my first sword-swallowing teacher. He used to talk to me about making it look like you fired it inside yourself.

As I mentioned in my story about losing my sword in Ukraine, my older brother tragically died by suicide. He shot himself. It was twenty-five years ago now. And that led me into my life as an entertainer and danger performer. So, when I heard Red talking about swallowing a rifle, I thought I could swallow a rifle and cheat death and, in a strange way, honor my brother and how he chose to die. That's very strange, but it's kind of a therapeutic thing for me, you know? Because I'm a clown, I do it in a funny way.

We altered the gun to be a sword-swallowing rifle. And so, I swallow the whole barrel, and the handle and the trigger are sticking out of my throat. Then I take a bow and I have a hidden cannon of confetti. I make it look like I pull the trigger, and confetti shoots out of my butt—like clown guts look like confetti. There's a bang sound effect, and then I take the gun out and say, "That's gun control."

—**Eric Broomfield**, a.k.a. **Jellyboy the Clown**, whose stunts also include connecting a neon sword to a Tesla coil, attaching a functional chain saw to a swallowed sword to cut a watermelon in half, and attaching a rabbit puppet to the end of a sword that he controls while the blade is down his throat.

TARGET GIRLS WITH STOMACHS OF STEEL

I'm the only one that's ever had my assistant sword swallowing as I throw knives around her. I did it first with Kryssy Kocktail and then with Lynn Wheat. Lynn learned to swallow swords for a show at Circuba 2016. Adam Realman taught her real quick, and we went down there and we're the only knife throwing act. They haven't seen sword swallowing either. So there she is at the board, sucking this sword down and I throw ten knives around her real fast, and then I reach in and pull the sword out. The audience goes nuts. And no one has ever repeated that.

—**Dr. David Adamovich**, a.k.a. **The Great Throwdini**, the world's fastest, most accurate knife thrower. He and his target girls might be the first knife thrower and sword swallowing team since Fred and Betty Bancroft—though it's unknown if Betty ever swallowed swords while Fred threw knives around her.

The Great Throwdini throws knives around Target Girl Lynn Wheat as she swallows a sword at the National Circus of Cuba. *Courtesy of Dr. David Adamovich (Throwdini) and Target Girl Lynn Wheat*

THE BIG SWALLOW

In 2001, right after we had both first learned to swallow swords, Roderick Russell and I put together the Sword Swallowers Association Int'l and dreamed up an idea to create a new Guinness World Record by getting multiple sword swallowers together for a record setting convention.

On Friday, August 30, 2002, nineteen of the world's top sword swallowers—seventeen men and two women—set the Guinness World Record for the "Most Sword Swallowers Swallowing Multiple Swords" by swallowing fifty swords together at the first annual Sideshow Gathering and SSAI Sword Swallowers Convention in Wilkes-Barre, Pennsylvania. The record event was emceed by master showman Ward Hall, officially witnessed by James Taylor of *Shocked and Amazed!*, and filmed by international media, including CNN's Jeanne Moos.

The record-setting sword swallowers were Dai Andrews, Natasha Veruschka, Red Stuart, Johnny Fox, Tim Cridland (Zamora), Todd Robbins, George the Giant McArthur, Erik Sprague (Lizardman), Keith Nelson, Thomas Blackthorne, Pétur Gisli Finnbjörnsson (Pétur Pókus), Jewels Strouzer, Bill Berry, Chad Clos (Frack), Jesse House (Ses Carny), Michael Todd (Malakai), Danny Snyder (Damien Blade), Roderick Russell, and me, Dan Meyer.

Three years later, nine sword swallowers pushed the limits again by breaking this Guinness World Record at the 2005 Sideshow Gathering by swallowing fifty-two swords at once: Red Stuart (25 swords), Natasha Veruschka (11 swords), me (7 swords), Keith Nelson (3 swords), Travis Fessler (2 swords), Matt Cassiere (1 sword), Charles Knight (1 sword), Roderick Russell (1 sword), and John Metz (1 sword).

Such records had never been set before in the 4,000-year history of sword swallowing. Our dream came true—twice!

—**Dan Meyer**, President, Sword Swallowers Association International

Many swords were swallowed simultaneously at the 2002 and 2005 Sideshow Gathering. *Courtesy of Dan Meyer*

SWORD SWALLOWING AND SIDESHOW GLOSSARY

back lot, backyard: Location behind the circus big top that was "off-limits" to the general public, which contained the dressing rooms, ring livestock tents, wardrobe and costume departments, doctor's wagon, tailor's wagon, and performers' rest areas in the backyard of railroad-transported circuses.

bally, ballyhoo: A free teaser show given outside a sideshow to attract a "tip."

big top: Main canvas tent of a circus.

blade glommer: Sword swallower.

blockhead: A sideshow act in which a performer drives a nail, spike, ice pick, scissors, running drill, or other object into the nasal passage, originally performed as part of a human pincushion act. The act appears as early as 1906 in a manuscript by Walter Deland. The act was made famous by Melvin Burkhart, who began performing it in 1929, but it was too "strong" for many of the audiences of the day. It went over well in Ripley's Odditorium in New York in the late 1930s, where Robert Ripley dubbed Burkhart "The Human Blockhead," a nickname he wore proudly. Many current performers replicate his act (sometimes line for line) as an homage.

blow-off: An extra attraction, sometimes of an adult nature, added at the end of a ten-in-one show for an additional fee.

carny: Someone who works in a carnival. The term is also applied to the carnival itself.

cutting up jackpots: See jackpot.

dime museum, dime show: A collection of often-lurid and sensational curiosities, monstrosities, and freaks exhibited for a single low price of admission, usually a dime. P. T. Barnum opened Barnum's American Museum in 1841, and it cost only a dime to enter.

the drop: A sword swallower's act of holding a sword in the throat by using the muscles of the esophagus, then relaxing these muscles to allow the sword to drop down the throat.

donniker: A portable bathroom, Porta-Potty.

fakir: Wandering Middle Eastern or South Asian ascetic, mystic, dervish, or monk who sometimes performed fakir stunts such as sword swallowing, fire eating, bed of nails, or snake charming.

gaff: Gimmicked or rigged sword or prop often used by magicians or illusionists to imitate sword swallowers. A "gaff" can also be a crafted "creature" such as a "Fiji mermaid" to pull people into the sideshow. The term "gaff" comes from the "gaff" fishing tool used to pull fish in; in sideshow terms, a "gaff" can be used to pull people into the sideshow.

grind, grind show: A sideshow pitch that continually repeats itself for a constantly changing audience.

hilt: Sword handle.

jackpot: Tall tales and anecdotes told by circus/sideshow performers of life with the circus/sideshow. "Cutting up jackpots" is the expression given to swapping these stories.

joey: Circus clown, after the first circus clown, Joseph Grimaldi.

mark: Local townspeople who become sideshow audience/customers. Also rubes or towners.

midway: The row of attractions located "midway" to the circus big top.

mud show: Circus that sets up its canvas big top on grass lots, which often become mud lots over time.

neon: Neon tube swallowed by some sword swallowers to illuminate the throat and chest.

pommel: Metal knob, protrusion, or disc on the end of a sword hilt that fastens to the tang of the blade and adds to the sword's balance and aesthetics by functioning as a counterweight to the blade while holding the sword and hilt in place.

rube: Local townspeople who become sideshow audience/customers. Also marks or towners.

sandwich, sword sandwich: Multiple swords swallowed "sandwiched" together at the same time.

shimmy shawobble, shimmy shwabble: Sword swallower Alex Linton's feature act, where a serpentine sword or plated pin bent into a series of S curves is swallowed down the throat, making the Adam's apple visibly wobble from side to side as the serpentine sword or S-pin slides up and down the throat.

SSAI: Sword Swallowers Association International

steel slurper: Sword swallower.

talker: The person who "talks" in front of an attraction in order to attract "marks" and "turn a tip." When done outside on the "bally," he is known as an "outside talker" (never "barker"). When done inside the tent, he is known as an "inside talker" or "lecturer."

ten-in-one (10-in-1): A carnival midway show with ten attractions inside one show (sideshows could have more or fewer than ten attractions, but they were still called "ten-in-ones").

tip: Sideshow term for a crowd of prospective customers who gather to hear a "bally" pitch. An "outside talker" will "work a tip," "build a tip," "hold a tip," and "turn a tip" so that customers pay their money to enter the sideshow, ideally without losing the crowd's interest and "blowing a tip."

towner: Local townspeople who become sideshow audience/customers. Also marks and rubes.

APPENDIX

SWORD SWALLOWERS BY CIRCUSES, SIDESHOWS, AND VENUES

This list gives a glimpse of where and when sword swallowers performed from the late 1800s to current day. Names included that don't appear earlier in this book can be found at the SSAI site, swordswallow.com.

JOHN ROBINSON CIRCUS SIDE SHOW

1869: Unnamed sword swallower
1881: Signor Forestell
1899: Iola
1900: Iola
1905: Marie DeVere
1907: Mlle Amy
1908: Mlle Amy
1909: Mlle Amy
1911: Great Lorenzo
1912–1915: Show did not go out
1916: Delno Fritz, Maud D'Auldin
1919: Marguerite Davis
1920: Marguerite Davis
1923: Fred Marineau

HARRY DAVIS EDEN MUSEE FAMILY THEATRE, (HARRISBURG, PENNSYLVANIA)

1892: Chevalier Cliquot
1893: Delno Fritz
1894: Delno Fritz, Maud Churchill

CLARK STREET, STATE STREET GLOBE, KOHL & MIDDLETON'S DIME MUSEUMS (CHICAGO)

1892: Cliquot at Globe Dime Museum Chicago
1894: Dick Adams at State Street Globe Museum
1894: Victorina at Clark Street Dime Museum
1895: Delno Fritz at State Street Globe Museum
1895: Delno Fritz at Clark Street Museum
1902: Prof. De Roche at Middleton's Clark Street Museum Chicago
1908: Milo Milse with Mrs. Edith Clifford

BUFFALO BILL'S WILD WEST SHOW

1899: Victorina
1903: Professor Charles E. Griffin in Europe
1904: Professor Charles E. Griffin in Europe
1904: Mighty Ajax in Europe
1905: Professor Charles E. Griffin in Europe
1906: Julian Putzjewitsch, Prof. Charles E. Griffin in Europe
1907: Professor Charles E. Griffin
1911: Delno Fritz, Maud D'Auldin

WORLD'S COLUMBIAN EXPOSITION CHICAGO WORLD'S FAIR, 1893

1893: Buffalo Bill's Wild West Show, sword swallowers unknown
1893: Carl Hagenbeck's Circus, sword swallowers unknown

NINTH AND ARCH DIME MUSEUM (PHILADELPHIA)

1895: Delno Fritz
1896: Delno Fritz
1897: Delno Fritz, King Sabro
1899: Victorina
1900: Victorina
1901: Victorina
1903: Mlle Amy
1905: Marie DeVere
1908: Marie DeVere
1909: Marie DeVere

AUSTIN & STONE'S DIME MUSEUM (BOSTON)

1895: Chevalier Delno Fritz
1896: King Sarbro
1897: Delno Fritz, Mlle Maude de Aldine
1901: Victorina
1902: Victorina
1905: Marie DeVere
1906: Marie DeVere
1907: Marie DeVere
1910: Marie DeVere

HUBER'S 14TH STREET MUSEUM (NEW YORK)

1893: Chevalier Cliquot
1894: Delno Fritz, Maud Churchill
1895: Delno Fritz, Maud Churchill
1896: Delno Fritz
1896: King Salvo
1899: Mlle Victorina
1900: Mme Victorina
1903: Neeme
1903: Mlle Amy Murphy
1904: Mlle Amy Murphy
1905: Marie DeVere
1908: Edith Clifford and the Cliffords
1909: Edith Clifford and the Cliffords

FRANK A. ROBBINS CIRCUS SHOW

1898: Charles Griffin
1909: Marie DeVere
1910: Marie DeVere
1911: Marie DeVere, Lady Marguerite Margaret Davis
1912: Marie DeVere

GOLLMAR BROTHERS CIRCUS

1907: Mille Clifford
1908: Mlle Clifford
1909: Nellie Clifford
1910: Edith Morris
1911: Mlle Edith Clifford
1912: Mlle Edith Clifford
1913: Mlle Edith Clifford
1914: Mlle Edith Clifford

MIGHTY HAAG CIRCUS

1911: Mlle Amaza, Mrs. EJ Kelly
1912: Great DeVuell
1913: Mlle. Amaza; Mrs. EJ Kelly dies
1914: Lady Margurite Davis

SIG SAUTELLE CIRCUS

1912: Walter Sibley
1913: Marie DeVere
1918: Marie DeVere

SELLS-FLOTO CIRCUS

1922: The Great Lorenzo
1924: Cuban Mack
1938: Mimi Garneau

AL G. BARNES CIRCUS

1915: Delno Fritz, Maud D'Auldin
1920: Delno Fritz, Edna Price
1922: Bob Roberts
1923: Delno Fritz, Miss Edna Price
1925: The Great Laurie
1926: The Great Laurie
1927: Ethel Price, Edna Price
1929: Maurice Eugene
1938: Mimi Garneau

BARNUM & BAILEY CIRCUS

1896: Delno Fritz
1897: Delno Fritz
1897: Edith Clifford in London
1898: Delno Fritz, Mlle Edith Clifford in Europe
1899: Delno Fritz, Mlle Edith Clifford in Europe
1900: Mlle Amy in Germany
1901: Edith Clifford joins in Vienna, tours Europe
1902: Edith Clifford, Rob Roy
1903: Edith Clifford, Rob Roy
1904: Edith Clifford, "Veno" Nelson C. Barned
1905: Edith Clifford
1906: Edith Clifford
1907: Marie DeVere
1908: Edward Smith
1909: Edward Smith
1910: Edward Smith
1911: Edward Smith
1912: Edward Smith
1913: Edward Smith
1914: Edward Smith
1915: Slivers Bowden
1916: Edward Smith
1917: Edith Clifford
1918: Edith Clifford
1919: Edith Clifford

CHICAGO WORLD'S FAIR, 1933–34

1933: Mimi Garneau
1933: Edna Price
1933: Joseph Grendol
1933: Chester Dolphin
1933: Prince Yucon
1934: Joseph Grendol
New York World's Fair, 1939–40
1939: Edna Price
1940: Edna Price

RIVERVIEW PARK, CHICAGO, ILLINOIS

1921: Marie DeVere
1943: Rita Roselle
1953: Jim Lucky Ball
1956: Jim Lucky Ball (manages Dick Best's sideshow)
1958: Estelline Pike
1959: Estelline Pike
1960: Estelline Pike
1961: Estelline Pike
1964: Estelline Pike, Jim Ball, Judy Ball
1965: Estelline Pike, Jim Ball, Judy Ball

HAGENBECK-WALLACE CIRCUS

1903: Two unknown Indian sword swallowers
1906: Mlle Amy Murphy
1906: Edith Clifford
1912: Delno Fritz, Maud D'Auldin
1913: Mlle Amy Murphy
1914: Mlle Amy Murphy
1920: Millie Dearcy
1921: Milly Dearcy
1922: Milly Dearcy
1923: Milly Dearcy
1923: Prince Milo Laurie
1933: Senor Laraway
1934: Senor Laraway
1935: Prince Charles Prester
1937: Prince Charles Prester

ROYAL AMERICAN SHOWS

1933: Joseph Grendol
1934: Chester Dolphin
1946: Lucky Ball

1947: Lucky Ball
1948: Alex Linton
1948: Estelline Pike
1949: Estelline Pike
1950: Estelline Pike
1951: Estelline Pike
1951: Jim Lucky Ball
1952: Estelline Pike
1953: Alex Linton
1954: Lady Louise Long
1955: Estelline Pike
1955: Jim Lucky Ball
1955: Lady Patricia Zerm
1956: Jim Lucky Ball
1957: Estelline Pike
1958: Stan Marye
1960: Estelline Pike
1960: Jim Lucky Ball
1960: Sir Thomas Thomas
1964: Sir Thomas Thomas
1967: Billy Costello

KELLY MILLER BROTHERS CIRCUS

1950: Tommy Thompson
1962: Stan Marye
1963: Stan Marye
1965: Jim Scott
1967: Rosemary Puente

DAILEY BROTHERS CIRCUS

1946: Lady Patricia Zerm
1947–1949: No sword swallower
1950: Janet Roselle and guest Milo Laraway
1976: Red Trower

COLE BROS. AND CLYDE BEATTY-COLE BROS. CIRCUS

1908: Mlle Amaza
1927: Edna Price
1927: Stoney St. Claire joins show
1928: Stoney St. Claire
1929: Stoney St. Claire
1930: Stoney St. Claire
1931: Stoney St. Claire
1932: Stoney St. Claire
1933: Stoney St. Claire
1934: Joseph Grendol

1936: Alex Linton
1936: Charles Prester
1937: Charles Prester
1938: Mimi Garneau
1939: Maurice Eugene
1940: Joseph Grendol
1941: Leatha Smith
1942: Leatha Smith
1943: Leatha Smith
1944: Mlle Lethea Smith
1945: Leatha Smith
1946: Leatha Smith
1947: Leatha Smith
1948: Leatha Smith
1949: Leatha Smith
1950: Leatha Smith
1950: Alex Linton
1951: Leatha Smith
1950s: Capt. Don Leslie
1959: Alex Linton
1960: Alex Linton
1961: Alex Linton
1962: Alex Linton
1963: Alex Linton
1964: Alex Linton
1965: Alex Linton
1966: Alex Linton
1966: Francis Doran, Rick Dennis
1967: Francis Doran, Rick Dennis, Jackie Lynn Looney
1968: Jackie Lynn Looney, Rick Dennis, Baron Bill Unks
1969: Jackie Lynn Looney, Rick Dennis, Baron Bill Unks
1970: Baron Bill Unks
1971: Baron Bill Unks
1972: Baron Bill Unks
1973: Baron Bill Unks
1974: Baron Bill Unks
1976: Francis Doran
1978: Jackie Lynn Looney, Rick Dennis
1979: Jackie Lynn Looney, Rick Dennis
1979: Lady Sandra Reed
1981: Circus donated to Florida State University
1981: Jackie Lynn Looney works with John Bradshaw
1981: Renamed Cole Bros. Circus

RINGLING BROS. AND BARNUM & BAILEY CIRCUS

1890: Annie Roy
1891: Annie Roy
1892: Annie Roy
1899: Professor Charles E. Griffin
1900: Professor Charles E. Griffin
1901: Professor Charles E. Griffin
1902: Professor Charles E. Griffin
1903: None listed
1907: Ringling Brothers buys Barnum & Bailey Circus but tours separately
1907: Capt. Fritz Lecardo
1908: Edward Smith
1909: Edward Smith
1910: Edward Smith
1911: Edward Smith
1912: Edward Smith
1913: Edward Smith
1914: Edward Smith
1915: Edward Smith
1916: Edward Smith
1917: Edward Smith
1918: Edward Smith
1918: Ringling Brothers and Barnum & Bailey Circus become combined show
1919: Edith Clifford
1920: Edith Clifford
1921: Edith Clifford
1922: Mighty Ajax
1923: Delno Fritz, Miss Edna Price
1924: Delno Fritz, Edna Price
1924: Delno Fritz, Miss Edna Price
1925: Delno Fritz, Miss Edna Price
1925: July: Delno Fritz dies
1926: Rubel, Edna Price
1927: Mighty Ajax, Edna Price
1928: Balmung, Edna Price
1929: "Glendol" (Joseph Grendol)
1930: Edna Price
1931: Edna Price
1932: Edna Price
1933: Edna Price
1935: Joseph Grendol
1936: Mimi Garneau
1937: None listed
1938: Mimi Garneau
1939: Mimi Garneau
1939: Miss Patsy Smith
1940: Alex Linton
1941: Miss Patricia Katts
1942: Miss Patricia
1942: Curly Frisbie, Edward Willis

1943: Miss Patricia, Mrs. Speedy Smith
1944: Miss Patricia Katts, Miss Louise Long
1945: Lady Patricia Zerm
1945: Alex Linton
1946: Alex Linton
1947: Alex Linton
1948: Lady Patricia Zerm
1949: Alex Linton
1950: Lady Patricia Zerm
1951: Lady Patricia Zerm filmed Greatest Show on Earth
1952: Greatest Show on Earth movie released
1952: none listed
1953: Lady Beth Betty Bancroft
1954: Lady Beth Elizabeth J. Bancroft
1955: Ricky Richiardi
1956: Ricky Richiardi
1956: Alex Linton
1956: Last show under canvas
1957: Estelline Pike at Madison Square Garden
1958: Estelline Pike, Jim Lucky Ball at Madison Square Garden
1959: Estelline Pike at Madison Square Garden
1960: Estelline Pike at Madison Square Garden
1961: Estelline Pike at Madison Square Garden
1962: Estelline Pike at Madison Square Garden
1963: Estelline Pike at Madison Square Garden
1964: Estelline Pike at Madison Square Garden
1965: Estelline Pike at Madison Square Garden
1966: Estelline Pike at Madison Square Garden
1966: Sir Thomas Thomas
1967: Estelline Pike at Madison Square Garden
1968: RBB&B Sideshow eliminated
1969: Francis Doran's neon tube burst in Houston, Texas
1973: Lady Sandra Reed

HUBERT'S 42ND ST DIME MUSEUM (NEW YORK)

1919: Marie DeVere
1926: Marie DeVere
1927: Marie DeVere
1928: Mighty Ajax
1938: Alex Linton
1939: Alex Linton
1940: Nereida Caswell
1947: Alex Linton
1948: Alex Linton
1950: Charlie Lucas
1951: Charlie Lucas
1952: Charlie Lucas
1953: Charlie Lucas
1954: Charlie Lucas
1955: Charlie Lucas
1956: Charlie Lucas
1956: Alex Linton
1957: Alex Linton
1957: Estelline Pike, Jim Lucky Ball
1958: Estelline Pike
1959: Estelline Pike
1960: Estelline Pike
1961: Estelline Pike
1962: Estelline Pike
1963: Estelline Pike
1964: Estelline Pike
1965: Estelline Pike

CONEY ISLAND, NEW YORK

1910: Prince Milo Milse (Dreamland)
1916: Marie DeVere (Dreamland)
1917: Mighty Ajax (Dreamland)
1918: Mighty Ajax (Dreamland)
1919: Mighty Ajax (Dreamland)
1920: Mighty Ajax (Dreamland)
1921: Mighty Ajax (Dreamland)
1923: Mighty Ajax, Marie DeVere (Dreamland)
1924: Mighty Ajax (Dreamland)
1925: Mighty Ajax (Dreamland)
1926: Mighty Ajax (Dreamland)
1927: Mighty Ajax (Sam Wagner's World Circus Sideshow)
1927: Marie DeVere, King Charles Roy (Dreamland)
1928: Mighty Ajax (Sam Wagner's World Circus Sideshow)
1932: Dreamland Circus Sideshow: Mighty Ajax

1937: George Hamid's Playland Circus: Edna Price
1937: Sam Wagner's World Circus Sideshow: Edna Price
1938: Robert Moses attempts to ban sideshow ballies
1941: Sam Wagner's World Circus Sideshow closes
1944: Mammoth Wonder Show: Mighty Ajax
1944: Luna Park Wonderland Circus Sideshow: Mighty Ajax
1944: Luna Park damaged by two fires
1945: Luna Park closed
1960: Sir Thomas Thomas is sword swallower with Dave Rosen Side Show
1980: Dick Zigun founds Coney Island USA
1986: Sideshows by the Seashore founded by Dick Zigun
1989: Sideshows by the Seashore—Lady Diane Falk
1990: Sideshows by the Seashore—Lady Diane Falk
1991: Sideshows by the Seashore—Lady Diane Falk
1991: Sideshows by the Seashore—Baron Bill Unks
1991: John Bradshaw Sideshow—Tisha Vudie

JAMES E. STRATES SHOWS

1940s: Ray "Heavy" Case
1958: Stan Marye
1959: Stan Marye
1960: Stan Marye
1965: Lady Louise Chavanne
1966: Lady Louise Chavanne
1967: Lady Louise Chavanne
1968: Lady Louise Chavanne
1969: Sandra Reed
1974: Lady Sandra Reed
1975: Lady Sandra Reed
1970s: Jimmy Rapp

HOXIE BROS. CIRCUS

1961: Johnny Nugent
1962: Henry Thompson
1963: Henry Thompson
1964: Henry Thompson
1965: Ricky Richiardi

1966: Ricky Richiardi
1967: Ricky Richiardi
1968: Ricky Richiardi
1969: Ricky Richiardi
1970: Eric Tauber, Joe Abrams
1971: Eric Tauber, Joe Abrams
1972: Eric Tauber, Joe Abrams
1973: Eric Tauber, Joe Abrams
1974: Sir Francis Doran
1975: Sir Francis Doran
1976: Sir Francis Doran
1976: Baron Bill Unks
1977: Baron Bill Unks
1978: Baron Bill Unks
1979: Baron Bill Unks
1980: Baron Bill Unks
1981: Sammy Johnson

WORLD OF WONDERS SIDESHOW

1959: Lady Patricia Zerm, Stan Marye
1960: Estelline Pike
1961: Francis Doran, Estelline Pike
1962: Francis Doran, Estelline Pike
1963: Francis Doran
1964: Francis Doran, Estelline Pike
1965: Francis Doran, Estelline Pike
1966: Francis Doran, Estelline Pike
1960s: Dingi
1967: Francis Doran, Estelline Pike
1968: Francis Doran
1969: Lady Patricia Zerm, Francis Doran
1970: Lady Patricia Zerm, Francis Doran
1971: Lady Patricia Zerm, Francis Doran
1972: Lady Patricia Zerm, Francis Doran,, Mike Burford
1973: Lady Patricia Zerm, Francis Doran, Lady Sandra Reed, Eddie Miller
1973: Jimmy Rapp learns to use Francis Doran's swords
1974: Lady Patricia Zerm, Rick Dennis, Jimmy Rapp
1975: Lady Patricia Zerm, Rick Dennis, Jimmy Rapp, Sammy Johnson
1976: Lady Patricia Zerm, Rick Dennis, Jimmy Rapp
1977: Jimmy Rapp, Red Trower
1978: Jimmy Rapp, John Stevens, Eddie Miller
1979: Jimmy Rapp, John Stevens, Red Trower
1980: Red Trower

1980: Johnny Meah
1981: Johnny Meah
1982: Johnny Meah
1983: Johnny Meah
1984: Johnny Meah
1985: Red Trower, Jackie Lynn Looney
1986: Red Trower, Jackie Lynn Looney
1987: Johnny Meah
1988: Johnny Meah
1989: Johnny Meah, Red Stuart
1990: Johnny Meah, Red Stuart, Capt. Don Leslie
1991: Johnny Meah, Red Stuart
1992: Johnny Meah, Red Trower
1993: Johnny Meah, Red Trower, Butch Schutte
1994: Johnny Meah, Lady Diane Falk, Butch Schutte
1998: Red Trower, Keith Nelson
2000: Matthew Bouvier
2001: Matthew Bouvier
2002: Matthew Bouvier
2003: Ward Hall retired; show did not go out
2004: Johnny Meah, Red Stuart, Tommy Breen, Matthew Bouvier, Todd Robbins, Chelsea NoPants
2005: Red Stuart, Tommy Breen, Matthew Bouvier, Charon Henning, Alex Kensington
2006: Red Stuart, Lady Diane Falk, Tommy Breen, Chelsea NoPants
2007: Red Stuart, Lady Diane Falk, Tommy Breen, Johnny Meah, Chelsea NoPants, Brett Loudermilk
2008: Red Stuart, Lady Diane Falk, Tommy Breen, Matthew Bouvier
2009: Red Stuart, Lady Diane Falk, Tommy Breen
2010: Red Stuart, Lady Diane Falk, Tommy Breen
2011: Red Stuart, Lady Diane Falk, Tommy Breen
2012: Red Stuart, Lady Diane Falk, Tommy Breen, Penny Poison
2013: Red Stuart, Lady Diane Falk, Tommy Breen
2014: Red Stuart, Lady Diane Falk, Tommy Breen
2015: Red Stuart, Tommy Breen
2016: Red Stuart, Tommy Breen, Dizzy Diamond
2017: Tommy Breen, Dizzy Diamond

2018: Tommy Breen, Dizzy Diamond
2019: Tommy Breen
2020: Tommy Breen
2021: Tommy Breen
2022: Tommy Breen
2023: Tommy Breen
2024: Tommy Breen

Seeking information on sword swallowers and dates they performed with various circuses, sideshows, and other venues. Please contact: DanMeyerswords@gmail.com

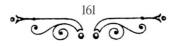

BEHIND THE CURTAIN

The information in this book came from a wide variety of sources. Many of them are included below, but our research also included interviews with living sword swallowers, surviving family members, other researchers, and conversations the authors have had over the past two decades.

"A Kindred Subject." *Missouri Republic*, April 27, 1873.

"A Performer's Present." *Los Angeles Herald*, October 1, 1888.

"A Remarkable Lawsuit." *Pittsburgh Daily Post*, January 10, 1876.

"A Sword Swallower Out of Work." *Alexandria Gazette*, October 31, 1894.

Advertisement. *Baton Rouge Gazette*, April 17, 1819.

Advertisement. *Natchez Gazette*, March 17, 1819.

Advertisement. *Portland Daily Press*, May 11, 1874.

"Al G. Barnes Circus." *Billboard*, October 23, 1920.

Anderson, Jon. "Sideshow Artist Takes Main Stage." *Chicago Tribune*, February 27, 2001.

Archibald, John J. "The Greatest Sideshow on Earth." *St. Louis Post-Dispatch*, September 20, 1985.

Arnold, Cathleen. "Haven for the Almost Human." *Cincinnati Enquirer*, July 6, 1975.

"The Art of Sword Swallowing." *Manchester Evening Chronicle*, June 24, 1899.

Associated Press. "Fat Lady and Sword Swallower Take Their Troubles to Court." *Iola Register*, October 7, 1942.

Associated Press. "Grapes Do Grow in Florida." *Arizona Daily Star*, September 4, 1966.

Associated Press. "Hiccup All Wrong. Sword Swallower Won't Use Neon Tubes Again." *Southern Illinoisan*, October 12, 1959.

Associated Press. "Sword Swallower Dies When Biggest Stunt Backfires." *Montana Standard*, June 6, 1936.

Associated Press. "Sword Swallower Won't Go to the Pauper's Grave." *Naples Daily News*, September 19, 1972.

Baba, Ali. "Carnival Caravans." *Billboard*, June 5, 1920.

Barringer, Felicity. "THE INAUGURATION: Inaugural Notebook; Many Drummers in History's March." *New York Times*, January 18, 1993.

"Body for Science." *South China Morning Post*, March 24, 1939.

Britton, Paul. "Tributes Paid to the Great Stromboli—Bolton's Famous Showman and Circus Performer." *Manchester Evening News*, April 21, 2019. https://www.manchestereveningnews.co.uk/news/greater-manchester-news/great-stromboli-daniel-lynch-death-16151487 (accessed January 25, 2024).

"Boyd & Linderman Shows at Perth Amboy, N.J." *Billboard,* July 3, 1926.

Budd. "Coney Island Chatter." *Billboard*, August 22, 1914.

Burdette, Dick. "They'll Charm You Wittily at Fun Fair." *Orlando Sentinel*, November 18, 1976.

Burke, George H. "Looking Backward in Paterson." *Morning Call* (Paterson, NJ), June 13, 1932.

Byrd, Sigman. "Leatha's Sword Swallowing Finale Was Swell; She Glowed Bright Red All the Way Down." *Houston Press*, November 6, 1947.

"Canton Woman a World-Famous Sword-Swallower." *The Repository*, November 21, 2010. https://www.cantonrep.com/story/news/2010/11/22/canton-woman-world-famous-sword/42248750007/# (accessed August 31, 2023).

"Carmichael Gets Four-Year Term." *Macon News*, December 4, 1956.

"Carnival Thrills Adults, Kiddies on Opening Night." *Morning Examiner* (Bartlesville, OK), May 2, 1933.

"Carnivals" *Billboard*, October 28, 1939.

"Champion Sword Swallower, Mlle. Edith, Says It's Easy." *Evening Ledger* (Philadelphia), May 9, 1916.

"Champion Sword Swallower Tells of Her First Attempt." *Washington Herald*, May 4, 1918.

Chapman, John. "Remember the Sideshow! Lady Sword Guzzler Points Out That Freaks Are Best People." *New York Daily News,* May 5, 1957.

Chapman, John. "When Does Season Open?" *New York Daily News*, September 15, 1963.

"Charles A. Prester." *Fort Pierce Tribune*, September 27, 1990.

"Christy Bros.' Side Show." *Billboard*, April 13, 1929.

"Circus Gossip." *Billboard*, April 8, 1911.

"Circus Gossip." *Billboard*, January 18, 1913.

"Circus in the Army." *Daily Herald* (Biloxi and Gulfport, Mississippi Coast), August 20, 1941.

Clinton, Audrey. "A New Circus with Old-Fashioned Dreams." *Newsday* (Suffolk edition), May 30, 1986.

Clune, Henry W. "Seen & Heard: Swords before Breakfast." *Democrat and Chronicle* (Rochester, NY), January 3, 1939.

Copland, James, MD, ed., John Darwall, MD, and John Conolly, MD. "Case of Polyphagia." *London Medical Repository and Review 3* (July–December 1826).

Crock, Duane. "It's No Gag. He Swallows Swords." *The Gazette* (Cedar Rapids, IA), May 11, 1979.

"Curiosity Show Will Be at Fair: World of Mirth Circus Sideshow to Be Midway Feature at State Fair." *News and Observer* (Raleigh, NC), October 6, 1941.

"Curious Feats." *Star of the Valley* (Newville, PA), August 22, 1868.

"Dancing under Difficulties." *Evening Telegram*, April 21, 1873.

"Danny Lynch: Fire Eater and Sword Swallower Known as 'The Great Stromboli' Who Appeared in *The Elephant Man*." *Daily Telegraph*, June 15, 2019.

Davis, Mark, and Andy Wallace. "Daniel Pratt Mannix 4th, 85, Adventurer and Author." *Philadelphia Inquirer*, February 2, 1997.

"Death from Swallowing a Sword." *Manchester Courier*, February 3, 1849.

"Death of the Great Blondini, aged 73." *Manchester Evening News*, November 21, 1996.

"Deaths in the Profession." *Billboard*, July 25, 1925.

Deggans, Eric. "He Speaks Fluent Carny." *Tampa Bay Times*, September 13, 2003.

Dykes, Ray. "On the Prowl." *The Albertan*, July 15, 1970.

"Eat Eight Swords. Lawrence Bowden 'of the Profession' Meet Hard Luck in Kenosha." *Kenosha Evening News*, December 29, 1913.

"Edna Price Showing at Chicago World's Fair." *Morning Call* (Allentown, PA), May 31, 1933.

"Elizabeth J. Bancroft." *Fort Myers News-Press*, March 23, 1985.

"Ex-Fire Eater, Contortionist Undergoing Training at RTC." *Great Lakes Bulletin*, April 25, 1958.

"Ex-Sword Swallower Still Pretty Sharp." *Akron Beacon Journal*, July 17, 1949.

"Famous Sword-Swallower Great Stromboli Dies at 92." *The Herald* (Glasgow, Scotland), April 26, 2019.

"The Final Curtain." *Billboard*, April 13, 1959.

Foley, Larry. "If It Tickles, You've Hit Rock Bottom." *Daily Telegraph*, September 5, 1954.

Folkestone Express, Sandgate, Shorncliffe & Hythe Advertiser, March 24, 1900.

"Former Local Woman Famous Stage Star." *Terre-Haute Tribune*, January 5, 1958.

Fowler, Gene. "The Rope Walker of Corsicana." TexasCoopPower.com, February 2018. https://www.texascooppower.com/texas-stories/history/the-rope-walker-of-corsicana (accessed July 5, 2018).

"Flying Hopes Go Bang." *Manchester Evening News*, October 23, 1983.

Gaillard's Medical Journal. Vols. 68–69, 1898.

"General Gossip." *New York Times*, December 5, 1874.

Gentlemen's Magazine, August 21, 1850.

"Gestures at Gettysburg." *Lancaster Eagle-Gazette*, July 5, 1938.

Gibson, Gregory. *Hubert's Freaks*. New York: Harcourt, 2008.

Govenar, Alan, dir. *The Human Volcano*. Dallas: Documentary Arts, 1997.

Griffin, Charles Eldridge. *Four Years in Europe with Buffalo Bill*. Lincoln: University of Nebraska Press, 2010.

Hall, Ward. *My Very Unusual Friends*. Self-published, 1991.

Harrison, Paul. "In New York." *Arizona Republic*, April 27, 1935.

Hartzman, Marc. *American Sideshow: An Encyclopedia of History's Most Wondrous and Curiously Strange Performers*. New York: Tarcher, 2005.

Hartzman, Marc. "Armless Man and Legless Man Join Forces to Help the Less Fortunate." AOL News, February 17, 2011.

Hartzman, Marc. "Johnny Fox: A Tribute to the King of Swords." WeirdHistorian.com, December 21, 2017. https://www.weirdhistorian.com/johnny-fox-a-tribute-to-the-king-of-swords/ (accessed September 15, 2023).

Hartzman, Marc. "Man Swallows 100-Year-Old Museum Exhibit." AOL News, November 17, 2010.

Hartzman, Marc. "Sword Swallowing, Spike Hammering, and Freaks at Johnny Fox's Freakatorium." *Backwash* 15 (2000).

Hayden, Bernie. "Sword Swallower Has Ups, Downs." *Daily Mail* (Hagerstown, MD), May 5, 1971.

"He's Full of Junk." *Brooklyn Times Union*, July 18, 1907.

"Heck's Wonder World." *Kentucky Post*, October 17, 1899.

Houdini, Harry. *Miracle Mongers and Their Methods*. New York: Curious, 2021.

Hudson, John. "Blondini's Tomb with a £500 View." *The Guardian*, August 7, 1975.

"Impressive Funeral for Bill Roberts." *Billboard*, June 20, 1936.

"In the Act." *Herald Express*, May 20, 1954.

"In the Asylum. Noted Sword Swallower Taken There Today—No Dispute over Property." *Paterson Evening News*, November 7, 1898.

Jackson, James O. "Red Fakir, Sword Swallower Reaches 100." *Miami Herald* (United Press International), January 26, 1972.

Jay, Ricky. *Learned Pigs and Fireproof Women*. New York: Villard Books, 1986.

Jenkins, Jim, Jr. "Mannix Portrays the Carnival Folks." *Richmond Times-Dispatch*, May 13, 1951.

Johnston, Scott. "Sword Swallower in Record Book, Live Life to Hilt." *Buffalo Evening News*, November 2, 1978.

"Joseph Hallworth: Vaudeville, Wild West Performer of Yesteryear." *Boston Globe*, June 27, 1958.

"Just Ask." *Star Tribune*, September 5, 1948.

Kellar, Harry. *A Magician's Tour: Up and Down and Round About the Earth*. Chicago: R. R. Donnelley & Sons, 1886.

"L. C. Delmore Engages Strong Array of Talkers." *Billboard*, February 2, 1929.

Langford, Lowell. "Actor Is a Sharp Fellow." *Tampa Times*, November 12, 1968.

Lewis, Arthur H. *Carnival*. New York: Trident, 1970.

"Lewiston Has Big Youngstown Opener." *Billboard*, February 26, 1944.

"Life in New York: Showing Some of the Foibles of Gotham Existence." *Atlanta Constitution*, September 30, 1883.

"Literary Notes." *Times Colonist* (Victoria, BC), September 8, 1928.

Lizotte, Thomas. "Walter's Way of Earning Living is Definitely 'Hard to Swallow.'" *Central Maine Morning Sentinel*, August 19, 1978.

"Local Events: The Hollenback Hop and Other Items of More Than Ordinary Interest." *Los Angeles Daily Herald*, February 6, 1890.

"Looks Up to Husband." *Tampa Times*, October 26, 1931.

Lorenzen, Deb. "He Gets His Point Across . . . and Down." *Waterloo Courier*, April 4, 1979.

Lummis, Charles F. *Mesa, Cañon and Pueblo*. New York: Century, 1925.

Lynch, Nancy E. "Sword-Swallower Likes the Dagwood." *Morning News*, July 23, 1974.

Madame Chinchilla. *Capt. Don Leslie: Sword Swallower, Circus Sideshow Attraction*. Fort Bragg, CA: Isador, 2010.

Malone, Tom. "This Bears Mention." *Morning News*, May 6, 1968.

"Man Admits Cap Pistol Holdup on State Street." *Bristol Herald Courier*, February 19, 1960.

Mannix, Daniel P. "Steel into Your Stomach." *True*, April 1951.

"Martin Murphy's Benefit." *San Francisco Examiner*, January 3, 1887.

"Maud Churchhill's Troubles." *Scranton Republican*, February 4, 1896.

McCarthy, Jude. "Costello, Michael ('The Amazing Blondini')." *Dictionary of Irish Biography*. https://www.dib.ie/biography/costello-michael-amazing-blondini-a2083 (accessed October 2, 2023).

McCormack, Patricia. "Estelline's No Piker." *Courier-Journal* (Louisville, KY), May 12, 1961.

McWhirter, Norris. *Guinness Book of World Records*. New York: Bantam Books, 1984.

"Midway Confab." *Billboard*, July 20, 1940.

"Midway Confab." *Billboard*, May 31, 1941.

"Midway Confab." *Billboard*, September 25, 1943.

"Miller's Traveling Museum." *Billboard*, January 10, 1931.

"Milse the Great Show at Parras." *Morning Echo*, August 9, 1910.

"Miscellaneous Paragraphs." *Daily Albany Argus*, April 4, 1868.

"Modern Sword Swallower." *Birmingham News*, September 18, 1935.

Moore, Solomon. "Sideshow No Longer." *Los Angeles Times*, July 11, 1997.

Mulholland, John. *Quicker Than the Eye: The Magic and Magicians of the World*. New York: Junior Literary Guild, 1932.

New Orleans Republican, March 11, 1873.

New Orleans Republican, September 6, 1871.

Nickell, Joe. *Secrets of the Sideshows*. Lexington: University of Kentucky Press, 2008.

"Night Crowds Good for Cole Show in Greater Cincinnati." *Billboard*, May 18, 1940.

"Novel Performance." *Mississippi Free Trader*, December 26, 1822.

"Only One New Production in the Theatrical Week." *New York Times*, March 15, 1903.

Pittsburgh Commercial, December 15, 1869.

Qureshi, Yakub. "400-Year-Old Giant Egg Is Star of the Show." *Manchester Evening News*, April 28, 2010. https://www.manchestereveningnews.co.uk/news/greater-manchester-news/400-year-old-giant-egg-is-star-of-the-show-602096 (accessed January 25, 2024).

"Rabbits to Share Honeymoon Suite." *Philadelphia Inquirer*, December 2, 1939.

"Ralph R. Miller Shows." *Billboard*, January 21, 1928.

"Ramo Samee." *Daily Mail* (Hull, UK), June 11, 1970.

"Raymonds with Beggs." *Billboard*, December 10, 1932.

Rayner, Polly. "No Time to Rattle Sabers." *Morning Call*, August 8, 1973.

Reed, Billy. "Lady Sword Swallower Has a Sharp Eye on Her Job." *Courier-Journal* (Lexington, KY), February 5, 1975.

Rehnberg, Victor, and Ed Walters. "The Life and Work of Adolph Kussmaul, 1822–1902: 'Sword Swallowers in Modern Medicine.'" National Library of Medicine, February 1, 2016.

Richards, Robert. "Wanna Be a Sword Swallower? Well Talk to Mr. Linton." United Press, December 17, 1947.

Rickard, D'arcy. "Swords Go Down for the Count." *The Advocate* (Alberta), December 30, 1982.

"Ripley's Believe It or Not! Starts on 20-Week Tour." *Billboard*, December 2, 1933.

Ross, Ted. "Tent Man One of a Kind." *Augustana Observer*, May 8, 1968.

"Russian Swordswallower." *Kensington News and West London Times*, January 8, 1943.

Sanchez, Edgar. "Magic under the Big Top." *Palm Beach Post*, December 3, 1978.

"Saturday Evening Post Writer Gets Story of Brooks' Hounds." *La Crosse Tribune*, November 7, 1948.

"Sena Sama." *Alexandria Gazette*, March 2, 1818.

"Sheridan Countian Deserted Lions for Sword-Swallowing." *Wichita Evening Eagle*, October 27, 1938.

"Shirley Temple Is Academy Star for 2 Days Beginning Wednesday." *Selma (AL) Times*, July 25, 1937.

"Side Show on R-B Abounds in New Acts." *Billboard*, April 16, 1955.

Slavit, E. Max. "Deep Throat at Legislature." *Pacific Daily News* (Agana Heights, Guam), October 27, 1988.

Smith, Ulysses. "Johnny Meah's Banner Career: A Sideshow Superstar's Life in Pictures." *Chicago Reader*, March 1, 2001. https://chicagoreader.com/news-politics/johnny-meahs-banner-career/ (accessed January 2, 2024).

"Somewhat Strange: Accidents and Incidents of Every-Day Life." *News and Citizen*, September 19, 1889.

Squatriglia, Chuck. "'Captain' Don Leslie—World Record Sword Swallower Lived Colorful Life." *San Francisco Chronicle*, June 21, 2007.

Staff, Frank. "Dickens the Conjuror, and a Mystery Solved." *Dickensian*, Spring 1943.

Steelcroft, Framley. "Some Peculiar Entertainments." *Strand Magazine*, January 1896.

Stone, Cordelia, dir. *Penn & Teller Go Public*. YouTube, 1985. https://www.youtube.com/watch?v=fRt2ZIHbJcM (accessed January 12, 2024).

"Swallow These Statistics." *Billboard*, September 9, 1939.

"Swallowing a Sword." *Nelson Evening Mail*, June 22, 1869.

"Swallowing Neon Tubes Is Safe If They Don't Crack." *Wilkes-Barre Record*, October 8, 1937.

"Swallowing Swords and Bayonets." *Detroit Free Press*, July 5, 1874.

"Swallows Swords: Pierce Is the Real Thing in This Line—He Likes to Eat Lamp Chimneys." *Bangor Daily News*, November 11, 1905.

"Sword Diet Did Not Agree." *New York Times*, January 21, 1894.

"Sword-Swallower and a Boy Prodigy Missing." *Los Angeles Times*, February 1, 1890.

"Sword Swallower 'Ate' One Too Many." *Daily News*, April 15, 1908.

"Sword Swallower Cut." *New York Times*, May 30, 1909.

"Sword Swallower Cut." *Variety* 37, no. 2 (December 12, 1914).

"Sword Swallower Cuts Throat." *Courier-Journal*, August 16, 1903.

"Sword Swallower Died from Use of Morphine." *Bismarck Daily Tribune*, July 17, 1913.

"The Sword Swallower: Examination of Signor Beneditti at the Jefferson College." *Philadelphia Inquirer*, May 26, 1874.

"Sword-Swallower Goes Too Far." *Miami News*, June 14, 1950.

"Sword Swallower Hit Circus Fat Woman." *Calgary Herald*, April 24, 1948.

"Sword Swallower Makes a Miscue; Well Known Here." *Times-Leader* (Wilkes-Barre, PA), January 1, 1915.

"Sword Swallower Peril." *Boston Globe*, October 16, 1894.

"Sword-Swallowers. How Professionals Train Themselves for These Daring Feats." *Manitowoc Pilot* (from *La Nature*), December 27, 1883.

"Sword-Swallowing." *Youth's Companion*, May 2, 1878.

"Sword-Swallowing in Earnest." *Cincinnati Enquirer*, April 13, 1878.

Witcombe, Brian, and Dan Meyer. "Sword Swallowing and Its Side Effects." *British Medical Journal* 333, no. 7582 (December 21, 2006): 1285–87.

Taylor, James. *James Taylor's Shocked and Amazed! On & Off the Midway*. Vol. 1. Baltimore: Dolphin-Moon, 1995.

Thomas, Gordon. *Bed of Nails: The Story of the Amazing Blondini*. London: Allan Wingate, 1955.

Travsd. "In the Swim with Chester Dolphin." *Travalanche*, June 3, 2021. https://travsd.wordpress.com/2021/06/03/in-the-swim-on-chester-dolphin/ (accessed November 8, 2023).

Trenton Evening Times, November 7, 1898.

"Turns from Hot to Hotter." *Oakland Tribune*, January 24, 1960.

"Under the Marquee." *Billboard*, May 5, 1928.

Uhrhammer, Jerry. "Lady Sword Swallower (One of Few) Puts on Impromptu Show for R-G Team." *Eugene Guard*, October 12, 1960.

United Press. "Fair Carnivals Wonder about 1943 Prospects." *Jackson (TN) Sun*, March 16, 1943.

United Press. "Swallowing Swords Is Simple, but Long Hours Get Al Down." United Press, January 6, 1948.

United Press International. "Hiccups Hospitalize Sword Swallower." *Tampa Times*, October 12, 1959.

United Press International. "Neon Tube Explodes inside Sword Swallower." *Miami Herald*, June 17, 1969.

United Press International. "Red Fakir, Sword Swallower Reaches 100." *Fort Lauderdale News*, January 27, 1972.

United Press International. "Rough on Digestion. Neon Tube Gives Sword Swallower Trouble." United Press International, February 23, 1960.

United Press International. "Russian Sword Swallower Hits 100, Tells of Life." *Sun Post News*, January 25, 1972.

"Vaudeville." *Billboard*, December 29, 1906.

"Ventriloquist Sues Backers of Film." *New York Times*, November 25, 1929.

"Visitors Have Party Tonight." *Orlando Evening Star*, February 28, 1933.

Volkenberg, W. D. van. "Coney Island Chatter." *Billboard*, June 28, 1930.

"Walker's Museum." *Boston Post*, December 6, 1903.

Walton, Lloyd B. "Life May Hang by a Fiber." *Indianapolis Star*, July 8, 1978.

Warren, Jack. "The John Robinson Ten Big Shows." *Billboard*, June 27, 1908.

What's My Line? CBS, April 4, 1954. https://www.youtube.com/watch?v=h8h9aCc8vqs&list=PLqsaqh5sqUxqkNGHbNWOy-9fK82pcv1jw-&index=100 (accessed September 3, 2023).

White, Randy. "Swallow Five Swords? You Said a Mouthful." *Fort Myers News-Press*, February 15, 1977.

"William S. Fritz, Famous Showman, Taken by Death." *Wilkes-Barre Times*, July 15, 1925.

Williams, Greg. "Arbus Revealed." *Tampa Tribune*, March 11, 2004.

Yarin, Jim. "Moses Berg: The Rope Walker of Corsicana." *Corsican Daily Sun*, January 30, 2016. http://www.corsicanadailysun.com/news/moses-berg-the-rope-walker-of-corsicana/article_8acccbd0-c6e0-11e5-80c1-f75b45428ce8.html (accessed July 5, 2018).

Yarin, Jim. "'Rope Walker' Responds." *Corsican Daily Sun*, January 24, 2016. http://www.corsicanadailysun.com/news/rope-walker-responds/article_88a8cb24-c163-11e5-92a3-9726c82adabf.html (accessed July 5, 2018).

INDEX OF SWORD SWALLOWERS, SHOWS, SHOWMEN, AND OTHER PERFORMERS

ACKNOWLEDGMENTS

There are less than a few dozen full-time professional sword swallowers actively performing around the world today. That's roughly one out of every 300 million people. Of this incredible rare group of humans, we'd like to thank the many whom we had an opportunity to speak with for sharing their stories: the Amazing Zilla, Jim Ball, Brianna Belladonna, Bill Berry, Tommy Breen, Eric Broomfield, Brad Byers, Ted Campbell, Ses Carny, Geoffrey Cobb, Diane Falk, Travis Fessler, Pétur Gisli Finnbjörnsson, Tyler and Jill Fleet, Natalie Grist, Frank Hartman, Heather Holliday, Jesse House, Franz Huber, Fred Kahl, Lynx Kim, Alex Magala, George "The Giant" McArthur, Mighty Torrent, Keith Nelson, Harley Newman, Cyrus Pynn, Nick Penney, Asia Ray, Adam Rinn, Edward Robinson, Jim Rose, Sati, Jax Silvertree, Erik Sprague, Chris Steele, John Strong, Red Stuart, Lydia Treats, and Natasha Veruschka.

Several non–sword swallowers (including relatives of sword swallowers) offered information, images, and suggestions that we greatly appreciate. Thank you, David Adamovich, Dori Ann Bischmann, Carolyn Bass Burns, Dean Gurney, Cyndi Price, Tim O'Brien, Trav SD, James Taylor, and Rob Way for all your invaluable help.

Dr. Brian Witcombe, thank you for providing your expertise, and for celebrating sword swallowing and educating audiences about it around the world for nearly two decades.

Warren and Karla Raymond, thank you for sharing so many wondrous images from your phenomenal collection, as well as for your knowledge of performers and the history of sideshow.

Max Bolno, Tod Benedict, Jack Chappell, and Pete Schiffer, thank you for all your guidance and enthusiasm for this project.

You have all made this a better book.

Finally, thank you to every other sword swallower out there, past and present. Your dedication, presentation, and fearlessness will always live on through the wonder and amazement of others.

ABOUT THE AUTHORS

Dan Meyer grew up a child of ridicule, teased and beat up by bullies, who vowed to one day do real magic and change the world. Today, he's known as the world's leading expert on sword swallowing as president of the Sword Swallowers Association International, founder of World Sword Swallower's Day, and winner of the 2007 Ig Nobel Prize in Medicine at Harvard for medical research on sword swallowing. Meyer has been called the "world's top sword swallower" by Guinness World Records and Ripley's Believe It or Not! for his 40 world records and death-defying stunts, as featured in Ripley's cartoons, books, and museums and seen by 800 million viewers on over 100 TV shows, including 15 Got Talents and the finals of *America's Got Talent*. He was also the Golden Buzzer winner on Sweden's *Talang* and has performed live in 60 countries. A global TEDx speaker, Meyer enjoys inspiring audiences to cut through fear and do the impossible in their lives. His viral TED Talk "Cutting through Fear" is now the most translated TED Talk in the world. He lives in Mesa, Arizona.

Marc Hartzman is, according to ABC News, "one of America's leading connoisseurs of the bizarre." George Noory from Coast to Coast AM said he's "as bizarre as Robert Ripley." Marc considers both high praise. Hartzman is the author of *American Sideshow: An Encyclopedia of History's Most Wondrous and Curiously Strange Performers*, *We Are Not Alone: The Extraordinary History of UFOs and Aliens Invading Our Hopes, Fears, and Fantasies*, and eight other books, along with nearly 100 sideshow-related articles for AOL Weird News, *Bizarre* magazine, and *Mental Floss*. He has also discussed oddities on CNN, MSNBC, Ripley's Radio, History Channel's *The UnXplained*, the Travel Channel's *Mysteries at the Museum*, and dozens of podcasts. More on his love for the strange and unusual can be found on his site, WeirdHistorian.com. Outside of these projects, Hartzman earns a living as an award-winning advertising creative director. He lives in New Rochelle, New York.